Dilemmas of Culture in African Schools

Cati Coe

Dilemmas of Culture in

Youth,

Nationalism,

and the

Transformation of

Knowledge

The University of Chicago Press

Chicago and London

Cati Coe is assistant professor of anthropology at Rutgers University.

The University of Chicago Press, Chicago 60637
The University of Chicago Press, Ltd., London
© 2005 by The University of Chicago
All rights reserved. Published 2005
Printed in the United States of America

14 13 12 11 10 09 08 07 06 05   1 2 3 4 5

ISBN: 0-226-11129-6 (cloth)
ISBN: 0-226-11131-8 (paper)

Library of Congress Cataloging-in-Publication Data

Coe, Cati.
    Dilemmas of culture in African schools : youth, nation-
alism, and the transformation of knowledge / Cati Coe.
        p.   cm.
    Includes bibliographical references and index.
    ISBN 0-226-11129-6 (cloth : alk. paper)—
    ISBN 0-226-11131-8 (pbk. : alk. paper)
    1. Educational anthropology—Ghana.   2. Education
and state—Ghana.   I. Title.
    LB45.C64 2005
    306.43′096—dc22

                                            2005002897

♾ The paper used in this publication meets the minimum
requirements of the American National Standard for
Information Sciences—Permanence of Paper for Printed
Library Materials, ANSI Z39.48-1992.

CONTENTS

ACKNOWLEDGMENTS

THIS WORK would not have been completed without the support and encouragement of numerous people and institutions. In Akuapem, I extend my heartfelt thanks to the two families with whom I stayed for allowing me to share their lives and for their patience with my foreign foibles: the family of Ofori Boahene and Nana Asieduaa Antwi Boasiako I and their children, and Gladys Ohene and her family. My brother Kojo Oppong and sisters Rosemary Abu, Doreen Abu, Gertrude Oppong, Betty Abu, and Patience Ohene shared their perspectives on the teaching profession and their schooling experiences. Without Mr. Yɛboa-Dankwa, a strong advocate of his town, I would not have had the opportunity of working in Akuapem. Without his niece Ms. Gladys Owusu-Agyakwa, I would never have been introduced to the families with whom I stayed; and I will always be grateful to her for coming to my aid in a time of emergency at home. My mother's friends Sam and Irene Woode and Charles and Joanna Laryea were my families in Accra, and I thank them for letting me stay with them when I needed time away.

I also want to thank the teachers who allowed me to enter their classrooms and the headteachers of their schools: I cannot name them here, but they are in my thoughts. The people who gave me insights through conversations and interviews are too numerous to mention. I am happy to defer to the wishes of many to remain anonymous; those who wished to be named are listed at the beginning of the list of references. I appreciate the openness of several students and their families to my questions. Nana Asieduaa gave me access to chiefly activities in Akropong, as did Teacher Darko in Larteh and Nana

Amma Aboagyewa to Abiriw and Okere Guan courts. I also wish to thank those who served as mediators for me at various points of research and helped me represent my work: Mr. Yɛboa-Dankwa, Stella Dede Djan, Professor Kwamena-Poh, Gladys Ohene, Sandra Akosua Yirenkyiwa, Kofi Akuffo, and Mensah Abavon. Joe Bramson helped with videography, getting a tripod for the regional and national competitions and videotaping a kindergarten competition.

At the district education office, Mr. Devoh was especially generous with his time, letting me observe his workshops, giving me rides on his motorcycle, and providing materials. I was given access to local educational statistics and was always welcomed at the office. Reverend S. K. Aboa, Fred Agyemang, and Professor Michael Kwamena-Poh shared their materials, books, and ideas freely with me and were influential in shaping the historical aspects of my research. My thanks to all those who communicated with me in Twi, and especially to Reverend Kobina Ofosu-Donkoh in Philadelphia and Afari Amoako in Akropong for teaching me the grammatical and finer points of the language. Afari Amoako and I worked on the initial translations and transcriptions together; Reverend Ofosu-Donkoh very kindly proofread both the Twi text and the translations. I am immensely grateful to both.

This work was financed by a travel grant from the Ford Foundation Workshop on the Problematics of Identities and States at the University of Pennsylvania, which allowed me to spend two months in Ghana in 1997; a Fulbright (IIE) grant, which supported my year of fieldwork in 1998–99; and a fellowship from the University of Pennsylvania, which freed me to write up my findings for publication. The staff of USIS-Accra got me a residency permit, gave me access to their equipment to make copies of videotapes of cultural competitions to give to teachers, and solved my computer problems. The interaction with other Fulbright researchers was important: Joy Gorman provided me with important policy documents from her own research on Ghana's educational reform of 1987; Jesse Shipley and I were able to compare notes about Ghana's cultural policy and institutions; and I visited Lauren Morris MacLean at her research site, a village in Brong-Ahafo.

One of the most important institutions to me (and not only because it was the closest, right in Akropong) was the Akrofi-Christaller Memorial Center for Mission Research and Applied Theology. I thank the staff for allowing me to stay in their hostel for my eight-week visit in 2002. My initial understanding of the Basel missionaries and Christianity in Ghana was strengthened and challenged by the perspectives and materials available at the ACMC.

At the Cultural Studies Unit in Accra, I thank Mr. Apraku, Nana Sakyi, and Mr. Aguri for letting me photocopy materials and videotape the national competition. They kept me well fed during the national competition and shared their insights in informal conversations. Mr. Klah at the Curriculum Research and Development Division (CRDD) at the Ghana Education Service gave me access to syllabi. At the University of Ghana at Legon, Professors Robert Addo-Fening, S. D. Asiama, A. Mawɛre-Opoku, Kwabena Nketia, Mary Yirenkyi, and Asiedu Yirenkyi were extremely helpful and insightful, sharing their own memories as well as their own research with me.

Over the years, many scholars have nurtured me and helped me understand and express more clearly my findings: Ann Anagnost, Deborah Augsburger, Regina Bendix, Lee Cassanelli, Kamari Clarke, Virginia Dominguez, Ilana Gershon, Michelle Gilbert, Carol Greenhouse, Kathleen Hall, Amanda Holmes, Clare Ignatowski, Margaret Mills, Catherine Newling, Rachel Reynolds, Jeffrey Shultz, Amy Stambach, and Kristina Wirtz, as well as the anonymous reviewers of the manuscript. I am grateful to all of them for providing models of how to be a scholar of integrity, intellectual curiosity, and human generosity.

Members of my family each approached this project in his or her own way: my father with his far-reaching knowledge, sharp mind, and proofreading pen; my mother with insights from her own experiences in Ghana in the mid-1960s and 1979–82, giving me more of a sense of the *longue durée*; and my sister, who joined me for three weeks in Ghana, with her sensitivity to the need to protect both her own and my personhood.

I am not sure that people in Akuapem would consider this story a pot of gold, buried in the field and joyfully discovered. To most, if not all, of them, learning how culture was taught in the schools was not a form of important knowledge like cultural traditions themselves or the history of the town's migrations. Nonetheless, there is much that I treasure in my interactions with others who were as mortal and slipperily positioned as myself during this journey, and I offer this book as a testament to that.

THE DAY of the circuit cultural competitions began misty and cool. When I arrived at Demonstration Primary School at eight o'clock, students and teachers were busy with the preparations in the school's courtyard, which was enclosed by a covered veranda on one side and white-washed classroom blocks with black shutters on the other three. Children were sweeping the patios and the red dirt of the courtyard. The younger ones played clapping games or walked around holding hands, waiting for the competition to begin. Teachers were supervising the setting up of a canopy at one end of the courtyard to provide some shade against the harsh rays of the midday sun. It was 1997, in the town of Akropong, Aku-apem, and I had been in Ghana for only three weeks. Later I would learn not to arrive so early. Coordinating all the participants, setting up rented canopies, and coaxing a crackly sound system to work meant that school cultural competitions usually began late in the morning.

INTRODUCTION
Dilemmas of Culture
in African Schools

But today, with thirteen schools—eight primary schools and five junior secondary schools from Akropong and neighboring Abiriw—set to perform in six different categories, the competition had to begin as soon as possible, or we would be there until dark. Students from these schools crowded into the courtyard, finding spots to sit with their friends, and the judges and dignitaries began arriving, making their way to the chairs on the covered veranda. By ten o'clock, we were ready to go.

The first competition category was dance-drama, in which students related a narrative through drumming, singing, and dancing, without any talking. Abiriw Pres-byterian Primary School presented a dance-drama on water pollution, demonstrating how improper care for streams results in illness. In Lady Brown Primary School's piece, "Unity," students showed that they could not break the brush of a broom when all the pieces of straw were tied together and could only raise a Ghanaian flag when they all came together. Akropong Presbyterian Primary

Figure 1. A pregnant teenager dying from complications, dance-drama performance, Akropong circuit cultural competition, June 1997

School's presentation, also on unity, showed squabbling political parties being dispersed by soldiers. "An opponent is not your enemy. A better Ghana is the answer," read the sign that the performers held up at the end. Most of the dance-dramas seemed to be in this didactic vein, designed to point out the nation's problems and how they could be resolved. Of the five dance-dramas performed by junior secondary school students that day, two concerned teenage pregnancy, two instructed parents to "Send Your Girl Child to School," and one enacted the dangers of drug abuse. In both of the dance-dramas on teenage pregnancy, the pregnant girl died in a dramatic scene, clutching her stomach in pain before lying down in the dust of the courtyard (fig. 1). Only two dance-dramas departed from this kind of message: students from Demonstration Primary School told the story of how King Solomon decided which woman was the mother of a baby, and Seventh Day Adventist Primary School students enacted a funeral, in which children clad in red and black cloth got up one by one to dance. The last to join in was a little boy, who won the hearts of everyone with his level of skill. "This one is pure traditional," commented the teacher sitting next to me, implying that the presentations of national development and Christian narratives were not.

The audience grew during the course of the day. Though primarily composed of teachers and students, some older women came in from town to sit under the canopy. Other women did a brisk business selling fruit, peanuts, and bread on the fringes of the crowd. Between performances students in the audience, who had crowded forward to see better, were driven back by a teacher yelling loudly and swinging a switch. After the dance-dramas boys from the different schools performed drum language, a performance art in which the tonal phrasing of speaking is imitated on a set of high- and low-toned drums. The tension on the boys' faces was palpable, and members of the audience were appreciative and eager to evaluate the performers. Drum language, unlike dance-drama, is a genre with symbolic significance performed outside of school during funerals and in chiefs' courts. "It's a great art," said a teacher behind me after an inept performance. Then came poetry recital, in which a girl from each school dramatically recited a poem of condemnation or sorrow about some aspect of contemporary Ghanaian life, using her attire, gestures, and voice to move the spectators to shame or pity. Finally, as dusk approached, there was choral singing, in which students sang nationalist songs, dressed neatly in their school uniforms with clean white socks and shiny black shoes or in *kente* cloth, made of strips of brightly woven silk. As the competitions ended, students began to leave, hungry and weary from sitting in the sun all day. The judges stood up to give their verdicts in each artistic category, and students cheered for their school when its victory was announced, a guarantee that its team could continue to the district competition, with a chance to move on to the regional and national levels.

Despite my exhaustion from the seven hours of competition in Akropong, the next day I attended another circuit competition a few towns over, in Adukrom, compelled by what I had seen. To me, the competitions represented a triumph of government cultural programming. Not only were schools and students participating in these events, but the school-children were spreading public service messages on behalf of the nation. Because the performances seemed so similar in their didacticism and focus on national problems, the cultural competitions seemed to mark the success of the particular definition of culture that the government was promoting. "Culture for development" seemed to have become a way of speaking about culture broadly shared by teachers and students. As I attended other school cultural competitions in 1999 and 2002, I saw fewer "aberrant" performances in the form of biblical stories or the reenactment of traditional customs; that shared understanding seemed to be gaining more adherents (see appendix A for a list of dance-drama themes from the cultural competitions). Schools thus seemed to be the perfect vehicles for promoting state ideology about culture.

But that was not the whole story, as I found out during the year I spent in Akropong (Aug. 1998–Aug. 1999). The relationship between the state and schools is more complicated than I had first assumed.

Schools and States

Studies of the state have shown how its agents seek to render visible the people and areas under their domains in order to control them. They seek to rationalize, standardize, and clarify social life in order to better manage it through social engineering and planning, such as teaching farmers scientific agricultural methods, creating well-ordered cities and sewage systems, surveying populations, and mapping the land (Cohn 1984; Scott 1998). Although many studies of the state do not mention schools in these interventions, historically the expansion of mass education is closely linked to the expansion of the state. Not only does the provision of mass education, as a public good, help justify the legitimacy of the state to govern and accumulate power, particularly in postcolonial states (Chatterjee 1999), but it also helps the state control its populace by appropriating knowledge and power associated with local social institutions. With the expansion of mass education, children spend more time in school. As a result, they generally have less opportunity to learn local knowledges, closely tied to complex local social relations and ecologies. Curricula and textbooks standardize knowledge, and teachers, experts in that knowledge, disseminate it. Schools are one of the most sustained zones of contact most people have with the state, and they become a way for the state to attempt to reach and shape its populace. In the late nineteenth century, schools helped turn "peasants into Frenchmen" and sufficiently overcome regional identifications to create a sense of the nation (E. Weber 1976; but see Reed-Danahay 1996).

Anthropologists and folklorists have explored the emergence of a sense of national belonging and national sentiment in the nineteenth and twentieth centuries around the world (Anderson 1991; Handler 1988; Herzfeld 1997). The nation was a new locus of identification that was neither natural nor self-evident, but was constructed with the help of literacy (Anderson 1991) and the popularization of folkloric, linguistic, and historical scholarship (Verdery 1990; Wilson 1976). Culture and local language became the primary signifiers for identifying and representing the modern nation, and in the process of generating a national identity, cultural traditions were remolded for national use: objectified, sanitized, and reified. Particularly in Africa, performing and musical arts became a way for the state to represent the nation (Apter 1996; Askew 2002; Turino 2000). Both mass education and cultural reification became central features of the modern institution of the nation-state.

However, scholars who have examined the nationalist use of tradition have not paid sufficient attention to the way that state-sponsored cultural interventions focus on schools. In fact, many nationalists sought to popularize their ideas about culture by reforming school curricula. To cite one particular nation-building moment, the Norwegian folklorist Ole Vig (1824–57) wanted to transform the elementary school for lower-class children into a folk school that used landsmål, or Norwegian peasant dialects, rather than Latin. He campaigned for textbooks that would include myths and proverbs, as well as history, geography, and nature study, and contain literary selections in Norwegian and Swedish folk dialects and in Old Norwegian and Old Danish. Likewise, Johann Gottfried Herder (1744–1802), whose theories animated later European nationalism, preached on the reform of German elementary education, and at Weimar, where he functioned as the duke's minister of education, he was able to put into practice some of his ideas, such as replacing the Latin curriculum with instruction in the mother tongue (Hayes 1927). Thus, the teaching of a national or folk culture in schools often accompanies nationalist sentiment and the extension of state-sponsored schooling to non-elite children. But the phenomenon remains curiously little studied. Bradley Levinson (1999) argues that anthropologists neglect schooling as an object of study because we tend to take the effects of schooling for granted and because we are reluctant to study modern, bureaucratic institutions even as we increasingly study policy, development institutions, and the state. If studies of nationalism and the representation of culture took schooling into account, it would become clear how those nationalist representations are transformed as they are incorporated into an institution with its own traditions, associations, and dynamics.

For schools are not fully state institutions. Participant observation and ethnographic research methods, with their fine-grained focus on people's lives, reveal that other meanings adhere to schools: the personal hopes of students and their families become embedded within them. Local goals and conceptions change the function and meaning of schools, as studies of schooling in rural France (Reed-Danahay 1996) and revolutionary Mexico have shown (Rockwell 1994; Vaughn 1997). Education, as one of the state's obligations to its citizens, is also a means by which citizens critique and put pressure on the state to provide for them. Schools thus become places where the relationship between a state and its citizens is negotiated, with each side seeking to influence the other.

State projects entail visions and intentions that aim to be powerful but may never be fully realized (Thomas 1994). Standardization projects ignore the complex interdependencies by which people make their way (Certeau 1984). Schools attempt to standardize and objectify vernacular knowledge, codifying tradition in classroom lessons into facts that take the form of lists and definitions. But that very standardizing process undercuts itself. Rather than appropriating vernacular knowledge, standardization generates a new field of knowledge—a school knowledge that has different connotations and meanings than vernacular knowledge. Ultimately, both forms of knowledge exist side by side, each with its own associated meanings and social institutions. Thus, even as the state attempts to claim and appropriate the meaning of culture through schools, the meaning of culture bisects and becomes multiple, slipping from the state's grasp. In Ghana what this means is that as culture is taught in schools, local elders and chiefs are esteemed for their knowledge and practice of the most "authentic" culture, while an objectified and nationalized culture taught in schools is devalued, considered suitable only for children and adolescents.

As I learned over the year 1998–99, school cultural programming in Ghana is multivocal, producing messages that contradict the state's notion of the meaning of culture. The government lays the groundwork for the production of national culture through events like school cultural competitions, but what is produced there is far from what was intended. Teachers and students have adapted those spaces to create their own meanings and practices. To be sure, those meanings and practices are not completely new—except as they are newly combined. But the social relations of power from which they arise, above all, chieftaincy and the church, are precisely what the state seeks to displace or appropriate. Agency is not simply a mode of resistance to powerful discourses—like those produced by the state or other political entities such as the church and traditional chiefs. Rather it is a capacity for action that specific discourses create and enable (Mahmood 2001). Thus, people draw on discourses that compete with those of the state in order to create meanings other than what the state intends within the very spaces that the state creates.

The Meaning of Culture

I define culture differently from most Ghanaians. For me, culture encompasses the everyday, habitual practices of people, including practices of Christianity and schooling and "Western" ways. It is contextual and flexible: we enact it in specific settings among specific people. For instance, there is a school culture in Ghana in which certain practices of dress and modes of speaking have become natural and expected. In this study, how-ever, I do not use the term "culture" in the way contemporary anthropolo-gists and folklorists understand it. Rather, I am concerned with the ways people think about and enact their own ideas of culture, some of which are concepts that scholars have discarded but that have found new life among various publics (Kirshenblatt-Gimblett 2000). While scholars might like to keep these two meanings of "culture" distinct—one for popular con-sumption and one for the analysis of social life—the history of feedback loops between academic scholarship and publics in Europe and Ghana makes this a frustrating and ultimately problematic task. As a result, I will be using culture (without quotes) to refer to the way that Ghanaians imag-ine and fight over the cultural, rather than to signal my sense of culture, in-culcated through my training, as something we embody and enact, usually unwittingly and sometimes unwillingly, every moment of our lives.

David Whisnant (1983), in his study of the creation of a folk high school and folk festival in Appalachia, makes a distinction between a cul-tural intervention, which presupposes a selection, arrangement, and ob-jectification of cultural elements, and everyday tradition, in which people "resist and accommodate, keep and let go" (262). As the state became in-volved in the promotion of culture in Ghana, its interventions legitimized and normalized selected parts of the totality of everyday cultural life. Cul-ture became thing-like, "bounded, continuous, and precisely distinguish-able from other analogous entities," such as economics and politics (Han-dler 1988, 15). Culture was idealized and imagined in certain ways, with some things marked as cultural and others not (Dominguez 1992). In this way culture was abstracted from ongoing social practice and could be dis-played in contexts such as museums and national festivals. Experts in cul-ture were created and maintained.

But interventions and representations cannot be critiqued simply on the grounds that they freeze living forms and depict reality in incomplete ways. All cultural practices are the products of contestations between var-ious groups, involving representations, reifications, and points of rigidity (R. Foster 1991). Essentializing culture is not solely the domain of elites or the nation-state. Rather, "social life consists of processes of reifications and essentialism as well as challenges to these processes" (Herzfeld 1997, 26). What we see as the complex flow of cultural practices in everyday life is the result of past contestations, essentialisms, and representations.

Following in the path cut by missionary Christianity, all the discourses of culture currently operating in Ghana render culture a distant or abstract thing and a selection of the totality of everyday and ritual practices. It has little concreteness or points of fixture in people's everyday lives. It is always "out there," referring to specific activities or practices, not "what we do." People in Akuapem feel that culture occasionally touches their lives: at ritual ceremonies, festivals, and school cultural competitions. For many Ghanaians, culture means "Ghanaian culture," which can be avoided if one wishes, or in which one can participate on Saturdays or specific festive occasions.

Cultural Programming in Schools: The Case of Ghana

This study examines, historically and ethnographically, the production of national culture in Ghana through schools. This little-studied phenomenon illustrates the reach of the state as it seeks to transform the minds and bodies of its young citizens through the widespread institution of schooling and with the emotional pull of culture. However, precisely because the state's interventions rely on two institutions—culture and schools—that carry so much social significance and emotional weight, the limits of its reach also become clear as citizens bring their own understanding of the role of those institutions to the state's project. Cultural programming in schools thus becomes an important site for exploring the interaction between a state and its citizens.

The Ghanaian state is not unusual in promoting culture by this means. Many African countries incorporate culture into their school curricula: oral literature in Kenya (Opondo 2000; Samper 1997), performing arts in independent Namibia (Mans 2000), "cultural activity" in South Africa under the African National Congress (UNESCO 1995), and theater in Burkina Faso (UNESCO 1981). In the name of multicultural education and diversity, ethnic traditions and students' home customs are celebrated sporadically in schools in the United States and Europe. School cultural competitions are organized regularly in Botswana, Guinea, Uganda, Bolivia, and New Zealand.[1] These interventions raise questions about the reasons why schools become involved in this domain and about the kinds of negotiations that take place between teachers and students faced with incorporating forms of knowledge and practice with particular social and symbolic significance into an institution with a very different purpose and association.

Ghana is an especially good place to study the politics of culture and schooling. It has had a long history of cultural programming, and as a result, it influenced other British-ruled African colonies and African countries. Teachers at the government secondary school of Achimota and colonial officials in what was then known as the Gold Coast, for instance, wrote articles for teachers' journals in Nigeria and Zanzibar (Zachernuk 1998; Jonathan Glassman, pers. comm., May 2000). In 1957 Ghana became the first country in sub-Saharan Africa to gain independence from a colonial power, and as a result, its first prime minister, Dr. Kwame Nkrumah, felt a special obligation to work toward the cultural, political, and economic liberation of all of Africa. Nkrumah invited others from the continent to work in Ghana to learn from its nationalist movement, and one of those who came was Robert Mugabe, the future president of Zimbabwe. From his experience of working as a schoolteacher in Ghana (1958–60), Mugabe drew inspiration from Nkrumah's party organization to create a youth wing for his own movement; like Nkrumah's Young Pioneers, it used drama and dancing to generate emotional enthusiasm among young people (Turino 2000). Nkrumah set up the Institute of African Studies at the University of Ghana, which was devoted to research and teaching about African culture, performance traditions, and history. He also established the Arts Council (renamed the National Commission of Culture in the 1980s), whose mission was to collect folklore traditions, promote local artists, and educate the public about Ghana's cultural heritage.[2] Thanks to Nkrumah's vision, the country has a fifty-year history of cultural programming, although it has risen and fallen with the financial resources and power of the state.

The NDC (National Defence Council) government of Ghana, in power from 1981 to 2000, reinvigorated the push to promote "Ghanaian culture." (The NDC is an outgrowth of the Provisional National Defence Council, PNDC, a regime that took over in a military coup in 1981 and then converted to a civilian political party. To stress the continuity between the two regimes, many political scientists who study Ghana, as well as Ghanaian newspaper columnists, refer to the (P)NDC government, and I follow their example in this study.) The (P)NDC wrote a new cultural policy. It established a cultural education unit within the Ghana Education Service—the implementation arm of the Ministry of Education—to organize cultural competitions and activities within schools. As part of the extensive Educational Reform Programme launched under the auspices of the World Bank in 1986, "cultural studies" was introduced as a separate and requisite subject in all primary and junior secondary schools, which was considered basic education. By developing, preserving, and promoting a "national culture," the Ghanaian government hoped that children would develop attitudes and skills useful for development, national unity, and social cohesion. The Ministry of Education and Culture's "Policy Guidelines for the Educational Reform Programme" stated, as one of seven principles for the

reform of basic education: "Every Ghanaian needs a sense of cultural identity and dignity. Ghana has a cultural heritage of individual ethnic cultures
and promoting a unified Ghanaian culture will ensure a sense of national
identity and make the nation stronger and more unified. This will help the
pupils to be proud of themselves and their society. A proper cultural identity will help free our minds from dependency on the cultures of other
people" (Ghana 1988b, 3). Even though the main opposition party, the
New Patriotic Party (NPP), was elected to power in 2000, many of the
(P)NDC government's educational and cultural policies remained intact
through that transition — a phenomenon we will see occur repeatedly in
Ghana's long history of state interest in promoting things cultural in
schools.

Although Ghana may be at one end of the spectrum in its organization
of policy, state agencies, and schooling in Africa, the same push and pull
between schooling and culture and between the state and its citizens is to
be found throughout the continent. As in other African countries, vernacular traditions were labeled "cultural" and representative of the past
during the colonial period in the Gold Coast. Subjecting African tradition
to colonial norms resulted in its rehabilitation by nationalist and anticolo-
nialist movements during the struggle for independence. Furthermore, African postcolonial states, in order to shore up their legitimacy, often attempt to appropriate and undercut the power of alternative political
authorities. Culture, to the extent that it is associated with these local poli-
ties, can be used symbolically in this political struggle. Schools in Africa,
as much a part of the colonial legacy as the objectification of culture, are
associated with access to colonial power, entry into state employment, and
the rejection of conventional ways of living. For this reason, as part of their
rehabilitation and appropriation efforts, African states have inserted culture into school curricula and extracurricular activities, but this effort is
made problematic precisely because of schooling's historical associations
with Christianity and cosmopolitanism. The current popularity of charismatic Christianity across Africa heightens the polarization between Christianity and culture (Gifford 1998), and to the extent that young teachers,
as well as students, are charismatic Christians, they are unlikely to support
their government's efforts to promote culture in schools. In illustrating
these complex historical, political, and social processes, Ghana provides a
rich case study for understanding how a national culture is created and
contested in schools in an African postcolonial state.

The postcolonial intervention to create a national culture raises several
questions. I seek to understand the strategies of the state and the tactics of

its citizens in the production of national culture, both how the state aims to promote a particular meaning of culture and how Ghanaians work within the spaces that the state constructs to generate different meanings and practices. One line of inquiry investigates the forces behind the state's promotion of Ghanaian culture in schools. How has culture become the property of the state? How has the state's role in the transmission and up-keep of culture been naturalized? Why have schools become part of the state's efforts to claim culture as its own to present and promote? The second line of inquiry considers whether the government's claim that culture is the property of the state is contested. How do teachers and students transform school cultural programming according to their own under-standings and identities? What meanings and identities are ultimately pro-duced through Ghana's cultural programming in schools? In short, this study examines how culture is appropriated by the state through cultural interventions in schools but reclaimed by its citizens. School cultural pro-gramming is a lens by which to study the negotiations between citizens and the state as each seeks to define culture.

Although I had the option to study educational and cultural policy by following the operations of cultural officers and educational bureaucracies in the capital city of Accra, I decided that these questions could be better answered by examining how the top-down program was carried out in schools in one area. Located on a low-lying ridge about thirty miles north-east of Accra, Akropong is a town that serves simultaneously as the district capital for the Akuapem North district in the Eastern Region and as the capital of the traditional Akan kingdom of Akuapem (see maps 1 and 2). Akropong allowed me to see both schools and cultural activities in action, more than in rural areas of Ghana but at some remove from the national and regional centers of state activity.

Houses and Histories in Akuapem

It is hard to read the history of a strange place at first. I could not date the styles of architecture in Akropong the way I could in Philadelphia. I saw houses with tin roofs built around a central courtyard near the center of town, old crumbling mansions with two or three stories built farther out, and then the newer mansions, painted white, symbols of success but some-times uninhabited, on the outskirts of town, hidden among the farms they were displacing. The old Presbyterian cemetery in Akropong, established in the nineteenth century, was situated right behind a new market, begun in 1994 after a conflict between Akropong and the neighboring town of Abiriw destroyed the old market on the border between the two towns; the

Map 1. The
Republic of
Ghana

stillness of the long grass and the cemetery's white gate contrasted with the
hustle and bustle of the small market. The streams, so important in the past
for water and as sacred places, were hidden in the valleys and less used after running water began to be piped in. The main (tarred) road took one
to the capital city of Accra or Koforidua, the capital of the Eastern Region,
in an hour or two.

Migration has long pulled people away from the town. But most remain
fiercely loyal to their hometown. They return home for festivals and funerals on weekends, and this is where they will build a house if they can.
Local and ethnic identities remain far more salient in Akropong than national sentiments. Although Akropong people have long engaged with
outside forces and cannot ignore the power and resources of the state, for
them the hometown is the locus of sentiment and identity. The seventeen
towns on the ridge compete with one another, and conflicts between them
have been heightened by the inhabitants' knowledge of their town's history, told with an awareness of ethnic identity and past injustices. Akropong is also a destination for migrants. There has been a long history of

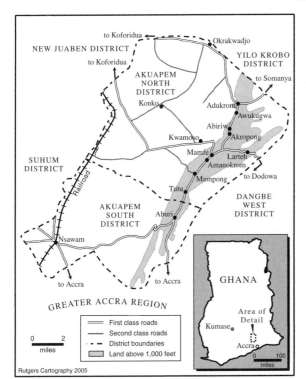

Map 2. Akuapem North and South districts

Ewe people living in Akropong, and people from the north and outside the country come through and settle as traders, amulet sellers, and laborers. Teachers from other parts of southern Ghana come to teach in the schools and the teacher training college. Akropong is the largest town in Akuapem, in part because of the concentration of schools and district offices there, with the town of Larteh almost as big, its old buildings a sign of its one-time wealth from cocoa. To give an approximate sense of the size, the census of 1984 reported that Akropong had a population of 8,479, and Larteh a population of 6,459 (Ghana 1989b).

It is tempting to read the history of the area as a sedimentation of successive political entities. First there were Guan settlers, thought to have come in the sixteenth century, whose priests served as both political and spiritual leaders; next were Twi (Akan)-speaking conquerors, who were dominant in the seventeenth and eighteenth centuries; then came missionaries and British colonial officials in the nineteenth century, the latter replaced by Ghanaian bureaucrats after independence in 1957. But rather than serializing these different political entities, it is more appropriate to see them as resources that can be reactivated in the present. For instance, Akuapem can be read both as the traditional Akan kingdom of Akuapem and as two administrative units of the modern state. These political structures coexist alongside one another, sometimes harmoniously and sometimes in tension.

To view Akuapem as an Akan traditional kingdom, one must focus on the seventeen towns that are organized hierarchically within it. The paramount chief, or *ɔmanhene*, comes from Akropong, the capital; the chiefs of other towns hold various political offices and command their own military divisions. To draw an American analogy, it is as if the mayor also served as state representative: an important chief is simultaneously head of his town and a member of the kingdom's governing structure. The kingdom's governing structure is separate from the state governing structure of national representatives and district administrators, although the two are supposed to work cooperatively.

British colonial administration was only felt in Akuapem toward the end of the nineteenth century. Because of the policy of indirect rule and reliance on traditional political authorities, the boundaries of the traditional kingdom became coterminous with the colonial administrative unit of the district. This history means that multiple political allegiances are active and in play within the same space. In Ghana the central government attempts to gain a popular base through traditional chiefs and thereby takes sides in chieftaincy disputes, while chiefs compete to bring government resources to their local areas (Brokensha 1966; Ladouceur 1979; Peasah 1975). The postcolonial state has inherited the relationship between the British and the traditional kingdom: although it asks the chiefs to be partners in development, it effectively undercuts their authority. The state intervenes in chieftaincy disputes, requesting stability and peace in the cause of development, even as its political parties contribute to the instability by aligning themselves with various chiefly factions. In Akuapem this state of affairs has lately led to a fissuring of the Akuapem kingdom, disputes over land, and the creation of more chiefs.

An important element in this fissuring is the increasing politicization of the two main ethnic groups in the area (Gilbert 1997). Akan and Guan peoples mark their ethnic differences in terms of religion, modes of descent, and language. The grievance between the Guan towns and Akropong dates back to 1994, when a conflict between the Guan town of Abiriw and the Akan town of Akropong over land use and ownership, a tense topic in Akuapem with its shortage of fertile land, erupted into violence. The situation has been exacerbated by efforts to unite the scattered

Guan communities across northern and southern Ghana, a process of ethnic revival and unification that began at least as early as the 1960s but intensified in the 1980s, with a major role being played by residents and chiefs in the Guan town of Larteh. Although not formally recognized by the national government, most of the Guan towns have seceded to form their own traditional kingdoms. The Akuapem traditional state now de facto encompasses only two towns, Akropong and Amanokrom, and factions in two others, Mamfe and Aburi. By 1998 things had reached such a fever pitch that the chiefs and queen mothers of many Akuapem towns did not show up at the annual Odwira festival to swear their allegiance to the paramount chief.

Currently, Akuapem is administratively divided into two districts, Akuapem North, headquartered in the traditional capital of Akropong, and Akuapem South, headquartered in the former cocoa-marketing — and thus relatively new — town of Nsawam. In an effort at decentralization, the state has made the assemblies and offices of these districts, including the offices of education, responsible for collecting and disbursing local taxes and fees. In 1997 the Akuapem North district was charged with serving a population of 102,971, almost half of whom (48 percent) were children (Ghana 1997). The primary and junior secondary schools they attend are further divided into administrative units called circuits. At times these units have shifted in response to the fissuring of the traditional state. Schools in the Akan town of Akropong and the Guan town of Abiriw, for example, are in the same circuit. But in 1998–99 the Abiriw schools chose to participate in the circuit events (in sports and the kindergarten cultural competitions) of Adukrom, a Guan town. By 2002, when tensions between Guan towns and Akropong had cooled, Abiriw was again participating in Akropong circuit activities.

How representative of Ghana is Akropong? As in other southern towns, many of the inhabitants are Christian and educated; the two generally go hand and hand. But Akropong and Akuapem in general are not typical in the sense that they are known in Ghana for their particularly long history of involvement with Christianity and education. Both Christianity and education are associated with the loss of traditional culture, but they also account, in the minds of Ghanaians, for the politeness and social delicacy of Akuapem people. Akropong is neither a big urban area, rich with trade and employment opportunities, nor a rural area, producing food for other areas. Rather, it is dependent on its connections to both sectors. Minivans constantly take people and goods back and forth to Accra, Koforidua, and parts beyond. People living in Akropong wait for money from relatives working in the cities of Tema, Accra, and Koforidua, and are dependent on food from the valleys to the west or from food-producing areas even farther away. Akropong is caught in the middle of the urban-rural divide in Ghana, with the eyes of its young people turned to the cities and the older people remembering the ways of farming life. Akropong highlights certain tensions that have relevance to Ghana as a whole: the political maneuvering between chiefs and the state, the structural tensions of an economy that is built on farmers but rewards urban dwellers and those close to the state, and a strong allegiance to one's hometown.

In many ways the economy of Akropong is education. For a century or more, since the Basel Mission's establishment of a seminary in 1848 and a boys' boarding school in 1867, many of the local people have earned a living by selling cooked food and produce to teachers and students, taking care of the college as groundskeepers or guards, or working as servants for the missionaries and teachers. In not a few cases, the salaries of teachers are a source of cash for local relatives (Brokensha 1966). So are remittances from Akropong's educated youth, the people most equipped to succeed in their migrations to cities and overseas. Because schools are thought to be of better quality in Akropong and other towns on the Akuapem ridge than in other parts of rural Ghana (Ghana 1997), many parents working in the cities or on farms send their children to the area to be schooled; this inflow accounts for the high percentage of children in Akuapem (Brokensha 1966). Through this kind of exchange, old people, taking care of their grandchildren, can help persuade their working children to provide for them.

Many studies of Ghanaian education are based on schools in the capital city, Accra (Masemann 1974; Peil 1995; but for an exception, see Sefa Dei 1993), and do not give a representative picture of the state of education in Ghana. Its rural schools have considerable difficulty attracting teachers, who often prefer to stay in urban centers with amenities like electricity and running water and opportunities to earn money on the side. Most schools on the Akuapem ridge have a full complement of teachers day in and day out. Even so, those schools are not considered as good as the ones in urban areas like Koforidua, Tema, and Accra, and only a few of their graduates go on to prestigious secondary boarding schools, although many continue their education in other ways, such as through apprenticeships in car mechanics, hairdressing, and tailoring.

Eleven of the fifteen districts in the Eastern Region held district-level cultural competitions in 1999, and only five districts competed in all six artistic categories at the regional competition; Akuapem North district succeeded in doing both. Thus, in comparison to other districts in the Eastern Region, schools in the Akuapem North district participated more fully in school cultural competitions, although, as is true of most districts, only half of the second-cycle institutions chose to participate at all (six of the twelve possible secondary schools and teacher training colleges). This high rate of participation is due in great part to the cultural studies officer in the district education office, Mr. Devoh, who works hard at organizing cultural competitions. Civil servants, including teachers, are generally dispirited about their work, a phenomenon that makes Mr. Devoh's dedication and activity all the more remarkable in the face of the somnolence of the district Center for National Culture, whose two employees do little to promote cultural activities in the locality (unlike its counterpart in the regional capital of Koforidua, which regularly organizes afterschool and vacation cultural activities for schoolchildren in the vicinity). Because cultural activities in Akropong schools were regularly being organized and schools were operating smoothly, I had the opportunity to see the object of my study in action.

The Process of Making Meaning

I did not do ethnographic research in the classic sense. My aim was not to study the town of Akropong as a community or to do an ethnography of a school. Rather, I wanted to examine how an educational policy in general was configured. The nation was the scope of my study; schools in and around Akropong were my lens. My topic was both large and ephemeral, its web stretching in many dimensions—from the nineteenth century to the present, from Akropong to Accra—but its articulation flickered in and out, just as one can see the work of a spider only from certain angles—when it is covered in drops of dew or as the sun strikes it. Like the anthropologist Johannes Fabian (1971), who unhappily admitted, "I still seem to traverse, rather than follow insights" (206), I felt that the more I tried to track this articulation, the more I was finding the path by crossing it unexpectedly. Although this may be true of all ethnographic studies of the nation and policy (Handler 1988; Shore and Wright 1997), it was the flickering articulation of cultural programming in Ghana that gave me the first intimation that the government's cultural intervention might not be as powerful as it seemed at first blush.

My metaphor of the flickering spider's web had its equivalent in the Akuapem metaphor of buried treasure. In Akuapem important knowledge is not easily acquired; it is secret and well hidden. One day when I was sitting around chatting with my Twi teacher, his cousin, and an elderly neighbor, the cousin asked how my research was going, and I told him that it was hard to get people to talk to me. He said that people were secretive because of the long history of war and slavery in Akuapem: secrets had allowed Akropong to survive as a town. While one might engage in intense, hard work, he assured me, its reward would come unexpectedly. A few weeks later, I was toying with the idea of leaving a few months before the school year ended, and my Twi teacher urged me to stay, telling me the story of Ananse the Spider, who was locked up for ten days as punishment for some mischief he had done and escaped two days before he was to be set free. When he was caught again, he was given life imprisonment. Switching metaphors, I argued, "Why bother to finish weeding the field if the field isn't worth weeding at all?" Quick on his feet, he replied that in the part of the field that was left, I would find the treasure, like a buried pot of gold. My Twi teacher and his cousin persuaded me to have the patience to look for the hidden meaning, for "the underneath of things" (Ferme 2001).

During my three trips to Akuapem, I stayed either in Akropong or in neighboring Abiriw, the two towns where I was most well known. Jonas Kwesi Yeboa-Dankwa, a folklorist and linguist from Abiriw, took me to his hometown during the summer of 1997. He introduced me to teachers in several schools, and through him, I was able to gain permission to enter their classrooms before pursuing more top-level approval from the district education office. On my return, in 1998, I stayed with two different households in Akropong. My first family was composed of a queen mother, an important person in the chiefly apparatus of Akropong; her husband, a former principal of Presbyterian Training College; and their many children, aged ten to twenty-four, four of whom were teachers or teachers-in-training. The queen mother had an active social life, attending and organizing festivals, funerals, and functions. As a queen mother, she could not leave the house alone. Consequently, one or more of her children would accompany her when she went out, and I was often invited to tag along as part of the entourage. My second family was run by another woman with a powerful personality, the headteacher of a primary school, who lived with her adult son and several other young adult dependents, among them a student at Odesuafo Junior Secondary School and a student at Gyahene Secondary School. The school she ran was one of the two primary schools I came to know best, having spent time there observing a classroom in 1999 and rehearsals for school cultural competitions in 2002. During a two-month stay in May–June 2002, I lived in a hostel run by a theological institute affiliated with the teacher training college in Akropong.

One of my priorities was to observe the teaching of culture in school classrooms. Because culture had a place on the national syllabi of primary schools (equivalent to grades 1–6) and junior secondary schools (grades 7–9), I visited each of the thirteen primary and junior secondary schools in the Abiriw/Akropong circuit, spending a day at each school. During each visit I observed at least two classes, primarily in Ghanaian languages, and less frequently in religious and moral education, music and dance, and vocational skills, and talked to principals and teachers about their school, the educational reform, and the teaching of culture. Unfortunately, despite my attempts to dissuade them from doing so, many of the schools put on a show or lesson for me, and I could never be sure that the teachers were teaching something that they would not otherwise teach.

Because of this experience, I decided to spend at least a week at two primary schools and one junior secondary school where I had strong personal contacts to see what place cultural studies had within the routine schedule (see table 1). After this week of observation, I maintained contact with the schools, dropping by to see the teachers, to drop off presents or copies of photos, or just to say hello. On the streets of Akropong or in church, I would meet teachers from these schools, and we maintained friendly, cordial contact. I also observed a Ghanaian languages class at each level of the three-year teacher training college and at the two secondary schools. In order to learn about the history of cultural programming in Ghana, I also frequented the archives in Accra and Koforidua and interviewed seventeen elderly and middle-aged teachers in Akuapem, including some at the schools I visited and observed, about their personal experiences of school and culture.

The activities surrounding the cultural competitions, which in 1998–99 involved secondary school students (grades 9–12), proved to be an invaluable source of information. I attended the workshop Mr. Devoh, the district cultural officer, gave for school representatives and followed him on his visits to the schools to give further instruction about the competition, occasionally getting a lift on his motorcycle. My friends in the primary schools introduced me to teachers in the secondary schools, and for the three weeks before the district competition, I attended as many rehearsals as possible at the three schools I had chosen to focus on—two boarding schools and one day school (table 1). I videotaped the one-day district competition in Akropong, the three-day regional competition in Koforidua, and the three-day national cultural competition in Cape Coast, and interviewed teachers, students, and judges involved in each, sometimes during the competition and at other times making arrangements to

Table 1   Schools featured in the text

School	Total students	Classes observed			Cultural competition rehearsals[a]	
		Year/type	Period	Number of students	Genre	Sessions
Primary						
Kenkan	216	Year 5	2 weeks	36 (16 boys, 20 girls)	Choir; poetry recital	1
Nhoma	432	Year 5	1 week	37 (10 boys, 27 girls)	Choir; dance-drama; drum language	4
Obikyere	289	Years 1–6	6 classes	34–52 students in each class (almost equal number of boys and girls)	Choir; drum language; poetry recital; dance-drama	3
Junior secondary						
Osuafo	196	Year 8	1 week	33 (20 boys, 13 girls)		
Adesua (Larteh)					Poetry recital; drum language; dance-drama	1
Secondary						
Abe (boarding)	ca. 1,000	Akan language classes, years 9–12; art class, year 12 (form 3)	5 classes	6–25 students in each class (almost equal number of boys and girls)	Choir; dance-drama; drum language	13
Gyahene (boarding)	ca. 900	Akan language classes, years 9–12	3 classes	23–41 students in each class (mainly girls)	Choir; dance-drama; drum language	5
Horeb	ca. 250				Poetry; dance-drama; drum language	2

Note: All school names are pseudonyms.

[a] Rehearsal sessions lasted between two and four hours. I attended two-thirds of each secondary school's rehearsals, but only a third of those for each primary and junior secondary school.

visit them later. After the district competition I invited performers from each of the three schools I had followed to participate in focus group discussions. Taking the advice of one of my "sisters" in the queen mother's household who was concerned that the girls would not speak in the boys' presence, I formed separate groups for the boys and girls. The number of students in each group ranged from seven to seventeen; the average size was eleven. The focus groups worked well because the presence of so many students stimulated conversations among them about topics I had not even considered, despite watching the rehearsals. At the regional competition I made contact with teachers from other schools in the Eastern Region. As a result, I was able to visit another secondary school later, Begoro Secondary School, where I gave the staff a copy of my videotape of the competition, edited according to their request, and talked with a mixed group of thirty boys and girls in the presence of the teacher. Even though these students were clearly hesitant to speak freely to a perfect stranger (a foreign one at that) and in front of a teacher, the meeting was useful; it demonstrated how common the feelings expressed in the focus group discussions in Akuapem were.

Only later, in 2002, was I able to observe younger students rehearsing for school cultural competitions. I initially intended to concentrate on the two primary schools and one junior secondary school where I had done classroom observations. As it turned out, the junior secondary school did not plan to participate that year. But at the other schools, though the students I knew had graduated, and there had been some turnover among teachers, those who knew me from before welcomed me. Fortunately for me, another primary school across the street from my hostel was also busy rehearsing, and after introducing myself to the headmaster, I was able to wander over to the grounds whenever I heard the sound of drumming and singing. Some schools in the area were able to hire a skilled dancer from the district Center for National Culture to help train their students, and he invited me to accompany him for a rehearsal in a junior secondary school in Larteh (table 1). I videotaped circuit competitions in three towns along the ridge—in Larteh, Akropong, and Adukrom—and talked with judges, teachers, and students during these events. I did not conduct any group discussions with primary school students because I felt that they were too young to provide useful information, but several girls aged eight through eleven from one of the primary schools I had observed befriended me, and we engaged in many informal discussions about the progress and meaning of the rehearsals as I stopped to watch them play in the street or when they came by to visit me at the hostel. I followed my informants' lead in the language of our conversations and interviews: some of my interviews were in English and others were in Twi with English words sprinkled in, particularly in my conversations with secondary-school students. The names of students, schools, and most of the teachers given in the text are pseudonyms; teachers who wished to have their names attached to their statements are listed in the interview section of the references.

My research took me up and down the Akuapem ridge; to Accra and Koforidua, to consult the national and regional archives and interview educational and cultural officials; and to Cape Coast, for the national cultural competition. Because I was constantly moving between levels—from school to school, between different sets of schools and towns, between schools and education offices, from district to regional and then national competitions with different officials and schools involved at each level—I was always meeting new people, making the task of explaining myself and gaining trust a constant issue. The benefit of all my movement was that I was gaining exposure to the big picture in which the teaching of culture unfolded, with a sense of the different layers of this intervention.

Despite my running to and fro, my approach was certainly ethnographic, to the extent that participant observation was my primary research strategy. I focused on understanding the lived experiences of people in Akuapem and their feelings about government cultural programming. My view was holistic in the sense that I sought to understand the connections of state interventions with events and relationships that might initially seem to be quite far from the topic at hand. The growing strength of charismatic Christianity and the history of the Basel Mission were some of the issues that people in Akropong felt were central in their lives and important to understanding their town. This process of understanding how people see their own world requires making relationships over time. Although I engaged in formal research activities, such as interviews, focus group discussions, and classroom observations, my richest insights came from unexpected informal conversations. Visiting schools and attending church services and festivals became less and less an exercise in seeing what was going on in those places than in maintaining contact with people who might find me worthy of the information I sought. More and more, I simply shared whatever I was thinking about with people I encountered, and depending on the degree of closeness, they would respond with their personal stories and opinions about the cultural programming in schools. This approach was particularly fruitful during my 2002 trip, when visiting and catching up with friends provided confirmation for conclusions I had developed in the interval and prompted new insights.

One thing that worked in my favor in making these friends, mainly teachers and students, was my status as an *oburoni*, a term Ghanaians give to all foreigners who are of lighter skin color than they and to Americans of every shade, including African-Americans. It is a term deeply inflected by the colonial encounter and contemporary global inequalities. Being an *oburoni* meant that I was not a low-status young woman, and it offset my lack of the family and school connections that smooth so much social interaction in Ghana.

Much of what I had to learn in Ghana was about *how* to learn: how to ask, how to be present, and how to respond appropriately (Briggs 1986).[3] The process of fieldwork made me focus on some issues more than I initially expected—such as the local construction of knowledge and theories of learning—issues that I came to see as critically important in the teaching of Ghanaian culture in the schools. Everyday practices and conversations in Akuapem became my object of study not from neutral interest, but because they could serve as models for my own behavior. Akuapem people taught me to grapple with the issues that were central to their lives: with knowledge and power, the invisible and the unspoken. The rest of this book deals with the meaning made out of that process. The national culture project in its quest for dominance is translated and transformed, multifaceted and fragmentary, and my understanding of it is similarly so, built on a web of conversations over cooking, on the way back from church, or during recess on the veranda of a school.

Looking Ahead: The Structure of the Book

Part 1 of the book explores three questions: How did the state come to be involved in the promotion of culture? What kind of culture was it promoting and why? Why did much of the state's cultural programming become located in schools? Drawing on archival sources and interviews with teachers aged forty to ninety, I answer these questions historically.

Chapter 1 focuses on missionary understandings of culture. The Basel Mission, established in Akropong in 1835, had a contradictory relationship to local cultural traditions. On the one hand, missionaries brought with them romantic-nationalist ideas that linked language to the nation and provided opportunities for African Christians to document their own customs and history. On the other hand, their introduction of European ideas about labor and learning effectively separated schoolchildren and slaves from their families and communities, as they were brought under the patronage of the Basel Mission. Schooling was the primary route by which Akuapem people became Christian. African Christians used their literacy and experience of travel within the Gold Coast to create a national identity and to document traditions that they felt were compatible with Christianity. Through these efforts, they generated a sense of the nation long before the Gold Coast won administrative independence from Great Britain. Christianity in Africa thus helped constitute culture as an object of discourse and created a kind of educated person who could appreciate—but was less willing to participate in—particular activities that represented the African past, a mode of relating to culture that resonates for educated people to this day.

Schools in principle ceased to be Christian institutions in the early twentieth century as they were gradually absorbed into the administrative apparatus of an increasingly powerful British colonial state. But despite this heightened control, because of the affiliations of teachers and students, schools continued to be Christian institutions in practice. Chapter 2 reflects these developments, with special emphasis on the promotion of cultural traditions in schools, exploring the construction of the meaning of culture from British colonialism in the 1920s to educational reforms pursued in the 1980s. How did culture come to mean performance traditions—"drumming and dancing"—and what did that meaning of culture accomplish? Furthermore, how did schools come to be a primary site where that definition was produced? Through the complex interaction of teachers, students, and state arts organizations, in which the dreams of some educated individuals and the state concatenated, the state gradually became aware of the potential of schools to realize its cultural agenda. This chapter details how the colonial and postcolonial state became involved in the production of national culture through schools.

Part 2 uses my ethnographic research from 1997, 1998–99, and 2002 to explore how, despite its best efforts, the state has failed to attain its goal of creating and propagating a particular notion of culture that would solidify its authority. Why, in the spaces that it constructs, are different practices and meanings of culture being generated? Chapter 3 is the first of two chapters examining the disparate discourses that operate in Ghanaian schools and that result in different meanings being produced in schools than what the government intends. Chapter 3 analyzes three government discourses—culture for development, culture as the way of life of a people, and culture as drumming and dancing—that legitimize the state's use of culture, and two popular ones—culture as inherited from the ancestors and culture as the customs of traditional kingdoms—that highlight the power of alternative political authorities, particularly the power of chiefs and elders. Ghanaians seek to answer the question: to whom does culture belong? Their answers help shape how culture is actually represented in classrooms and competitions.

Chapter 4 examines, in particular, Christian discourses about culture, the most powerful counterweight to national discourses of culture in Akuapem. Charismatic Christianity demonizes what is marked as traditional culture, and thus its adherents find the government's cultural programming deeply problematic. Christian teachers and students are torn by the tensions between their religious beliefs and the state's mandated cultural activities. Some seek to resolve the problem of participation by aligning the goals of Christianity and national development to produce "development morality plays," dance-dramas of the type we saw earlier that focus on teenage pregnancy and drug abuse, which are construed as at once national problems and sinful activities that make one vulnerable to demonic influence.

While these two chapters focus on explicit ideological conflicts that emerge from the teaching of culture, the next two chapters focus on more subtle negotiations about the relationship between knowledge and power to examine the pedagogical contradictions of cultural programming in schools. Conceptually, the modern project of knowledge-transmission in schools involves a general, common, and basic training of all citizens of the nation, particularly of children and adolescents, for their future productivity. This notion of the school, however, goes against the more selective local transmission of cultural knowledge, which people learn only *after* they have gained a ritual-political position, usually after middle age. As states, through schools, appropriate traditional knowledge, they partially transform the meaning, location of expertise, and process of learning cultural knowledge. This chapter explores the strategies by which teachers convert cultural knowledge into school knowledge — or try to. Some are unable to do so because the school teaching of culture goes against local proscriptions against the sharing of cultural information with a general public. Because many teachers do not have expertise in cultural traditions, local elders and chiefs are ironically re-legitimated as the keepers of the most respected cultural knowledge.

Whereas chapter 5 focuses on teacher strategies during classroom lessons, chapter 6 examines students' strategies for learning during rehearsals for the cultural competitions. Scholars have increasingly discussed the disenfranchisement of young people in Africa. As a state-generated activity, the cultural competition gives us a lens for examining two questions. How does the state model young people's participation in the political process? And how are young people shaping their own participation in the nation?

As a mirror for the operations of the state, cultural competitions model a competitive, clientelist form of participation. Students, on the other hand, particularly those from the least prestigious of the three secondary schools I studied, sought to create collaborative, open contexts for participation, drawing on local means of learning performing arts. Through the cultural competitions, students had greater authority than they usually had, either in or out of school, but they experienced such authority as disempowerment because it signaled their exclusion from resources and opportunities the state provided.

I conclude that the state has been unable to use schools to teach cultural knowledge for the ends of national unity and legitimacy for two reasons. First, the Christian identities of students and teachers make the teaching of culture problematic because they commonly associate it with the demonic. And second, local notions of the relationship between age and cultural authority work to reinscribe the expertise of elders, rather than teachers and young people. The case of Ghana raises ramifications about the teaching of cultural traditions in schools elsewhere in the world, such as through multicultural education in the United States, a subject that I explore in the conclusion.

«   »

With the next chapter, I turn to the long history behind the state's appropriation of local traditions and the ideas that undergird and legitimate that effort. The deep historical sedimentation of discourses making culture central to the national polity makes one appreciate more fully the contemporary fractiousness about culture in Ghana: how can one raise questions about culture in the face of discussions that emphasize its importance to the nation for at least a century and a half? And yet Ghanaians do just that, drawing on this wealth of discourse to create different conceptions of what culture means for them. The nation is indeed a work in progress (Askew 2002). Let us turn now to the masons who worked on its foundations, African Christians.

How Culture
Became the Property
of the State

WHY DID the government of Ghana become involved in the promotion of culture? Asking that question leads us to odd places in the history of cultural nationalism in Ghana, such as to a classroom in Christianborg Middle School in Accra in 1876, run by the Basel Mission. In a school essay on the festival of Homɔwɔ celebrated in Accra, one student, G. Medegbo, began with an etymology: "This festival received its name from the Gã language: *hõmɔ* means hungry, and *yi wuɔmɔ—wuɔ yi* means to rejoice over; and thus the word *hõmɔwuɔ* means: the day of shouting joy over hungry."

"Every Nation Has Its Own Gifts"

Christianity, Schooling, and the Construction of Tradition

Theodore Flindt, another student, also connected Homɔwɔ to the Gã people: "This Homɔwɔ is use[d] on Gã Land. They used it as a new year or as Christmas." However, a student named Quartey thought it was celebrated throughout the Gold Coast colony: "This feast begins from the end of Aug. till Sept. 14th or 21rst. And this festival entertainment is done throw [through] the whole Gold Coast" (Basel Mission Archives, D-10.4, 7). In other essays written in 1875 or 1876, students described the "Gods and Fetishes of the Accra Natives" and narrated different "African Folk Tales" or Ananse stories (Basel Mission Archives, D-10.4, 6–8). Although Christianity has been implicated in the suppression of cultural traditions in Africa, these essays written in a Basel Mission school in the Gold Coast hint at a more complex tale, in which missionaries and their African students found African culture, like the festival of Homɔwɔ, a suitable object of discourse.

In southern Ghana, towns tended to convert to the religion of the missionary group that arrived first, so Cape Coast and Kumase, for example, are associated with Wesleyan Methodism, and Brong-Ahafo with Catholicism. Each mission had a slightly different attitude to the local languages and customs it encountered. This chapter confines itself to the Basel Mission because of its importance in Akuapem as the first on the ground in the area. But Presbyterianism is the default religion there because the mission was replaced by the United Free Church of Scotland during World War I. Akuapem also has Roman Catholic and Methodist congregations; they are mainly made up of migrants from other areas of Ghana. Newest of all are the charismatic churches, which are becoming more and more popular and changing the way God is worshiped even in the Presbyterian congregations (chapter 3).

The Basel missionaries to the Gold Coast brought with them a romantic-nationalist conception of Africans as analogous to "the folk" of Europe. In the nineteenth century, European scholars and writers romanticized the folk as the embodiment of a national heritage with which the elite had lost touch, spurring the study of linguistics and folklore. Likewise, the Basel missionaries considered each African ethnicity to have a national spirit, most visibly revealed in language. Similar to the way romantic nationalism played out in Europe, the Basel missionaries saw the recuperation of the past and vernacular language as necessary to pave the way for Christianity and nationhood.

This project of cultural documentation and reification was predicated, however, on getting people to abandon their customary ways of life. As part of their romantic vision, the Basel missionaries wanted to recreate European village life in the hilly, rural area of Akuapem. Their vision of village life led them to condemn African customs as immoral and fraudulent, and they required new converts to break with their communities and families. The separation of African converts from their lifeworld was accomplished through the creation of a distinct community for Christians and through schools, in which children became the charges of the mission. In their essays students stressed their personal lack of knowledge even as they described the rituals and stories associated with the gods of Accra: "I myself have not seen it [a particular ritual] but it was relate[d] to me by some body," wrote Samuel Patrick; and Christian Emmanuel Briand wrote, "I can not related [sic] the history about them all; because I don't know" (Basel Mission Archives, D-10.4, 6). As Thomas Turino (2000) points out in the case of Zimbabwe a century later, "the people who became most acutely aware of their own distance from indigenous lifeways" but appreciated it nonetheless "were missionized Africans and especially members of the middle class" (34).

Once African cultural practices were rendered distant and abstract, some African Christians began rehabilitating those practices that they deemed worthwhile and compatible with Christianity as they sought to create an African nation. Although these African Christians had different

criteria and chose different practices for recuperation, the notion that traditional folkways could be selectively evaluated, with customs distinct and
disconnected from one another, was very much a product of the missionary endeavor in the Gold Coast, and part of colonial practice more generally in Africa (Askew 2002). The missionary project and its interpretation
by African Christians thus generated a particular kind of "modern person,"
one who was separated from traditional lifeways but engaged in studying,
documenting, and evaluating those practices.

But what was the relationship between the linguistic and ethnographic
documentation of African Christians and the policies of the postcolonial
state? Scholars have struggled to define the relationship between church
and state in Africa. Anti-colonial thinkers consider the missionaries the
handmaidens of the colonial state. Like missionaries elsewhere in Africa,
the Basel missionaries in the Gold Coast laid the groundwork for
identifications based on language and ethnicity, which Johannes Fabian
(1983) argues were necessary for administrative purposes. Missionary work
required the protection and support of colonial powers. Particularly in the
areas of education and other social services, missionaries built and managed the infrastructure and personnel that became incorporated into the
emerging colonial state, particularly after World War I. Thus, in many ways
the colonial state inherited structures that the missionaries had set up, although this transfer of authority was hotly contested. At the same time,
scholars have become more sensitive to the tensions and contradictions
within the imperial mission (Stoler and Cooper 1997). For instance, missionaries, settlers, and colonial officials in South Africa held far different
models of colonialism, which resulted in conflicts between them (John
Comaroff 1997). Likewise, the Basel missionaries, as citizens of Germany,
Switzerland, and Denmark, found themselves in tension with first Danish
and then British colonial officials. They promoted the teaching of Twi and
Gã languages over English, and fostered a form of cultural nationalism that
at times articulated with an urban, elite nationalism whose target was the
British colonial government. The missionary endeavor created a sense of
the nation based on language and ethnicity long before the reins of governance were actually handed over to anti-colonial nationalists (Chatterjee
1999). At the same time, the missionary project generated a notion
of modernity based on a rejection of the lifeworld of tradition, a notion
that has most recently been in conflict with the state's project of cultural
nationalism.

People in Akuapem were continually pushing me to examine the history of the Basel Mission, something that I initially felt was peripheral to

my project. Many were proud of the long history of Christianity in the area and felt that the establishment of the mission—along with the seminary and teacher training college it founded—made Akuapem distinctive and worthy of recognition. The Basel Mission may also have come up in our conversations frequently because they saw me as having a similar social position to a Basel missionary, as an outsider with whom to forge new linkages with people and resources. In any case, as the various discourses about culture swirled around me, I found that I could not understand the strong emotions and the stances Akuapem people took toward culture—in the different ways that they selectively defined it—without knowing this part of their history.

"An African Folk-Spirit": Romantic Nationalism and the Basel Mission

Anxieties about national unity and prominence have often sparked interest in folk cultural traditions, although this interest has had different forms in different historical periods. Romantic-nationalists in early-nineteenth-century Europe concentrated on the link between the nation, vernacular language, and folk traditions, and argued that the nation's welfare was bound up in its respect for its oral traditions and myths (Alver 1989; Falnes 1933; Wilson 1976). Considered closer to nature, more attuned to their emotions and instincts, and embodying the past, peasants were romanticized as keepers of national values, and their cultural traditions were collected as artifacts of their nation's past glory (Abrahams 1993). Within an evolutionary framework, the folk embodied the childhood of the nation or race; their customs contained survivals from the nation's heroic past, from which, romantic-nationalists declared, the nation had declined into artificiality and spiritual decay in its old age. Collectors and scholars inspired by romantic nationalism felt that the revival of the nation was intimately related to the revival of the past in the form of folk traditions and language, but also felt the need to codify, synthesize, and sanitize these vernacular, peasant traditions for bourgeois consumption (Zipes 1987). Johann Gottfried von Herder (1744–1803), whose theoretical work inspired many historians and folklorists in the nineteenth century, felt that culture and language were a product of a generative mystical folk-character or folk-spirit; the nation was thus considered to be a spiritual unity, and nationalism akin to a religious feeling (Cocchiara 1981; Hayes 1927). Some romantics even felt that the nation was part of a divine plan, in which each people had a distinctive task to accomplish on earth (Simon 1960). For many romantic-nationalists the enthusiasm for mythology and paganism coexisted with Christian belief. The Danish mythologist N. F. S. Grundtvig, who inspired the folk high school movement in Scandinavia, saw a strongly developed national spirit as a necessary condition to receiving the word of God, using the Jewish people as an exemplar (Simon 1960).

Scholars have argued that these romantic-nationalist ideologies about tradition expressed tensions arising from class stratification and increasing industrialization in nineteenth-century Europe (Abrahams 1993; Mosse 1964). Rural peasants were romanticized as the true inheritors of the national past, not the urban, middle-class bourgeoisie with their "foreign" languages and alien lifeways. Yet it was the bourgeoisie themselves who made the critique, at a time when they were being squeezed by the Industrial Revolution. They desired a spiritual revolution that would revitalize the nation and their position without revolutionizing its structure; they romanticized nature in order to provide an alternative to an industrial modernity.

These ideas about the relationship between the folk and the nation in Europe influenced the civilizing missions of Christianity and colonialism in Africa, just as explorations of the New World and descriptions of "savages" had inspired the romanticism of Rousseau and others in the eighteenth century (Cocchiara 1981). As studies of imperialism and metropolitan class relations have shown, peasants at home were analogous to primitives abroad, and missionaries adapted the institutions and strategies they used among lower-class people at home for use in the colonies, and vice-versa (Beidelman 1981; Comaroff and Comaroff 1991; Stoler and Cooper 1997; Thorne 1997). Thus, in the early twentieth century, a time when New Romanticism inspired festivals recreating folk rituals, dances, and music in Germany (Mosse 1964), German Protestant missionaries were also organizing folk festivals in Tanzania in an attempt to wed Christianity to the folk-spirit of the African *Volk* (Fiedler 1996).

After the Napoleonic wars, in 1815, the Basel Evangelical Mission Society founded a seminary in Basel, Switzerland, to prepare men for service with existing Protestant missionary societies all over the world. The first graduates were deployed not only to the Gold Coast, but also to Cameroon, India, southern Russia, and North America. The Basel Mission grew out of the Pietist revival, especially Württemberg Pietism, a rural religious movement begun in the 1670s. The Pietism that characterized the Basel Mission combined religious emotion and deep thought. The aim was personal devotion to and relationship with Christ, in which individuals had a responsibility for saving souls and spreading the Kingdom of God on Earth. For Pietists the Bible was the sole source of divine truth. Thus, much

Basel missionary effort in the Gold Coast focused on teaching literacy so that the newly converted could read the Scriptures.

Pietism was popular among those whose economic and social position was threatened by industrialism and urbanization, especially during the nineteenth century. Pietists saw peasant villages as a necessary condition in the practice of Christian faith, and they established model Christian villages, made up of farmers and craftsmen, in Europe. Others migrated and set up new farming communities in Russia and America (Dah 1983).

Akuapem, 1835–1917: The Creation of an African Christian Community

Basel missionaries came to the Gold Coast in 1828 at the invitation of the Danish governor Richelieu. They came mainly from rural Switzerland and southern Germany and were villagers who combined farming with practical trades such as carpentry, house-building, shoemaking, blacksmithing, pottery, and hat-making (Agyemang 1978; P. Jenkins 1980). Motivated by a desire to atone for the destruction wrought by European countries through the slave trade, missionaries concentrated on training Africans in productive and practical skills, as well as on promoting trade. In the Gold Coast they established the Basel Mission Trading Factory, which was involved in the export of palm oil and other goods and helped fund their missionary activity. They also set up an artisan workshop in Christianborg, Accra, to train joiners, carpenters, blacksmiths, and masons; these craftsmen became much in demand throughout West Africa (Smith 1966).

But illness and death decimated these early arrivals. Andreas Riis, a Dane from Sleswig who arrived in the Gold Coast four years later, in 1832, was instrumental in moving the mission to the healthier climate of the ridge of Akuapem, a move that improved the missionaries' life expectancy.[1] Riis had heard of Akuapem through the best-selling publication of a German doctor named Isert, who had been in the service of a Danish trading company. A disciple of Rousseau, Isert had visited Akuapem in 1786 and ran a plantation there for a few short years before his death, in 1790 (Smith 1966, 26–31). Suspicious of urban life and Western influences, driven by Rousseau and romantic notions, Riis went to Akuapem in search of rural, village people "unspoiled" by contact with Europeans.

When Riis and his party arrived in Akropong, the capital of Akuapem, in 1835, they found the traditional state of Akuapem disrupted by political struggles. During the 1830s, faced with internal disputes over chiefly political succession, many of the inhabitants of the capital fled to their farms in the valleys and neighboring towns (Johnson 1972). Historians generally attribute Riis's lack of success in gaining a single convert during his first ten years to these political disturbances (Kwamena-Poh 1980, 1973). Akuapem's internal disputes were prolonged and fueled by competition among the Danish and British colonizers for influence over and control of Akuapem, a rivalry that ended when the Danes left the Gold Coast in 1850. Although the British had increasing influence thereafter, the presence of the British colonial government was not fully felt in Akuapem until the end of the nineteenth century (Kwamena-Poh 1972).

With the settlement of a group of West Indians in Akropong and Aburi in 1843 and a modicum of political stability in Akuapem after 1845, the Basel Mission slowly grew. Twenty-four West Indians, including six couples and their children, had been recruited from Moravian congregations, mainly in Jamaica, to serve as exemplars of black Christian life for the local Akuapem people. There were many tensions between the Basel missionaries and the West Indians over their contract, which committed the missionaries to take care of the West Indians for five years while they worked for the mission, and to pay for their transport back home, provided that they were in good standing with the church. Some left at the end of the term; others stayed, married, and continued to work, some in prominent positions, for the mission. The West Indians brought new seeds and plants to the Gold Coast: coffee, cocoa, tobacco, cocoyam, mango, avocado, and breadfruit (Oku-Ampofo 1981; Smith 1966). A primary school was set up for the West Indian children, and several in the first generation of West Indians served as teachers there. Present-day Akropong people attribute the conversion of their ancestors to the mere presence of the black West Indians. But their direct influence in this regard seems to have been limited.[2] The West Indians tended to feel superior to the Africans, even though two of them discovered that their mothers had been from Akuapem before being taken to the West Indies as slaves (Oku-Ampofo 1981). It was through the school set up for the West Indian children that the missionaries gained their first converts, all of whom consisted of their servant-students.

In order to populate their schools, the missionaries had to compete with others who had rights over children as their own sons and daughters, foster children, pawns, or slaves. Riis reported in 1847, "Girls we cannot get yet, since they are used as slaves, and people do not wish to miss their work" (*Missions Magazin* 92, Ghana Natl. Archives, EC 6/3). Missionaries had difficulty determining the differences between a non-Akuapem—mainly Ewe—slave and a slave incorporated into an Akuapem family, and between a slave and a debt-pawn, a relative of the debtor who served the lender's family until the debt was repaid (Haenger 2000). Furthermore, because slavery signaled a relation of dependency, the term *akoa*, generally translated simply as "slave," not only referred to male slaves, servants, and subjects, but was in fact a generic term for men because almost everyone was in a state of dependency relative to someone else (Reverend S. K. Aboa, pers. comm., 10 Feb. 2000; see also Rattray 1929, 35). A variety of people thus had rights to children's labor, with the result that students were constantly pulled out of the mission school unexpectedly. In August 1847 the missionary Widmann reported from Akropong that they lost one schoolboy who had been pawned away; the missionaries paid the debt for another boy who was under a similar threat so that he was able to continue his schooling (*Jahresbericht* 1848, 132–42, Ghana Natl. Archives, EC 6/3).

Because of the ambiguity of children's status in the missionaries' eyes, they attempted to establish exclusive rights over their students. They became increasingly involved in the local labor market, buying slaves and redeeming the debts of pawns with a view to establishing rights over their students that Akuapem people would respect. In 1851 the Basel Society's general inspector, Joseph Josenhans, concerned about the problem of obtaining another cohort for the new seminary established in 1848, advised: "If children cannot be obtained in any other way, the freedom of slave children can be bought for a couple of thalers. One would, however, have to arrange by means of a contract witnessed by an authority that the children remain at the institution up to a certain age, and that neither parents nor relatives have the right to remove them any sooner. If in this way we were able to obtain a good number of native teachers [as these children might become], then we would not need to increase the quantity of European workers so much" (quoted in Haenger 2000, 19 n. 15).

Between 1859 and 1867, in missions across the Gold Coast, Basel missionaries bought the freedom of some 150 children and enrolled them in their schools (Debrunner 1967). During the cocoa boom from the 1890s to the 1920s, the pawning of children increased as Akuapem families searched for capital to purchase lands for growing cocoa. The lack of labor for cocoa and food farms also led to the buying of children, illegal by this time. As a result of the sudden removal of students from schools during the cocoa boom, the writer S. E. O. in Mamfe argued in the pages of the Basel Mission's newspaper, *Kristofo Sɛnkekafo* ("Christian Reporter" or "Christian Messenger") that parents should sign a paper saying that they gave control of their children to teachers (Feb. 1917, 12 [2]). Missionaries attempted to gain exclusive rights to the labor of children in order to prevent relatives from removing children from school to raise capital, serve as collateral for a debt, or work in the household.

In the process, missionaries redefined their relationship to their students, and schooling became equivalent to servitude to and labor for a patron. The students lived with the missionaries and were their servants. An early Akropong catechist and teacher, Theophilus Opoku, described what living with the missionaries felt like in his autobiography, printed in *Kristofo Senkekafo* as part of his obituary in 1916. Born in 1842, Opoku was from a powerful family. He was the son of the principal ɔkyeame, or speech mediator, for the ɔmanhene (paramount chief) in Akropong and the sixth and last child of the ɔmanhene's niece. Because the boy had trouble with his legs, his father allowed him to choose his own future, and he decided to go to school; he began school in 1850 or 1851. He stayed with the missionary J. A. Mader (Akropong, 1851–77), along with another boy, who later died during advanced studies in Basel. Opoku described himself as a disobedient servant: "Because I saw my father's house, his village, his wives and his children, his slaves and debt-pawns, his coming and his going, it made me proud, as a person of importance. One day when I did something wrong and my benefactor [the missionary Mader] punished me, I rose up speaking against him, saying, 'Am I your slave that you punish me like this? I will return to my father's house'" (*Kristofo Senkekafo*, May 1916, 11 [5]: 51).[3] Nevertheless, Opoku continued to stay with Mader, and he was baptized in 1856.

J. G. Auer, a schoolmaster from Württemberg who instituted many educational reforms when he was a missionary in the Gold Coast (1858–61), reported in disgust that "the Seminary was handy for the missionaries since it provided cheap servants" (quoted in Debrunner 1967, 149). The system of houseboys lasted a long time. In 1946 the class senior was the houseboy of the principal at Akropong Practice School (Reynolds interview, 24 Sept. 1998). For children who were pawns or slaves, schooling gave them the opportunity to experience a change of patrons; for royal children it made them feel like subordinates or slaves.

The missionaries not only separated children from their families but also separated adult Christians from their relatives by forming wholly new model villages or hamlets. One of the missionaries' first steps upon settling in a town was to ask the chief for land, where they built a separate neighborhood for Christians, usually known as Salem. This strategy made sense to the local people because strangers and migrants to towns generally settled in their own neighborhoods, such as the Muslim zongo. Neighborhoods were populated by different lineages and had their own leaders who served as their liaisons with the chief of the town. The Basel missionaries, however, separated themselves and their converts from the rest of the town for different reasons. As Noel Smith (1966) writes in his history of the Presbyterian Church in Ghana, "Life in the native town seemed to the missionaries to be the antithesis of ordered and disciplined Christian community living" (49). Furthermore, the missionaries, paternalistically, saw a separate neighborhood for Christians as a way to prevent the backsliding of converts. When a chief in another town criticized the Basel missionaries for creating separate communities, Reverend E. Nothwang replied, "Our Christians are still children to be nursed, so that they will not fall, therefore they dwell in separate quarters" (quoted in Debrunner 1967, 174). In Akropong converts generally did not enter the chief's palace; they wore European dress rather than cloth; and they did not marry non-Christians (Middleton 1983). Once living in their own community under the strict control of church elders, Christian Africans felt they did not have to obey traditional religious regulations, such as abstaining from work on days sacred to the spirits (see Addo-Fening 1980).

The missionaries' model of a European peasant village required that they rigorously denounce and oppose all African traditions that seemed antithetical to Christianity. They were especially hostile to traditional priests and considered their religion a sham that had to be exposed. One striking example is the aforementioned Mader, who in his "private feud against the 'fetish' priests" went so far as to flog one who opposed the preaching of the Gospel, and who (no doubt deliberately) scandalized the townspeople by having students from the seminary fetch black soil from the sacred grove in Akropong for the school farms (Smith 1966, 90–91). Many of the articles in *Kristofo Sɛnkekafo* (which the Basel Mission published in both Gã and Twi editions off and on between 1883 and 1917), documented the conversion of traditional religious priests or the destruction of their credibility and sacred objects.[4] These attacks were met with resistance from practitioners and priests of traditional religion.[5] When there was no rain for some time, the traditional priests would blame the missionaries and Christians for working on their farms on prohibited days and for building houses with stone and the wood of the Odum tree, both of which were prohibited in Akropong. The friction with the priests eventually soured the relationship between the missionaries and chiefs, which began under initially friendly terms; the two sides grew increasingly hostile toward each other as the missionaries realized that the chiefs were closely allied with the traditional priests and the chiefs recognized the missionaries' threat to their authority in the attacks on child pawnage and the traditional priests (Brokensha 1966; Haenger 2000).

Although the missionaries made the school the mode for separating children and Christian converts from the "heathen" town and its ways, parents and wards contested their claim for total authority over their children's lives. Schooling had a very different social meaning for local people and the missionaries. Where the missionaries conceived of schooling as the first step in a total conversion process, children and their relatives saw it as a way of attaining European power and of coming under the missionaries' patronage as mission workers. Despite the Basel missionaries' conservatism, respect for peasant life, and antipathy to industrialization, their promotion of cocoa growing and trade brought Akuapem into further contact with the West. They thus introduced the very changes associated with "modernity" into the Gold Coast that they were trying to avoid at home (B. Meyer 1999b). African Christians clearly saw a connection between literacy and access to the new markets. "There is little doubt that in the early encounters of African peoples with missionary Christianity, African converts believed that in responding to the Christian message they were accepting a total package — Christianity and European civilisation" (Bediako 1995, 35). Reverend Widmann reported in his diary in 1843 that the elders were happy about the missionaries preaching and opening a school; they requested that their children be taught the English language, for in that way, they thought, "the children would get European goods too" (quoted in Kwamena-Poh 1980, 52). The schoolchildren even came to expect the missionaries, as their new patrons, to provide them with presents and cloth on Christmas, and the chief of the town of Akropong, Krontihene Boafo, removed his son from school temporarily when no clothes were distributed (Dieterle letter, 17 Feb. 1848, Basel Mission Archives, D-12, 1). Schools, in the eyes of people of Akuapem, served as an entry point to Western knowledge and skills, goods, and employment in the post office or some other government agency.

The creation of a separate community of Christians and schoolchildren was therefore the result of the interaction between Akuapem social and labor relations and the missionaries' project to reproduce a European village in the hills of Akuapem. From the 1850s onward, catechists and teachers flowed out from the seminary, setting up mission stations and schools in other towns (Smith 1966). In the boarding school (also called Salem) that opened in 1863 in Akropong, the "best" students were prepared as catechists, teachers, and ministers, and the rest were trained to be artisans. Thanks to this school, many blacksmiths, shoemakers, carpenters, and tailors were practicing their trade in Akropong by the late nineteenth century. The Basel Mission also maintained an artisan training workshop in Christianborg whose graduates set up workshops in Akuapem and traveled all over West Africa.

By the 1880s Akuapem was densely occupied with farming villages, many involved in the production of palm oil (Johnson 1972). By the 1890s cocoa, which had to be grown in virgin forest, was leading Akuapem farmers to establish themselves farther and farther away. The lucrative production of cocoa was financed by palm oil, rubber, and the earnings of migrant craftsmen and clerks (Hill 1972, 1963). In the first decade of the twentieth century, towns in Akuapem were deserted as nearly everyone became involved in growing, buying, and transporting cocoa. Missionaries and pastors complained that cocoa wealth was leading to immorality and frivolous spending, but the cocoa farmers also used their profits to build churches and houses in their hometowns in Akuapem (Kwamena-Poh 1980). Akuapem African Christians were thus quite mobile from the 1880s onward. As teachers, pastors, and artisans, they often worked in strange towns, where they had to gain acceptance from local people. As cocoa farmers, they were moving in companies into lands farther to the west. By 1911 Theophilus Opoku, writing in the pages of *Kristofo Senkekafo* about the cocoa boom, could say: "Akuapem people are not Asante, nor Asante Akyem, nor Kwawu nor Akyem, nor Fante. They are Akuapem, but they are also not Akuapem. They have become 'half' [*damusa*]. What does this mean? It means that they are from Akuapem, but they have also bought land all the way to Asante and all the other nations [*aman*] mentioned, building houses and pulling all their wives and children there. They are called Akuapem people, but if you look for them in Akuapem, you won't find them" (31 Mar. 1911, 6 [3]: 30–31).[6] Opoku here assumes a definition of peoples based on traditional kingdoms (*aman*, singular *ɔman*) like Asante, Akyem, and Akuapem. But through literacy and labor migration, Basel missionaries and African Christians began to construct a broader identification—the nation of Twi-speaking peoples—using the same word—*ɔman*.

Local Languages and History: The Basis of the Nation

Like their counterparts in southern Africa who were cultural brokers in organizing cultural symbols into a written language and history (Vail 1989), the Basel missionaries devoted much time to studying and documenting the local languages in the areas where they initially settled, Twi in Akuapem and Gã in Accra.[7] Extrapolating from the description of the day of Pentecost in the Bible, they felt that Africans should hear and read the words of God in their own language. Furthermore, they felt that language was "the noblest creation of an African folk-spirit" (Halldén 1968, 12). In 1853 Reverend J. G. Christaller was commissioned to study the Twi language; in 1859 he published the four Gospels and the Acts in Twi, and by 1868 he had translated the entire Bible. This was followed by a grammar in 1875, a collection of Twi proverbs in 1879, and a dictionary in 1881. Many of these studies were cowritten with two Akropong converts, Jonathan Bekoe Palmer and David Asante.[8] Asante also translated the catechism in 1872, *Events in World History* in 1874, *The Human Heart* (Onipa Koma) in 1875, and a number of storybooks for the schools. Reverends Opoku, Ofosu, and Koranteng also translated or composed many of the songs in the Twi hymnbook (Reynolds n.d.). Meanwhile, Reverend Johannes Zimmermann was engaged in similar activity for the Gã language of Accra.[9]

As was true of linguistic studies then being done in Europe and elsewhere in Africa, the study of Twi led to the documenting of local customs and history. Soon after his arrival in Akropong, Christaller asked African catechists to record the historical traditions of Akuapem in Twi (Jones 1998). With the help of Palmer, Asante, and others, Christaller collected source material in local history and notes on traditional religions.[10] Twi language readers used in Basel Mission schools, with very few changes from the first edition in 1891 to the later editions of 1922 and 1950, included world history, folktales, and Twi proverbs, along with Bible stories and hymns. Thus, having students in Christianborg Middle School in the 1870s write essays about festivals, Ananse stories, and traditional gods was not an unusual occurrence. J. H. Nketia (1962) is truly on the mark when he observes, in his book on African cultural education, that the "church has been the greatest advocate of the study of our languages" (31).

By promoting vernacular languages, Basel missionaries hoped to foster unified "nations" built around a common language and history. It was for this reason that the Basel Mission began publishing *Kristofo Sɛnkekafo*, with Christaller as its first editor (1883–88, 1893–95).[11] In 1893 he stated that his mission on the Gold Coast and the aim of the paper was "the formation of Christian nations out of the tribes of the Gold Coast" (quoted in Agyemang 1978, 27). In a letter to Reverend Carl Reindorf (undated but probably written in late 1893), Christaller articulated further his notion of the relationship between vernacular language and nationhood:

> The English language ought to be for the natives of the Gold Coast what Latin has been for the nations of middle Europe in the middle ages. But Latin has only been too long the exclusive language of the learned in Europe. Now the Germans, the English and others have their books in their own tongue. I do not believe that all the Tshi [Twi] tribes will ever exchange their vernacular for the English language; I doubt whether the Gã people will do so, and if they did, it would be

unnatural.[12] A nation's best home is its own language. . . . Every nation has its own gifts and abilities, and although the leading men in a nation ought to thoroughly understand the conditions of other nations, they cannot deprive their own people of their peculiar nature in order to make them members of an other nation that had a different growth and history. (Quoted in Bearth 1998, 98–99)

Like romantic-nationalists throughout northern Europe at this time, Christaller considered the "colonial" language, whether Latin or English, a language of the elite. The language that would develop and unify the nation would be the vernacular, because only it embodied the genius or "peculiar nature" of the nation; all others would be "unnatural." As in Europe, there was a class basis for this concern: the elite ("the leading men" or "the educated people") of the Gold Coast should look outward to other nations but not reject the national spirit of "their own people."

At the same time Christaller envisioned a written language that would unify educated elites from the different "nations" with their different languages: "The tribes of the Gold Coast may become united by one common book language which must at the same time be cultivated, developed and refined so that it can take its place as a means of communication among educated people of the Gold Coast" (quoted in Agyemang 1978, 35). Reverend Mohr in the 1890s urged the Basel Mission to promote the Twi language in the cause of "unity of the greater whole" (Kwamena-Poh 1980, 224). Thus, the missionaries taught and preached in Twi even in areas where other languages were spoken. A promotion of the vernacular quickly turned into the promotion of the particular languages with which the Basel missionaries were familiar: Akuapem Twi and Gã.

Because the missionaries linked "nation" so closely to language, their formulation led to the sense that the "nation" was a nation of one language, for example, the Twi-speaking peoples. The phrase "*Twifo ɔman*" (the Twi nation) frequently appeared in the pages of *Kristofo Sɛnkekafo* between 1909 and 1917. This was a new way of thinking about "the nation" because "*ɔman*" previously referred to a traditional state like Akuapem or Akyem. To refer to "*ɔman*" as encompassing all Twi-speaking people, including Akyems, Asantes, Kwawus, and Akuapems, former enemies as well as allies, was a new conception of the nation.[13] The Basel Mission newspaper and other publications helped create an imagined community of the nation by standardizing Twi and Gã and generating a feeling of a shared African Christian public (see Anderson 1991). This conception did not correspond to the boundaries of colonial administration of the Gold Coast, still less to local commitments to family, town, or traditional kingdom, but rather created an entirely new field of identification.

A similar process happened with the Basel missionaries' interest in history. The national history they promoted was different from local understandings of history, which focused on a people's migrations, a town's founding and development, and the lineages of local chiefs.[14] The transformation of local, oral histories into a Christian national history is shown by the work of Reverend Carl Reindorf, of Gã-Danish ancestry, who was trained as a pastor by the Basel missionaries. In his *A History of the Gold Coast and Ashanti* (1889), Reindorf wrote a history of the "nation" within the colonial boundaries of the Gold Coast Colony and Ashanti, drawing on both the oral accounts gathered in various local towns and written sources (Wirz 1998). The historian Emmanuel Akyeampong wrote that nationhood meant, for Reindorf, a civilized, Christian nation, and "national development was a divinely ordained and ordered progressive process" (cited in R. Jenkins 1998, 103–4). Reindorf's book was serialized between 1893 and 1895 in the Gã editions of *Kristofo Sɛnkekafo*. The rewriting of vernacular histories into a Christian national narrative is reminiscent of histories inspired by romantic nationalism in nineteenth-century Europe, in which a strong "pagan" past was a necessary foundation to a unified Christian nation, the latter serving as the ultimate realization of the former (Simon 1960).[15]

This "pagan" past and its traditions were sometimes seen as a gift from God, who had blessed each nationality with its own national spirit. For J. J. Adaye of Akropong, who went to Theological Seminary (1868–72) and later taught in the middle school (Salem) in Akropong (Hall 1965), only a respect for their language would unite the Twi people into an African nation. In 1913 he wrote: "My plea is that it is very much needed that we get Representatives or a Society in Akuapem, Akyem, Kwawu, Asante, Asuogya, and Asante-Akyem. These representatives are there for the progress of all Twi people (both traditional religious practitioners and Christians) whose goal is that with great effort and sincere love for the nation they bring to light their Inheritance that is a gift from the hands of Nana Nyankopɔn Tweaduapɔn [the Almighty God] himself whom it pleases that we are Africans" (*Kristofo Sɛnkekafo*, Jan. 1913, 8 [1]: 4).[16] Adaye argued that these representatives should bring together the chiefs of the Twi people for greater unity and strength, unify the writing of the different Twi dialects, pay greater attention to Sunday school, and honor Christaller and Riis with festivals for their language study. But he saw the historical and cultural documentation of the Twi people as critical in bringing the disparate groups together. "We need to get a complete Twi history of every group so that one can see all the different Twi customs complete from their homes to their family groups to chieftaincy and state matters: our forefathers' religion, their different beliefs, their character, their different occupations" (ibid.).[17]

From the linguistic and historical cultural material collected by missionaries and mission-educated Africans, African Christians formulated new ideologies in an intellectual bricolage (Vail 1989). Twi-speaking African Christians educated by the Basel Mission tended to identify with other Twi-speaking peoples and a Twi nation, but their projects to unify the Twi nation dovetailed with the nationalist movement spearheaded by Fante and Gã intellectuals in the cities of Accra and Cape Coast, who generated a nationalism centered on the administrative unit of the Gold Coast Colony. Almost four years later, Adaye wrote for *Kristofo Senkekafo* a description of a meeting held in Kumase on 11 November 1916 of the Gold Coast National Research Association, whose aim was to research the different customs of the Gold Coast and Asante people, including their activities, way of life, and ancient history (Feb. 1917, 12 [2]: 20–21). This was a local branch of the organization founded by the Fante nationalist Casely Hayford in Sekondi, which was also established in Accra (by J. C. de Graft Johnson) and Cape Coast (by W. E. G. Sekyi) in November 1915. For its inauguration in Kumase, the group paraded through the streets of the town, joined by many schoolchildren from the various religious and government schools. While it is unclear what happened to this Kumase branch, its formation shows that teachers and ministers in provincial towns contributed to the growing nationalism, a movement that tends to be ascribed primarily to elite groups in Cape Coast and Accra who were closely involved in the workings of the colonial government. Thus, there was common ground between a "national" project that focused on Twi language ("ethnicity"), the project of Basel Mission teachers and pastors, and a "national" project of the elite groups in Cape Coast and Accra that took as its boundaries the reach of British colonial rule: the Gold Coast and Ashanti colonies. A linguistic nationalism articulated with a political nationalism.

In the pages of *Kristofo Senkekafo*, African Christians discussed fervently the importance of Twi language and particularly a "pure Twi" (*Twi kurenyenn*). Theophilus Opoku argued that those who were civilized did not borrow another people's language, that is, English (*Kristofo Senkekafo*, Oct. 1912, 7 [10]: 111–12), and that the language of the previous generations was being adulterated and lost, to the detriment of the nation's welfare (*Kristofo Senkekafo*, May 1912, 7 [5]: 51–55). Under the auspices of language study, African pastors and teachers wrote several articles between 1909 and 1917 documenting the structure and names of the seven

Akan families or clans; a smaller set of articles that discussed the names of Akan months, histories of towns, and warfare between states; and descriptions of traditional religious festivities. Studies of Twi language thus led to studies of verbal arts, history, and social structure.

The African Christians who wrote in the pages of *Kristofo Senkekafo* also began to question whether all African customs should be discarded in the search for civilization and Christianity. John Ayuw, a leading cocoa farmer from Mampong, wrote an article titled, "Is It Good That Our Customs Are Completely Lost?"[18] He contrasted the past with the present: "In ancient times when we lived in the Asante nation [*ɔman*], the Akyem nation, the Akuapem nation, and the Fante nation, then we held onto our customs tightly and we didn't denigrate them."[19] Some of these customs were important to keep, he argued, for example the *asafo* companies, whose drumming in times of war signaled danger and the location of friends and enemies. And some of the foreign customs should be dropped: "Fathers, let us keep our customs that are good for us and let us remove those of the Europeans that aren't good for us. One of our ancestors' customs that they used when fighting and struggling against one another is the talking drum [*atumpan*] that as for us these days, pardon me for saying, we say civilization has come so we don't respect this important thing" (*Kristofo Senkekafo*, Jan. 1915, 10 [1]: 7–8).[20]

Ayuw urged his fellow Christians not to reject their ancestors' traditions outright in the name of "civilization," but to evaluate both traditional customs and those of Europe critically according to their worth. Christaller, in his opening editorial in *Kristofo Senkekafo* in 1893, had promoted the study of history so that the nation "could compare its former and its present state, to disapprove and reject bad observances, and to rejoice in real improvements, to learn from the past, and to progress towards what is better": in comparing the present to the past, African Christians would see how far they had progressed (cited in Agyemang n.d., 36). But Ayuw was not interested in comparing the present to the past in a way that denigrated the past, only in recuperating those customs that he thought were "good for us."[21] As Turino (2000) concludes about Zimbabwe cosmopolitans, the focus on the decline of African traditions was more likely due to the personal trajectories of these African Christians, who had less and less occasion to speak and hear "pure Twi" after their schooling, than to an actual phenomenon of language decline in need of revival by educated Christians.

One sign that the recuperation of ancestors' customs was making headway was a series of articles in *Kristofo Senkekafo* in the early decades of the twentieth century calling for the use of African names, even for people who were baptized. A perusal of the newspaper shows that this exhortation was founded in practice. It printed notices in which people announced they were changing their names: in 1910 a farmer from Larteh living in Dodowa named Robert Nicholas Johnson changed his last name to Amponsah; in 1914 one David Asante Wilson of Effiduase in Koforidua dropped the "Wilson" from his name; in 1915 a Gottfried Frans Awere changed his name to Ɔfɛi Awere, "my real native name" (*Kristofo Sɛnkekafo,* July 1915, 10 [7]: 84). These changes paralleled earlier developments inspired by Fante nationalists, beginning in the 1880s, who similarly advocated the use of Fante names and good Fante customs (Kimble 1963; Sekyi 1997). Articles in *Kristofo Sɛnkekafo* in the early twentieth century speak to the growing nationalism of local elites—cocoa farmers, teachers, pastors, and clerks who were educated by the Basel Mission and could read and write Twi. The nationalism of this local elite group worked to generate greater respect for the customs of Twi-speaking nations.

African traditions and nationalism were able to enter into African Christian discourse and research through the focus on language and history. African Christians argued that traditions should be selectively revived, although writers had different criteria for determining their worth. In documenting vernacular traditions, missionaries and African Christians created a discourse about cultural practices, in which they were systematized, objectified, and evaluated. This discourse could emerge because African Christians became disconnected from local cultural practices in the process of becoming Christians, a change that could then be constructed as the past within their personal life histories. African Christians' understanding of tradition as a bounded object, with practices disconnected from one another so that they could be selectively recuperated, underpinned an intellectual bricolage in which they brought together two domains that they considered conceptually distinct, Christianity and tradition.

Furthermore, local histories, customs, and languages expanded to represent "the nation," in which there was slippage between a language-based nation ("the Twi nation," *Twifo ɔman*) and British colonial boundaries (the Gold Coast) and two different kinds of nationalisms. This tension between levels—does the nation refer to a traditional kingdom, a language-based ethnicity, or the country of Ghana?—continues to reverberate in contemporary Ghana. A romantic-nationalist view in which language symbolizes the national spirit served to both support and undercut a more elite nationalism based on gaining access to the governance of the administrative unit of the colony, a tension that postcolonial governments of Ghana have attempted to manage in their favor (chapter 3).

African and Christian: The Case of Ephraim Amu

The search for what being African and Christian meant took many forms. One form was growing nationalism within the church. By the 1880s African pastors in the Basel Mission had increased in numbers and were agitating for greater control and positions of power within the church, but the missionaries continued to treat them in a paternalistic, somewhat despotic, way. In 1913 E. D. Martinson resigned in protest over the limits to how high he, as an African, could rise in the church. He started an Anglican church in Larteh, later becoming an Anglican bishop (Kwamena-Poh 1980). World War I greatly helped the Africans' cause. In 1918 German missionaries were deported from the Gold Coast, and their mission was gradually taken over by the Unified Free Church of Scotland over the next two years. In the interim many of the congregations were under the authority of African pastors and financially self-supporting, and with African pressure, the Scottish mission allowed the church self-governance. By 1950 it had reached complete independence as the Presbyterian Church of Ghana. Although the Basel missionaries returned in 1926, the Scottish missionaries retained control over the educational system, particularly the training college, concerned that German missionaries would find a way to teach German nationalism to their students.

Despite this growing African nationalism within the church from the 1920s onward, there were fewer discussions about adopting African traditions than there had been in the early years of the twentieth century. Perhaps the struggle to convince Europeans that an African could be head of the church meant that Africans felt they had to prove themselves to be more European than the missionaries themselves. A discourse of cultural nationalism framed within Christian terms, under Presbyterian auspices and within the Presbyterian Church, was no longer active.

Several elderly retired teachers were willing to recall their earliest experiences in mission schools in the 1930s and 1940s for me. They emphasized the close association of Presbyterian mission schools with both Christianity and strict discipline. F. A. Gyampo, a frail retired art teacher and artist, described his experience of primary school in Larteh in the 1930s. The school, which was managed by the Presbyterian Church, "was where we first started learning about God" (interview, 12 Sept. 1998). School continued to be the way that children became Christian, which implied separation from their surrounding communities, signaled by wearing European clothes and not engaging in manual labor.

All teachers were trained by the church, not the government, and this meant that every teacher in a Presbyterian school was also a catechist for the Presbyterian Church. During this time pastors supervised teachers (Phelps-Stokes Commission 1922, 135). Reverend Okae-Anti, a Presbyterian pastor and teacher born in Tutu in 1913, described forcefully the church's control of schoolteachers, down to matters of dress, in the 1930s:

> Everything that was African was surprising. One thing is that, in our time, if they had let school out, and you yourself [as a teacher], you had free time, they had let school out, and you wore cloth in the African way at all, and you walked by on the street, and if the pastor or the reverend minister saw you, he called you, saying, "Teacher! come. Oh! I saw you passing here wearing cloth. Why?" It was surprising then. As for you, you didn't have an evil thought in your head. There wasn't anything evil in it, but the elders [of the church] took it to mean that as for you, a teacher, if you did something like an African, it was surprising. (Interview, 27 Nov. 1998)[22]

Reverend Okae-Anti's term "surprising" is clearly a euphemism. His account shows that the church prohibited or at least discouraged practices seen as African. A similar story, told by Kwame Ampene, a retired teacher, shows little change ten years later. He started teaching in 1946 in his town of Anyinasu in the Central Region. "You know," he said, "I remember when I started teaching in my own town during my first year of teaching, and because I loved music, I was using this drums, and I was—my premises was at the Christian quarters [Salem], so they would not allow me to use my drums because they were against drumming in the Christian quarters." He continued, "In those days, Presbyterian discipline was very, very strict. The least you would do, then they will either demote you, suspend you or dismiss you, because you are not Christian, because you are not following the Christian principles and so on" (interview, 3 Mar. 1999).[23] Reverend S. K. Aboa remarked on the filial feeling teachers had toward the Presbyterian Church in the 1930s and 1940s, a relationship to which some responded positively and others saw as overly controlling (conversation, 9 Oct. 1998). Ghanaians told me that Presbyterians were stricter in this regard than other denominations and then usually mentioned the name of Ephraim Amu to prove their point.

Within this context of strict discipline of teachers and control of their expression of "Africanness," Ephraim Amu was a cause célèbre, because his promotion of African drumming and dress led to his dismissal from Akropong Presbyterian Training College, where he taught. Ephraim Amu's movement from a church institution to a government school also reveals the growing power of the colonial government in relation to the church.

Ephraim Amu (1899–1995) went to Bremen Mission schools as a child and came to teach at PTC in Akropong in 1925. Deeply interested in church music, which then consisted of organ and choral music with European hymns translated into Twi, he began to compose religious songs in the early 1920s (Agyemang 1988, 27). His interest in African music was sparked by a call by the Scottish missionary Reverend Ferguson, then the principal of PTC, for students to sing "Yaa Amponsa," a popular but bawdy highlife tune, during a school assembly in 1927.[24] The students refused to sing it for fear of being expelled from the training college.[25] In response Amu wrote a sanitized version of "Yaa Amponsa" and taught his students to sing it.

From this beginning, Amu began to do research on African music, with help from two sons of the paramount chief in Akropong, Asante Akuffo and Boafo Akuffo, both expert drummers.[26] Although Amu's father had been a traditional drummer and singer, he had never played with his father (Agyemang 1988, 1). He picked five PTC students from traditional drumming families to teach him the art, and they used to play and practice together; later other boys joined them. Reverend Okae-Anti attended PTC (1931–34) during Amu's time and had been part of the drumming and flute (atɛntɛbɛn) group he had started (interview, 23 Oct. 1998). One day the eighty-year-old Reverend Peter Hall, born in 1851 in Akropong to Jamaican parents, the first moderator of the independent Presbyterian Church of the Gold Coast, who had fought against traditional religion his whole life, was on a stroll on PTC's campus and heard the drumming (Hall 1965). Learning that the drummers were college students, he is reported to have said, "Oh may the good God take me from this sinful world!" (Agyemang 1988, 63).

Amu's interest in wearing cloth was sparked not by the writings and activities of African Christians in the Basel Mission twenty years earlier, but by the activities and ideas of the West African Students Union (WASU) in England, which influenced generations of nationalist politicians in the Gold Coast, from J. B. Danquah to Kwame Nkrumah. In a magazine Amu read about the union's memorial service for Dr. Kwegyir Aggrey, the great Ghanaian educator and cofounder of Achimota College, in London in 1927. A photo in the magazine showed the Nigerian secretary of WASU, who wore Yoruba dress as he sang a Yoruba funeral song for the occasion. Amu was also moved by a statement by Dr. J. B. Danquah in the same magazine that Africans were abandoning their rich cultural heritage (Agyemang 1988, 58–59). Following the Yoruba student's example, Amu decided to begin wearing traditional cloth. Thus, Amu drew inspiration not from a local Christian nationalism that had been active twenty years earlier and then faded, but from an international African student movement that was very influential for the nationalists who led Ghana to political independence.

So long as Amu only conducted his singing band and college students in cloth, no one complained; attending church or conducting the choir in cloth was also acceptable. But in 1931 Amu led and preached a Sunday morning service in cloth. For this he was reprimanded by Reverend Hall: "We were quite taken aback to see you conduct Sunday service today in a native cloth which is so unbecoming of you, a teacher at the seminary where students are trained for the church's congregations and schools" (quoted in Agyemang 1988, 74). Amu decided not to preach at all if he could not preach in cloth. Two years later, thinking his request would be granted, Amu pleaded with the Synod Committee to rescind its decision and allow him to preach in "African attire" (quoted in Agyemang 1988, 89). The synod clerk's reply, dated 20 October 1933, was a notice of dismissal from PTC — not just because of his stubbornness about not preaching in "European dress," but also because "Mr. Amu has brought into the College different sorts of drums, horns etc., beating the drums and teaching some students how to beat the drums and how to dance" (quoted in Agyemang 1988, 90). The Synod Committee's stand against Amu's African dress, drumming, and music was made stronger by the arguments of some Kumase presbyters that the temptation to backslide would be too strong for the newly converted Asante Christians, who had just left behind traditional customs of human sacrifice, executioners, drumming, bells, and amulets. It was less the Scottish missionaries like Reverend Ferguson than the African Synod Committee members who decided that Amu's behavior was not appropriate for a teacher in the Presbyterian Church.

Despite the stir it created within the church, Amu's work had impressed many people by this time. In 1930 a group of young people in the Akropong Presbyterian Church had approached him to compose songs for them, and this was the beginning of the singing band movement, which spread rapidly among the Presbyterian churches, not only in Akuapem but elsewhere (Ofei n.d.; Okae-Anti interview, 23 Oct. 1998). The singing bands sang Christian songs in Twi with music based on African rhythms, something that had never been heard before in the churches.[27] PTC also put on annual concerts in which the repertoire was usually a mixture of songs, vignettes, choir singing, solos, duets, and an African drum and flute ensemble (Agyemang 1988, 79). The ensemble held the first African instrumental concert at the Palladium in Accra in 1933, and after the first piece the audience rushed the stage to shake Amu's hand (Okae-Anti interview, 23 Oct. 1998).

After Amu was dismissed from PTC in 1933, the secondary school of Achimota eagerly recruited him as a music teacher. Achimota was a newly established government school and therefore free of mission influence. Its founders were interested in educating African leaders who would not reject African customs; it was therefore a place that welcomed Amu's interests and expertise. Amu's transfer from PTC to Achimota signals the shift in the provision of education and the promotion of cultural nationalism from church to state. As the colonial state became more powerful, it increasingly appropriated some of the roles of the church. Although the churches continued to articulate their vision of modernity, they now did so in competition with the state, and the voices advocating a cultural nationalism within the church quieted.

Conclusion

The British colonial government had been giving grants to mission schools since 1874, finding it more cost effective than starting its own schools (McWilliam and Kwamena-Poh 1975). The Educational Ordinance of 1887 recognized two types of schools, "government," which were very few, and "assisted," which included all the mission schools. Despite the assistance, mission schoolteachers were usually paid less than government schoolteachers. Moreover, the mission schools' grants were conditional on certain requirements: they had to be open to all children, regardless of religion; to have an average of at least twenty pupils; to be staffed by certified teachers; and to include English reading and writing, arithmetic, and needlework in the curriculum. The Basel missionaries were unhappy with a policy that compelled their schools to place more emphasis on the academic, to the detriment of the vocational, and to English over the vernacular, even as they accepted government support (McWilliam and Kwamena-Poh 1975).[28]

By the beginning of World War I, schools had come under greater British colonial control, a process accelerated by the expulsion of the Basel and Bremen missionaries, although mission schools were still providing the vast majority of education in the Gold Coast. After the war, influenced by a wave of idealism and humanitarianism sweeping Europe, Britain took renewed interest in schools and social welfare in its colonies in Africa (Scanlon 1966). Governor Guggisberg (1919–27) opened the first government secondary school (Achimota), increased the grants given to schools (to 80 percent of their total budgets), and registered qualified teachers. From the 1920s until Ghana gained its independence, schools were under the care of both religious bodies and government authorities.

Although schools came more and more under state control and increasingly received state financing from 1874 to the 1950s, they retained their association with Christianity. Schools were intimately related to the missionary enterprise and the primary route by which people in Akuapem became Christians for a hundred years. Through schooling, people were separated from the lifeworld of their families, at the same time as through Twi literacy, they attempted to selectively recuperate some of the practices they had left behind. Basel Mission education created a class of people, who, through their travel as teachers, pastors, cocoa brokers, and cocoa farmers, began voicing a vision of the nation that went beyond the town or traditional state to a Christian Twi-literate public spread over a large area of the Gold Coast. But though the religious newspaper *Kristofo Senkekafo* gave them a place to articulate those views, as Africans took on more important roles in the church, the church leadership placed limits on the selective incorporation of African customs and practices, as we saw in the expulsion of Amu from PTC. The promotion of culture shifted to state institutions as Christianity became more and more defined in opposition to what were perceived to be African customs. Cultural nationalist sentiments also shifted from being articulated in Christian-oriented structures and publications to being stated within and against the British colonial government.

Missionary activities had contradictory effects in the Gold Coast. The Basel missionaries promoted vernacular language and history as necessary to Christian nationhood, but insisted on the model of a European peasant village for their converts' everyday life. In the Gold Coast they became agents of "modernity," rather than of conservatism as they had been in Europe, and the economic and social mobility of African Christians spoke more clearly to Africans than the missionaries' message of redemption and salvation. Because the missionaries felt that the study of Gold Coast histories, religious traditions, and languages was crucial to the development of a Christian nation, they helped constitute culture as an object of discourse, an object that was taken up and elaborated first by African Christians and then by colonial and postcolonial governments, just as their project of schooling was also increasingly taken over by the state.

CHAPTER 2

AFRICAN CHRISTIANS dissociated themselves from the bodily experience of everyday cultural practices at the same time as they made them into an object of discourse subject to evaluation. State officials, in many ways, inherited this project. But they also sought to naturalize new definitions of culture by making them part of Ghanaians' habitual experience. Jean and John Comaroff's explications of ideology and hegemony are useful as an analytic tool here. To them

Drumming and Dancing

The State's Involvement in Tradition

hegemony, as an understanding of the world that maintains current power relations, corresponds to Bourdieu's *doxa*: it is common sense. So well accepted is this understanding that it is barely acknowledged; hegemony is nonnegotiable and beyond direct argument, embedded in enduring forms and structures. Ideology, by contrast, is perceived as a matter of opinion and interest and therefore is open to overt contestation. What is hegemonic can become ideological and the object of discourse and debate, a transition that civil rights and environmental groups have made at various points in American history. Likewise, the ideological can become interred in habitual practices. The more successful the dominant ideology is, the more it will disappear into the domain of the hegemonic, "distilled into social forms that seem to have such historical longevity as to be above history" (Comaroff and Comaroff 1991, 30). What is so important about this concept is that it focuses our attention on the movement between the emergence of the ideological from the hegemonic and the disappearance of the ideological into the hegemonic. In that movement we can track shifts in social relations, personal identifications, and political arrangements.

In the history of the cultural in Ghana, we see at least two movements between the hegemonic and the ideological. In one, cultural practices emerged from the realm of everyday life to become an object of discourse, subject to overt articulation, reification, and contestation. Why did the state become involved in making culture an object of discourse? Cultural projects on behalf of the nation are due to the recycling of nineteenth-century European romantic-nationalist ideas, which held that each nation possessed a unique cultural heritage. There is an "international grammar of national culture with a checklist of items," such as a national museum, a national dance troupe, and national clothing (Löfgren 1989, 22; see also Dominguez 1992). In the nineteenth century, European nations not only embraced concepts of national folk culture but also considered institutions like national folk museums and archives absolute requirements. Thus, romantic nationalism, in defining what is essential for the nation, has justified state support for, expansion into, and appropriation of the cultural through state institutions and bureaucracies.

In this endeavor the state draws on practices that are part of the everyday lives of its subjects in an effort to appropriate that expressive power for national loyalty (Herzfeld 1997). By making the cultural explicit, the Ghanaian state attempts to lay claim to the nation in the face of competing political loyalties, such as to ethnicity or traditional kingdoms, that lived cultural experience helps validate. As cultural practices structured by local histories and relationships become a symbol for the nation, "the hallmark of festive behavior, its superabundance of symbols and meanings, [has to] be shrunk as much as possible to a handful of quickly and easily understood ideas" (Guss 2000, 13). In Ghana the state picked certain forms—particularly the performing arts and public display—as best able to legitimate its power. Because the phrase "drumming and dancing" is often used in Ghana as a synonym for culture, I use it metaphorically in this chapter to signal a range of arts, primarily performing arts but also arts and crafts, of which literal drumming and dancing are only two artistic forms.

In the second movement, this time from the ideological to the habitual, the state's presentation of culture as "drumming and dancing" became the dominant meaning of culture in Ghana. The national theater traditions of England, France, and the United States focused on citizens becoming an *audience* for national spectacles (Kruger 1992), but in Ghana schoolchildren have been turned into *performers* in national events. Through their performances, culture as drumming and dancing has become part of their bodily, habitual experience. Those performances have helped the schoolchildren internalize a new set of assumptions about themselves and their world, to gain a new subjectivity that makes sense within a world that they see as natural and real (Kavanagh 1995).

Why did the state choose to make schools a crucial vehicle for its cultural program? Development institutions and personnel may choose certain interventions because that is what they are best equipped to handle, not because it is the best solution to a particular problem (Ferguson 1994). States use schools as a primary mode of intervention in their cultural projects because these institutions are to a large extent within their control, already existing, and already organizing the routines and bodies of children across the nation. As government employees, teachers and principals can be brought under political pressure. Because schools became a site for the promotion of the state's definition of culture, teachers and students played a role in both the movement from the hegemonic to the ideological and the movement from the ideological to the hegemonic. While in Europe efforts at heritage revival were first undertaken by intellectuals who then pressured the state into a change of policy (Mosse 1964; Verdery 1990; Wilson 1976), in Ghana most initiatives to promote traditional culture have come primarily from the state.

However, for the state to attain hegemony over the meaning of culture and the mechanisms for its transmission, it cannot be seen as imposing its own policies on groups it has the means to pressure and control. Rather, those groups need to take the state's representation of the world as conforming to their own understanding of it (Gramsci 1988). During a brief period in Ghana's history, in the 1960s and 1970s, the representation of culture as drumming and dancing was hegemonic, though it is unclear whether this was because the state was galvanizing teachers and students into cultural activity or vice-versa. The interactions between state and teachers and students became a mutually reinforcing feedback loop, in which many teachers and students felt that state cultural programming spoke to or answered their own personal desires and identities. They recognized themselves in the cultural programs that the state organized and were moved to promote culture in their own environments of study and work, further encouraging the state to focus its organizing efforts on schools. University faculty advocated for and wrote certain policies as government ministers, at the same time as the state created and expanded educational institutions that not only gave greater weight and power to educated people's expertise but also helped shape the attitudes of their graduates. Through schools, the state and educated persons were engaged in the constitution of one another. Schools became a primary site for the naturalization and promotion of this meaning of culture because the projects of both educated people and the state came together in those institutions.

In the late 1990s teachers and students no longer demonstrate the enthusiasm about culture that they did in the documents and life histories analyzed here. Teachers see the cultural studies syllabus, in particular, as a top-down reform, imposed from above by government bureaucrats. Ghanaians seem more interested in learning English and French, useful for making connections in an economic system that is increasingly dependent on global flows, than in learning more about their own languages and culture. Many teachers tend to dismiss culture in schools as only "fun," noting that children become excited and "interested" during cultural activities (their words). As we will see, a very different structure of feeling reigned in the first few decades of independence, when many Ghanaians felt that government cultural programming awakened or responded to a new sense of cultural pride in which their personal mission corresponded to the government's project.

The Ups and Downs of the State in Ghana

After a short and intense nationalist struggle, the Gold Coast gained the right to internal self-government in 1951, and then won full independence in 1957, under the leadership of Kwame Nkrumah and his political party, the Convention People's Party (CPP). As the British Gold Coast, it had been praised as a "model colony" (Austin 1964). The mainstay of its economy has been cocoa, but gold mining and logging also serve as sources of foreign exchange. And tourism and remittances from abroad are becoming increasingly important. Ghana's political stability has mainly depended on the world market in cocoa: with the ups and downs of cocoa prices, so too have governments risen and fallen.

Kwame Nkrumah became increasingly autocratic during his tenure, consolidating power, imprisoning the opposition, and restricting freedom of the press. Toppled by a military coup in 1966, he was followed by a quick succession of regimes: the military National Liberation Council in 1966–69, the democratic Busia government in 1969–72, and the military Acheampong regime in 1972–78. Economic conditions worsened during the 1970s. Educated professionals, including teachers, left the country for other countries in West Africa, particularly Nigeria, and for the West. Imported goods became scarce, and food shortages were common. Instability within the military led to a coup in 1979 by Flight Lieutenant Jerry Rawlings, who then allowed a civilian government to be elected. Some two and a half years later, in 1981, that (Limann) government was toppled in another coup led by Rawlings, on the charge of corruption. The new government was headed by Rawlings and the Provisional National Defence Council. Although at first socialist and populist, the PNDC later became the darling of the International Monetary Fund and the World Bank and instituted structural and economic reforms. Under pressure from the international community, the military government began a process of democratization and transformed itself into a civilian political party, the NDC, which won both the presidential and the parliamentary elections in 1992 and 1996 but lost in 2000 to the main opposition party, the New Patriotic Party.

Remarkable as it might seem, through all these times of economic and political unrest and in a period when the state ceded much policy to international organizations, successive regimes continued to engage in cultural programming. Equally remarkably, cultural policies and practices demonstrated great continuity. Despite the several changes of government, each new regime recycled and expanded on the ideas of its predecessors. Thus, we see an increasing association of culture with drumming and dancing transmitted through the schools. These efforts point to the importance of exercising the power of the state through the domain of the cultural when other mechanisms for revealing the state's presence disappear. As Cris Shore and Susan Wright (1997) point out, "'Culture' is an increasingly important domain of governance through which modern states try to organize and control civil society. The scope of government and the techniques of governance have expanded notably into the 'cultural sector' precisely at the moment that the nation state's powers to control its own economic and political space have dwindled" (28). While their point explains the continuation of cultural interventions under unstable conditions, the overall strength of the state remains important. In the Ghana case, most postcolonial governments have wanted to do more in the way of cultural programming than they could accomplish.

The handover of states from colonial to postcolonial rulers has been characterized as a "passive revolution" in which the institutional structures of rule set up under colonialism continue after independence (Chatterjee 1999; Mamdani 1996). Because of the many continuities between colonial and postcolonial educational policies, I will first set the backdrop by looking at the elite school of Achimota, established by the British colonial government as an ideal model of African education.

"African in Sympathy": Educating an African Elite

The colonial authorities relied on two methods to teach a selected and reified African culture in schools. One, especially promoted at Achimota College, was to focus on arts, especially music and dance, performed during nonacademic times within the school schedule. This was one piece of an education for future African leaders that was primarily Christian and anglicized, so that they might be intermediaries between "civilization" and "tradition" (on similar French colonial policy, see Colonna 1997). The other method, left primarily to missionary schools, was to pair language and custom, which ended up strengthening ethnic awareness within a national polity (chapter 1). The second method is not unimportant, for mission schools educated far more people than Achimota did during this period, although Achimota alumni came to be represented disproportionately in the next generation of politicians and policymakers who formed the independence government (J. H. K. Nketia, conversation, 11 Jan. 1999).

In the 1920s and 1930s, liberal romantics in the British colonial service argued that Africans should respect their own traditions and customs (Zachernuk 1998). A colonial official in a Nigerian teachers' journal in 1934 "urged Yoruba to study their past, both to appreciate the present better and to develop, as Britain had, a sense of 'cohesion and national spirit.'" He lamented that schoolteachers "do nothing whatever to foster a pride in the past individuality of the race" (quoted in Zachernuk 1998, 495). In a similar vein, the anthropologist R. S. Rattray, in government employ in the Gold Coast, wrote that he told Ashanti people during the course of his research that "they will become better and finer men and women by remaining true Ashanti and retaining a certain pride in their past, and that their greatest hope lies in the future, if they will follow and build upon lines with which the national *sunsum* or soul has been familiar since first they were a people" (1923, 12). Colonial officials came to see African traditions as the basis on which the progress of the nation could be built, so long as Western ideas, institutions, and skills could be grafted onto them. At the same time, they racialized the concept of "the nation" and reified boundaries between ethnic groups.

Achimota symbolized a growth in the British colonial government's involvement in the provision of education in the Gold Coast. Schooling became part of the governmental dream of control and organization (Foucault 1979; Thomas 1994). Schools became crucial instruments for initiatives aimed at directing the future of the country and changing people's behavior and ideas. But in the 1920s and 1930s, the colonial government was not interested in mass education. Like colonial governments in other parts of Africa, it limited access to education and focused on the education of the sons and daughters of local elites (Ball 1983). Achimota was established in part because of nationalist pressure from local elites for secondary schools and universities.

Officially opened in 1927 as a coeducational boarding school, Achimota provided teacher training, technical training, and general secondary education. Its guiding principles were summarized in a committee report as follows: "Achimota hopes to produce a type of student who is 'Western' in his intellectual attitudes towards life, with a respect for science and capacity for systematic thought, but who remains African in sympathy and desirous of preserving and developing what is deserving of respect in tribal life, custom, rule and law" (Achimota College 1932, 14). Recall that urban intellectuals of the Gold Coast were at the forefront of nationalism at this time and making demands on the government (Kimble 1963). As a strategy for undercutting their demands, colonial officials criticized these intellectuals as cut off from their cultural roots and as caricatures of civilization. Through Achimota, the colonial government hoped to create a different local elite, one that would be respectful of both chiefs and the West. Achimota's founders were concerned that educated people were separating themselves from "the tribal organization which nevertheless remained the basis of their social and political life" (*Achimota Review* 1937, 6, Ghana Natl. Archives, CSO 18/6/62). If governing through indirect rule was to work, then the educated must be incorporated into the rest of society, but incorporated in a hierarchical way as leaders separate from but respectful of "the people," whom the British viewed as uneducated peasants untouched by modernity.

While the school's European staff were committed to teaching African customs, they were vague about which customs were most "deserving of respect," and they had difficulty in making those customs part of the habitual, bodily practices inculcated at Achimota (Coe 2002). Despite one teacher's statement that African culture was incorporated into the school's curriculum through local languages, agriculture, art, music, and history (*Achimota Review* 1937, 20), what was most highly indexed as African culture in the publications of Achimota and the memories of its students were the performing and visual arts.

At Achimota, as at other elite schools in West Africa (Gamble 2002; Kerr 1995; Osofisan 1974), African performance arts were used for entertainment purposes during celebrations and other extracurricular activities. Dramatic performances were among the features inherited from the Government Training College in Accra, which was incorporated into Achimota. Plays were performed on Saturday nights by the various houses in the school, with fierce competition between them. At first the plays were in the vernacular with simple plots and no written parts; the principal character was often a buffoon (*Achimota Review* 1937, 66–68; Agbodeka 1977). Sometimes the students sang one or two African songs at the beginning of the performance (*Achimota Review* 1937, 37).[1] Professor

Mawɛre-Opoku, who attended Achimota (1931–34) and later taught art there, recounted that on Founders' Day, each "tribal group" of Twi, Fante, Ewe, and Gã presented a dance new to their area. In addition, the students had "tribal drumming" and African nights two Saturdays a month. He defined "tribal drumming" as "taking lessons in drumming and dancing" (interview, 6 Aug. 1997). On "African night" the students were divided into the four principal "tribal groups." "For the Gãs, arrangements were made for [other] Gãs to come to talk and discuss things, to chat as one would in a village community, with experts from the Gã area" (Mawɛre-Opoku interview, 29 Oct. 1998). Or they would tell stories (Mawɛre-Opoku interview, 8 Dec. 1998).

The professor's memories are borne out by the comments of school inspectors in 1932: "Each people practices its own form of tribal dancing and song. We saw an exhibition of dancing given by each race and were much impressed by the enthusiasm and skill shown, and by the courage shown by the authorities in encouraging it. An African play in one or other vernacular is produced every year by each boarding-house on the college side, and by the senior girls" (Achimota College 1932, 36). Because the overall curriculum was primarily anglicized, "African culture" became located in the extracurricular spaces of the school, as entertainment, performing arts, and arts and crafts. It was the performing arts aspect of culture fostered at Achimota—rather than that of vernacular language or arts and crafts—that was elaborated and refined by the independence government of Nkrumah.

The Public Presentation of the Nation through Culture: The Nkrumah Years, 1957–1966

The rationale behind colonial attempts to teach culture centered on concerns that the divisions between the rural masses and the educated leaders of the country would threaten national unity. Although this anxiety about the elite continued to be articulated at various points in Ghana's history, its first leader, Kwame Nkrumah, was more concerned that ethnic, rather than class, rifts might divide the country. States commonly celebrate local cultural traditions, and yet this strategy risks dividing the nation from within, opening the way for local groups to claim that their distinctiveness warrants separate statehood or that the state favors a certain ethnic group (Herzfeld 1997; Turino 2000). Nkrumah, in seeking to appropriate cultural traditions and symbols in ways that were not divisive to the nation, used the approach, also used in Tanzania and Zimbabwe, of combining a variety of different ethnic artistic traditions in a single public display: a state-sponsored buffet of culture.[2]

Nkrumah did not articulate a clear cultural policy during his regime because he thought traditional culture had two tendencies divisive to the nation and resistant to change, thus militating against African progress: chieftaincy and "tribalism" (Hagan 1993). On the political front, the Convention People's Party (CPP) government was worried about the rise of ethnic nationalism. The late colonial period, after World War II, witnessed increased ethnic identifications. Challenges to the CPP's power during the 1950s came both from the Togoland Congress, which demanded an Ewe homeland under Ewe control, and from the National Liberation Movement, which alternated between asking for Asante autonomy within a Gold Coast federation and demanding complete secession (Allman 1990). This increased ethnic nationalism was not a residue of the past. Rather it was a response to a new political situation, in which the frame of reference had become the nation, and the growth of the central government meant that groups had to compete to have access to its resources (Geertz 1963).

When new states gained independence, central governments saw heightened ethnic identification as a threat to their power, because allegiances and alliances could be formed that could potentially overthrow the national government. However, as Partha Chatterjee (1999) wrote about India, the new nation-state "does not undertake a full-scale assault on all precapitalist dominant classes but seeks to limit their former power, neutralize them where necessary, attack them only selectively and bring them round to a position of subsidiary allies within a reformed state structure" (212). In similar fashion, Nkrumah attempted to undercut independent chiefs by taking away their judicial and administrative functions, to align chiefs with the national state, and to use symbols of chiefly authority to legitimate his own (Rathbone 2000). Nkrumah was not unusual in using culture to accomplish these goals. Other independent states in Africa similarly drew on cultural symbols to represent the nation (Adjakly 1985; Dedy 1984; Kaspin 1993; Samper 1997).

The tension between promoting cultural traditions and promoting national unity is demonstrated by a speech the Minister of Education and Information gave to the Akan Orthography Committee, which was working to unify the different orthographies and dialects of Akuapem Twi, Asante Twi, and Fante to form a standard Akan script: "No one would wish any Ghanaian to forget his mother tongue and his own traditions, which add so much to the cultural heritage of this country. . . . But this does not mean that the local loyalty can take first place. Over and above our affection for our village or family group or dialect area, we are Ghanaians first and foremost, and we are members of one nation. . . . The Government of

Dr. Nkrumah is there to encourage unity, not to magnify differences" (15 Aug. 1959, Ghana Natl. Archives, RG 3/1/74). Because Ghanaian languages were seen as potentially divisive to the nation, the Nkrumah government placed renewed emphasis on English, which gradually replaced Ghanaian languages as the medium of instruction (Chinebuah 1970). Rather than naming a single Ghanaian language as the national language, it decided to support several Ghanaian languages. The government aimed to divest linguistic and cultural markers of ethnic signification, but language was treated as more ethnically charged than other markers.[3]

The Nkrumah government considered dress and performing arts to be a more appropriate medium in this project of unity than language. Professor J. H. K. Nketia told me that Nkrumah was interested in "cultural identity" and was able to separate it from "ethnic identity." For instance, Nkrumah wore *kente*, a cloth sewn from woven strips, from the south, one day and *batakari*, a northern smock, the next, and these were "symbols of cultural identity, apart from ethnic origin" (conversation, 11 Jan. 1999). The wearing of Ghanaian dress, rather than European suits, by government ministers and Nkrumah was only one of many symbolic gestures, although it was one of the best remembered (Kwame Ampene interview, 3 Mar. 1999). In the view of Professor Mawɛre-Opoku, Nkrumah focused on promoting dancing and drumming because it appealed to Ghanaians across linguistic and ethnic boundaries; the professor himself considered it an ideal tool for creating national unity (n.d., 60).

Despite the CPP's repression of traditional practices deemed antithetical to "progress," it is remembered for bringing new attention to culture through traditional attire and artistic performances at national public events. Nkrumah appropriated the emblems of chiefs and traditional states to reflect the grandeur and power of both himself and the state (Hess 2001; Yankah 1985). Independence Day and Republic Day celebrations provided opportunities for the display of cultural artifacts as national symbols, separated from their dense relationship to local practices and meanings (see Turino 2000). In many ways Ghanaian traditions were substituted for English traditions on colonial holidays like Empire Day, where people had marched, saluted the flag, sung English songs, played soccer, and danced around the maypole (S. K. Aboa, conversation, 23 Oct. 1998). Nkrumah caused a stir by having an ɔkyeame (a speech mediator for a chief) perform the traditional rite of pouring libation to the gods and ancestors when the Duchess of Kent handed over independence to Ghana on 6 March 1957 (Pobee 1977, 120). The national celebrations also brought dancing by traditional religious priests (akɔmfo), and the Independence Day celebrations of 6 March 1958 in Kumase featured an *adowa* dance competition, a woman's festival featuring different traditional hairstyles, and a "traditional dress" contest for boys and girls (*Daily Graphic*, 10 Mar. 1958, 5, 10).[4] Nkrumah's selective representation of traditional culture differed from the representations of missionaries and colonial administrators. Public performances in national spaces were emphasized, designed to create national unity and emphasize the power of the state. Thus, while Nkrumah considered language more politically charged than presentation and performance, national public displays were clearly making political statements about the power of the state to incorporate and contain ethnic identifications.

Nkrumah considered the lack of African pride a product of colonial education; he wrote three pamphlets in Britain on the evils of European education and how it should be modified (Pobee 1977). But like many critics of schools, he felt that the solution would come through them as well (Coe 1999). The CPP government, when it gained power in the 1951 elections, was determined to jump start the progress of the country, and one of its first budgetary proposals concerned education. Under the Accelerated Development Plan for Education enacted in 1951, primary schooling rapidly expanded, thanks to the abolition of tuition fees (though parents still had to pay for textbooks and uniforms).

Nkrumah's government marked a change in the relationship between church and state. Although church managers continued to hire and pay teachers and supervise syllabi, equipment, and records at existing denominational schools, local district councils built new classrooms and schools as the Nkrumah government set about whittling away the church's control (McWilliam and Kwamena-Poh 1975, 83–84). The Education Act of 1961 prohibited schools from discriminating against students on the basis of religion and from requiring students to attend church. As Minister of Education Dowuona-Hammond, noted, in winding up the parliamentary debates on the Education Act in October 1961, all schools were now state-owned "because the teachers [were] paid by the Government"; the managers of the religious educational units were, in fact, "acting as agents of the Government" (quoted in McWilliam and Kwamena-Poh 1975, 100). As it turned out, many church managers and teachers were not so clear in their loyalties to the government as the minister suggests (chapter 4).

Nkrumah established two institutions that had a profound influence on the teaching of culture in the schools. One was the Arts Council, which promoted culture and arts all over Ghana; I will return to this institution later in the chapter. The other was the Institute of African Studies (IAS) at the University of Ghana, created in 1961. Nkrumah set up the IAS to promote the comparative study of Africa and the African diaspora—not just Ghana or West Africa, he emphasized—in "new African-centered ways," as he said in his speech on "The African Genius" at the institute's inauguration in 1963 (University of Ghana 1992, 12).[5] Scholars at the IAS were responsible for setting up courses in African studies—sociology, history, literature, musicology, dance, and drama—and conducting research in those areas. Their work should be "outward-looking," Nkrumah said, and they should "serve the needs of the people" through teaching and public speaking and by developing new forms of art (University of Ghana 1992, 17). The IAS and the affiliated School of Performing Arts have had immense symbolic value in teaching African history, music, and dance at the university level; culture became a form of expert knowledge to be learned through formal educational institutions.

Unfortunately, the university inherited the relationship between colonial anthropologists like Rattray and the colonial state, full of fractures and differing concerns (see Asad 1973). Like their colleagues in Nigeria (Nigerian Folklore Society 1987, 1985), the small group of scholars in the School of Performing Arts focused on the artistic and creative aspects of vernacular arts in their studies, thus promoting a view that culture is located solely or at least mainly in that domain (Adinku 1996; Egblewogbe 1975; Mawɛre-Opoku n.d.; Nketia 1974, 1963a, 1963b). Furthermore, by stressing the role of performing arts in increasing social integration and community, they laid the groundwork for the state's appropriation of performing arts to generate national unity. But some of the same scholars simultaneously articulated a more anthropological perspective. They took the position that culture encompassed more than drumming and dancing; it was the way of life of a people, a view that influenced a second generation of government policies. They and other intellectuals have been involved in "legitimizing, rationalizing, and disseminating more informal schemes of knowledge as incontrovertible expert judgment" (Boyer 2000, 461). Their close, albeit uneasy, relationship to the state has directed and helped transform, however unevenly, their intellectual activity into policy (see Chun 2000), generally supporting the government's attempt to use culture for national unification.

Under Nkrumah, the performing arts mode came to the fore on the national public stage as the best way to foster national unification. The mode of learning about ethnic customs through Ghanaian languages became less prominent—although it was still taught in schools—because of Nkrumah's concerns about the threat ethnic nationalism posed to his government. Up until this point, the teaching of "African tradition" to children had been relatively haphazard and isolated. Nkrumah was an organizer of a mass party, a man with grand visions for both his country and Africa. The national youth organization he set up in 1960, the Young Pioneers, had a profound impact on the form of cultural education in Ghana.

The Shoes and Scarves of the Young Pioneers, 1960–1966

Ghana's Young Pioneer (YP) movement was modeled on youth organizations in Eastern Europe, Israel, and the Soviet Union. It was meant to be, in the words of the Minister of Social Welfare, "an extensive school of citizenship . . . to instill into the youth of Ghana a high sense of patriotism, respect, and love for Ghana as their fatherland, whilst providing them with the opportunities for healthy association; further education, discipline, and training; and patriotic service to Ghana, during their leisure and recreational periods" (Minister of Social Welfare, draft cabinet memo, 1, Ghana Natl. Archives, RG 3/1/447). Leadership training activities, youth forums, voluntary workcamps, and youth festivals of art, music, and drama were planned so that "a true spirit of nationalism and service" would be inculcated into young people (ibid., 2). The minister took note of other youth organizations in Ghana, both secular and religious. According to Fred Agyemang, then working in the government Information Service, the Nkrumah government first tried to politicize the Boy Scouts, which had 7,000 members in 1960, but when its leaders refused, Nkrumah brought in the model of the Young Pioneers from Eastern Europe (conversation, 26 June 1999). The local organizers were usually young men with at least a middle school certificate; many had been Boy Scout or youth organization leaders. Local branches were set up; ideological institutes trained leaders in the urban areas of Teshie, Winneba, and Accra.[6]

Like many government organizations and initiatives, the Young Pioneer movement began close to the centers of government power, the national and regional capitals. It came to Koforidua, the capital of the Eastern Region, in 1961 (Eastern Regional Archives, ERG 1/14/11).[7] There, as elsewhere, YP members had afterschool classes on Monday, Wednesday, and Friday afternoons, where, in a four-week rotating national curriculum, they were taught an odd mix of subjects: state ideology, drumming and dancing, arts and crafts (including weaving), technological skills (such as radio mechanics and electrical engineering), and first aid plus the Young Pioneers' aims, code, and pledge.[8] This educational program tried to wed many diverse goals: patriotism, love of Nkrumah, awareness of his philosophy of Pan-Africanism and African Personality, the nation's technological development, and cultural display.

The Young Pioneer movement gained strength in Akuapem only when A. O. Nyante, an energetic man from Apirede, was appointed district organizer in January 1963.[9] He wrote to the regional office in the progress report for that month that they were studying drama, civics, folklore, and traditional drumming and dancing. In the next month's report, he said that the Akuapem Young Pioneers would make their debut at the independence celebrations in March, with a cultural competition in fɔntɔmfrɔm drumming and dancing among the boys and adenkum singing among the girls from towns all over Akuapem. Fɔntɔmfrɔm is a form of drumming widely used in the chiefs' courts, accompanied by a highly symbolic and charged dance by one person. It is a form of political communication, demonstrating loyalty, praise, and agreement, or their opposites; it is thus watched closely by those present. Adenkum does not have this political charge. Performed by women's singing groups, the songs are accompanied by gourds and clapping.[10] Although the Young Pioneers ended up not performing at the 1963 independence celebrations, Mr. Nyante reported that the attendance and enthusiasm at club house activities had increased as a result of rehearsals for the event (Mar. 1963 report, Eastern Regional Archives, ADM KD 33/6/215). The Akuapem members participated not only in local festivals, such as Odwira in Akropong in 1965, but also in national and regional celebrations, such as the Third Anniversary of the Republic celebrations in 1963 and the Eastern Regional Youth Festival in 1964, with competitions of cultural drumming and dancing, arts and crafts, physical and gymnastic display, and choral songs (Eastern Regional Archives, ERG 1/13/234; ERG 1/14/11; ADM KD 33/6/466). In other words, the Young Pioneers were made to serve two of the state's strategies: the creation of alternative "national" festivals and the attempt to appropriate local ones for national ends.

The official reports bear out what teachers and former youth members remembered of the YP curriculum. According to Mensah Abavon, the then-leader of the rival Boy Scouts in Akropong, the Young Pioneers marched on one day each week, studied Nkrumah ideology on the second, and drummed and danced on the third (interview, 30 July 1999). A former YP organizer in Larteh remembered that the students wanted to learn about "amammrɛ" (culture), and they were not learning about it at home from their parents and grandparents; the classes on drumming were particularly appreciated. Mr. Adi-Dako, then teaching at the Presbyterian Women's Training College at Aburi, recalled that the pupils were collected after school to practice music, marching, and dancing, but he considered it all done for the objective of "worshiping the hero," Nkrumah (interview,

29 Sept. 1998). Margaret Rose Tetteh, a teacher who joined the YP movement as a child in Akropong, remembered dressing up in cloth, learning how to dance and sing, and reciting the appellations of Nkrumah (interview, 19 July 1999). One of her contemporaries, another teacher, also remembered learning to dance and sing and march, but recalled the Pioneers being split into ethnic groups, with each group learning its own dances. Interestingly, despite the formal YP curriculum, with its odd combination of science, patriotism, African history, and culture, what former YP members to a person remembered most strongly were performances—reciting lists of Nkrumah's honorifics, dressing in cloth, marching in uniform, and drumming and dancing—activities that were made more significant by their public display at regional competitions and local festivals.

People I spoke to who had been adults in the 1960s saw the Young Pioneers as a sinister organization for two reasons. The first was that the movement had many of the trappings of a cult centered on the heroic figure of Nkrumah. One common complaint was that the Young Pioneers made Nkrumah a god by the use of slogans such as "Nkrumah never dies." One possibly apocryphal story I heard several times told how YP instructors gathered the children together, asked them to close their eyes, and pray to God for toffee. When the toffee did not materialize, they asked the children to pray to Dr. Nkrumah, whereupon the organizers showered them with sweets. The other cause of concern was the suspicion that YP members were encouraged to spy on their families. People could be detained in prison for talk against Nkrumah under the Preventative Detention Act, which began to be used in 1958. Three people from Akropong and neighboring Mamfe told me that their parents had prevented them from joining because of these political and religious concerns.

According to Mr. Abavon, who had been vehemently opposed to the Young Pioneers, most teachers and principals were members of the opposition party and against the Pioneers, but as government employees they could not say anything out of fear. As he put it, "Akyerɛkyerɛfo nni ano. Wɔyɛɛ adwuma, wotuaa wɔn ka nti na wɔnka hwee" (Teachers didn't have a voice. They worked, they were paid [by the government], so they said nothing; interview, 30 July 1999, my translation). But some found subtle ways of giving voice to their resistance. For example, Professor Addo-Fening, then a teacher at Tafo Secondary School in the Eastern Region, remembered that the teachers refused to help the YP organizer teach his class. Because the YP organizer was Gã and could not speak Twi fluently, he had difficulty controlling the students without the teachers' help (interview, 27 Sept. 1998). Mr. Reynolds, headteacher at Akropong Practice

School until 1963 and thereafter regional manager of education in the Ashanti Region, commented, "We didn't encourage it [the YP] in the schools. We didn't like it" (interview, 6 Oct. 1998).

Mr. Abavon had been asked to be Young Pioneer district leader for Akropong, but he refused. He and the Boy Scouts under him had a long-simmering conflict with the Young Pioneers, who had a similar uniform and scarf and, like the Scouts, marched in military formation. Mr. Abavon claimed that if the YP leader Nyante found students wearing Boy Scout badges at school, he would send them home, but that the Boy Scouts were supported by the headteachers at two middle schools, both themselves for-mer Scouts. The tensions between the two groups came to a head during the Independence Day celebration of 6 March 1965, when both groups marched in parade, their organizational flags and the Ghanaian flag flying high. In a scuffle after the parade, the Young Pioneers threw away both of the Boy Scouts' flags and, in retaliation, the Scouts burned the Young Pio-neers' flag. Mr. Nyante was on his way to the police station in Mampong to report the incident when he had a motorcycle accident. Mr. Abavon said it was an act of God because otherwise he would have been in trouble. If so, another occurred later. For the incident did finally get reported, and Mr. Abavon was supposed to appear in court on 24 February 1966, but was saved by the coup that toppled Nkrumah on that very day. After the coup the Boy Scout leader was given all the YP clothing, youth forms, and flags and burned them all; he kept Mr. Nyante's motorcycle. This was common after the coup: Young Pioneer property was everywhere seized and distrib-uted to other groups (Eastern Regional Archives, ERG 1/14/14). YP lead-ers and others associated with the CPP fled the country or moved to other towns, where they were not known for their connection to Nkrumah or his organizations.

Thanks to the opposition of Mr. Abavon and others, the YP had only limited success in Akuapem. According to Mr. Nyante's progress reports, the membership for all age groups rose slowly, from about 2,000 in April 1963 to about 2,500 in March 1964 and 3,000 in December 1965. In the 1965 report, as earlier, the overwhelming majority — some 2,000 mem-bers — were in the 8–16 age group (Eastern Regional Archives, ADM KD 33/6/215). According to the 1960 census, Akuapem had 11,030 school-going children between the ages of 6–14, so though the statistical age ranges in the two sets of data do not match up, it seems that at best only one in every five schoolchildren in 1963–65 participated in the YP, espe-cially if one considers that Mr. Nyante's figures were probably inflated.[11] Probably the majority of YP members were from the towns along the ridge, rather than from the villages in the valleys: the district commissioner berated Mr. Nyante for not visiting the villages of Kwamaso, Okrakwadjo, and Konko, where schools had invited him to come (Eastern Regional Archives, ADM KD 33/6/215). Moreover, the secondary school club seemed to be a branch in name only.[12]

Because headmasters felt pressured to start clubs (defined as a minimum of fifty-one children) in their schools, it is likely that some children did not voluntarily participate. But many children were clearly happy to join — to march and to look so "smart" in the shoes and scarves of the Young Pioneers. Both the cultural activities and the public presentations were attractive to students and made them want to participate. For adolescents, membership brought a more important advantage: an opportunity to study abroad; scholarships were given for studies and work camps in Eastern Europe, the Soviet Union, and East Germany (Ghana Natl. Archives, RG 3/1/590). Although many adults vilified the Young Pioneers as a political tool of Nkrumah and his CPP, a whole generation of children in primary and middle school in 1960–66 became enthusiastic about becoming public performers and learning to drum and dance. Professor Addo-Fening considered the Young Pioneers "very instrumental. . . . This was when it [drumming and dancing] began to be taken very seriously in the schools" (interview, 27 Sept. 1998). The YP movement showed that cultural programming oriented toward the "masses," unlike the "leaders" of Achimota, could successfully target schoolchildren, because these children were already organized under teachers and principals who could be pressured by political considerations.

The work of the Young Pioneers was paralleled and continued by the Arts Council, an organization that Nkrumah had set up even earlier, in 1957. Like the YP leaders, Arts Council instructors taught traditional forms of music and dance, drummed up enthusiasm for "African culture," and held competitions in arts and crafts and the performing arts. Both projects organized schoolchildren to perform drumming and dancing in public. Both projects at their inception were closely tied to the party organization, but the Arts Council was able to survive the end of Nkrumah's government. Two people who had been children in the 1960s still had difficulty differentiating between the work of the two organizations, but to the adults, the ideological content of the two projects differed greatly. The YP did not have local legitimacy because they were too closely tied to the socialist ideology and increasing autocracy of Nkrumah and seemed to prey on susceptible children. Although the Arts Council was a government agency, with national and regional centers, it initially targeted a different constituency—artists, rather than schoolchildren—and it was viewed as nonpolitical. Ghanaians were engaged in state projects of cultural nationalization differently during the same period of time, in which one organization seemed overly manipulative and the other spoke deeply to their own sentiments and identities.

The Arts Council, 1957–1978

In the 1960s and early 1970s, popular interest and enthusiasm for Ghanaian culture were sustained by the Arts Council, the government's primary way of supporting the arts in Ghana. The successive governments during these years, struggling with their own loss of power and economic difficulties (Chazan 1983), did not do much to promote culture at a policy level. But dedicated members of that institution continued to organize Ghanaian cultural activities and events. The Arts Council's drama and dance troupes, especially the national Ghana Dance Ensemble, stirred interest in drumming and dancing and became a resource for individuals and schools that requested equipment and training. Unlike the Young Pioneers, which drew on local cultural performance traditions such as *adenkum* and *fɔntɔmfrɔm*, the Arts Council nationalized culture, teaching the musical and movement arts of different ethnic groups—marked as such—and combining them in public performances. Like other government institutions, it was based in the capital with regional affiliates, so that in the early years, schools in Accra and regional capitals had the most access to its resources. The Kumase Cultural Center held dance classes as early as the 1950s and has maintained its strength (Mawɛrɛ-Opoku interview, 4 Aug. 1997), whereas the Eastern Region Arts Council began work in Koforidua only in April 1961 (Ghana Natl. Archives, RG 3/7/55). As in Tanzania, a bureaucracy bloomed to organize cultural production (Askew 2002). The institutional history of the Arts Council and its relationship to the Institute of African Studies is complicated and full of political maneuvering; I will simply detail how the Arts Council became involved with schools.

Initially, as in Tanzania and Zimbabwe (Askew 2002; Turino 2000), the Arts Council was more interested in adult artists than schoolchildren. The Eastern regional branch began by organizing arts festivals, forming clubs of musicians and other artists, and arranging classes "where young people [could] learn the ancient dances and drum language" (Eastern Region Monthly Report, Dec. 1961, Ghana Natl. Archives, RG 3/7/55). Cultural officers combed various towns and districts for artists and craftsmen during the early 1960s and organized folktale competitions, choral music concerts, and "cultural drumming and dance" performances, incorporating different ethnic dances. Later, they also organized dramatic performance and poetry recital competitions (Eastern Regional Archives, ERG 1/14/12).

The Arts Council became involved in schools not because the state decided they were the most suitable place for cultural interventions, but because when intellectuals—students, teachers, and university scholars—became personally invested in reviving cultural traditions, they turned to the institutions they knew best to carry out that work. Sometimes they felt that the schools themselves were part of the problem. Professor J. H. K. Nketia, of the Institute of African Studies, told Presbyterian schoolteachers at a conference in 1962 that educated people were most in need of cultural education precisely because of their schooling, which had alienated many of them from their fellow Ghanaians: "By cultural education I mean the simple process of passing on our cultural heritage not only in the traditional way, but also in schools and institutions of higher education so that the educated Ghanaian can become fully integrated culturally with his own society" (Ghana Natl. Archives, RG 3/1/217). For many of these intellectuals, teaching culture in the schools was part of a larger individual enterprise to promote culture: they also researched and wrote books on local customs and histories, and they organized cultural troupes and ethnic revival associations. In this emerging hegemony, educated people responded to and appropriated state efforts to nationalize culture as part of their efforts to promote tradition in general, at the same time as the state built on the enthusiasm and initiatives of teachers and students.

Letters to the National Arts Council in Accra show that teachers and students, from the late 1950s onward, organized dance and drama troupes in their schools on their own initiative, thereby showing that the conception of culture as drumming and dancing was quite dominant at this time. One young primary school teacher in Ada, the Volta Region, wrote to the National Arts Council in September 1960 to say that he had set up a cultural troupe with some schoolchildren and townsfolk "with the aim of promoting and encouraging drama, drumming, and dancing, because of my burning love for them" (Ghana Natl. Archives, RG 3/7/60). A student at Abuakwa State College, a secondary school in Kyebi in the Eastern Region, noted in October 1962 that he and his friends had started a cultural club at the school, where they were learning local *adowa* dancing and songs and gathering information on "some typical Akan traditions such as— Ohum, Akan marriage and the duties of the Queen Mother from grownups in the town" of Aburi, Akuapem.[13] They asked the Arts Council to help them buy drums to practice on (RG 3/7/60). This was one of many requests that flowed into Accra in the 1960s and 1970s for loans for (or sometimes of) musical equipment, usually when the school wanted to put on a cultural performance for its speech and prize-giving day. Drums are expensive, and the leather is easily broken; they thus constituted a sizable investment for a school that might want to use them only once or twice a year.

Some individuals coordinated their efforts with those of the Arts Council. Nana Asiedu Darko, a retired music teacher from Larteh, known to many as Teacher Darko, started a cultural troupe in 1964 at St. Andrews College, a teacher training college in Mampong-Ashanti, so students could learn the different performance traditions of *adenkum, mpinti, kete, adowa, fɔntɔmfrɔm,* and an Ewe dance form.[14] He had to bring in people from the outside because he himself did not know some of the dances and musical forms. The headmaster at St. Andrews was supportive and allowed Teacher Darko to buy whatever he wanted for the cultural troupe, so he bought drums for the school, including a northern *dondo* drum (interviews, 19 Feb., 9 Mar. 1999). Teacher Darko was clearly interested in representing the different performance traditions of Ghana, not just local ones. Transferred to Benkum Secondary School in his hometown in the 1970s, he organized a cultural troupe and cultural festivals for the secondary schools in the area of his own accord, and later participated in the National Drama Festival organized by the Arts Council in 1974–75. In this case Teacher Darko's individual efforts to organize cultural activities in schools eventually articulated with the activities of the Arts Council, where he was able to receive further recognition for his work.

The Arts Council soon picked up on teachers' and students' enthusiasm and began to deliberately organize cultural troupes in schools. The Eastern regional branch's quarterly report for July–September 1965 states that the chief education officer in Accra wanted cultural groups established in all the secondary schools and training colleges, and by the end of the year, the regional organizer had visited twenty-three schools and teacher training colleges in the Eastern Region to this end. During these visits the organizer told schools that clubs could focus on "folk dancing and drumming, music, drama, literature, fine arts and crafts" (Eastern Regional Archives, ERG 1/14/12).

Some school cultural troupes were fostered and encouraged by the many performances and demonstrations of the Arts Council's own standing troupe in Accra, which, under the direction of choreographer Robert A. Ayitey, toured the country. These "national" performances combined forms of music and movement associated with different ethnic groups. Women also drummed during their performances, challenging prohibitions about women touching drums. In November 1967 the troupe toured the Eastern Region, performing at eleven secondary schools and teacher training colleges. On this tour the first half of their performances was devoted to a series of "traditional dances" and the second half to a dance-drama called "Tears for a Stranger." Audiences, unfamiliar with this new storytelling form, sometimes responded to the dance-drama with shouts of "talk, talk!" This new artistic form, in which a story was "told" solely through dancing and gesture, was designed to make the drama comprehensible to audiences across a multilinguistic nation (Report on the Eastern Region tour, Ghana Natl. Archives, RG 3/7/146). At the 150th anniversary celebrations of Presbyterian Training College, held in December 1998 in Akropong, Frank Hayford, a professor of education at the University of Cape Coast, spoke about his experiences at the college in the 1960s. He recounted how he had seen the Ghana Dance Ensemble perform at PTC in February 1965, his third and last year, and had been "overwhelmed" and "moved to tears" because it was "so enriching" and "so different." In a report on a tour of the Western and Central regions in May and June 1970, one of the lead dancers, Mr. Ayitey, said that there was praise everywhere for the female drummers and "almost all the Secondary Schools and the Training College [asked] the company to come to their aid by teaching and helping them to know their cultural background" (Ghana Natl. Archives, RG 3/7/250).

Thanks to these tours, with their presentations of a "national culture" that combined dances and music from different ethnic groups, schools and teacher training institutions came to see the Arts Council, like the National Dance Company in Zimbabwe (Turino 2000), as the repository of the country's cultural knowledge. Thus, while students could learn local dances and musical forms from local adults, they turned to the Arts Council to learn about the traditions of other ethnic groups. For instance, after the national dance troupe's tour of the Eastern Region in 1967, Ghana Secondary School in Koforidua asked the Arts Council in Accra to send a dance instructor to refine their *adowa, kete,* and *agbaja* dances for a performance. Two instructors, Ayitey and a Miss Dziworno, came and stayed for two days. They taught the students drumming and then two dances, the Asante *adowa* and the Anlo-Ewe *gahu* (Ghana Secondary School to Arts Council of Ghana, 20 Mar. 1968, Ghana Natl. Archives, RG 3/7/146). In promoting this "national" version of culture, the Arts Council created a standard of cultural performance that made school cultural troupes more dependent on its particular cultural resources and expertise.

At the same time, because teacher training colleges and secondary schools drew students from all over southern Ghana, students could gain exposure to different performing traditions through one another. Informants indicated that, in a manner reminiscent of the multiethnic environment of Achimota, where members of different ethnic groups presented "their" own performance traditions to one another, students in these boarding institutions were able to participate in and learn drumming and dancing for extracurricular entertainment. A teacher in Awukugua remembered from his time at Peki Government Training College in the Volta Region (1967–69) that "every ethnic group had time to display its cultural heritage." On Saturday nights, for entertainment each ethnic group would perform *agoro*, or drumming and dancing (Osei-Awuku interview, 10 Aug. 1999). Mr. Appaenti, an Akan language teacher at the training college in Akropong, remembered a similarly structured entertainment at the School of Ghana Languages when he studied there a decade later, in 1979: on Thursdays each language group performed its own dances for the others (interview, 31 Dec. 1999). Thus, performing arts continued to be associated with ethnic- and language-based attachments even as the Arts Council created national productions that combined those different traditions of performing arts.

Both the Young Pioneer movement and the Arts Council activities were attempts by the state to make its ideology hegemonic. They were intended to disseminate as widely as possible how the contradiction between promoting a national identity and celebrating local and ethnic traditions was to be resolved: through state-sponsored performance. Both of these dissemination strategies relied on educated people to be successful. The YP movement targeted schools because children were considered susceptible to indoctrination, and teachers to political pressure, but with the fall of Nkrumah the movement, never popular with many parents and teachers in Akuapem, died, its equipment burned or appropriated by other organizations. The Arts Council began with a different purpose: to organize performances by traditional artists. But the interest exhibited by young people and their teachers for equipment and training caused it too to become involved with schools—particularly secondary schools and teacher training institutions—eventually more so than with artists. The Arts Council served as a model for the new aesthetic of a state-sponsored buffet of performance traditions incorporated into a single performance, which students then sought to imitate in their own performances. Through the feedback loop that educated people and the state generated between them during the 1960s and 1970s, culture as performing arts became a dominant meaning of culture, in which teachers and students became enthusiastic about "knowing their cultural background," in the words of dance instructor Ayitey, by learning to dance and drum.

"Promoting a Unified Ghanaian Culture": The (P)NDC Revolution

The (P)NDC government, which came to power in a military coup on New Year's Eve, 1981, was characterized by an expansion of the state in general and of its cultural programming in particular, in part because it agreed to a series of neoliberal economic reforms pushed by the World Bank and the International Monetary Fund in the early 1980s. Although neoliberalism is associated with the paring back of the state in favor of private enterprise, the state does not simply disappear as markets take over; the state continues to play a role (Clarke 2002). The government must actively construct political, legal, and institutional conditions under which the market can exist (Burchell 1996). Furthermore, the Ghanaian team that negotiated with economists from the IMF and the World Bank did not share their belief in the greater efficiency and productivity of market forces (Hutchful 2002). Far from undermining the state, the new policies in this case strengthened the state because the Ghanaian leadership used the increased flow of funds to recharge the state (Hutchful 2002). Thus, in Ghana neoliberalism was consistent with the aggrandizement and visibility of the state (Chabal 1992), and the primary effect of the 1981 revolution was the increased presence and power of the state in the Ghanaian landscape.

A World Bank–sponsored educational reform in 1986 brought several important policy shifts: it put more resources into the first nine years of education—defined as "basic education"—at the expense of secondary and university education; it reduced the mandatory total number of years of pre-university schooling; it made basic education more vocational so that those who did not go on to secondary school could be self-sufficient and self-employed; and it introduced school fees that increased with each level of schooling so that, outside of teachers' salaries that were paid by the government, schools could be self-supporting. This reform pushed through some initiatives that had a long history of being proposed—and resisted— in Ghana, notably vocational education and reducing the total number of years of schooling (P. Foster 1965).

With the larger restructuring of education sponsored by the World Bank, another reform was pushed through, although in this case not at the instigation of the bank. Two recommendations initially proposed in 1973 by the Acheampong regime were now fully adopted: replacing the four-year middle school course of study with a three-year junior secondary course, strong on vocational studies, and adding a new subject called "cultural studies" at the primary, junior secondary, and senior secondary levels. "Cultural studies," as envisioned by the Ministry of Education in 1974, would comprise "Religion, Music (including drumming and dancing), Drama, Arts and Crafts and Home Science" (Ghana 1974, 4, 5).[15] By 1979–80, 118 experimental junior secondary schools had been established, but the plan to transform middle schools into junior secondary schools was not fully implemented until the 1986 educational reform (Ghana [1995?]; Odamtten 1993, 60). The injection of funds from the World Bank allowed the state to implement policies proposed in earlier eras. Neoliberal educational reforms are consistent with a nationalist cultural education policy if we see the project of the Rawlings revolution as controlling and expanding the apparatus of the state.

A few years before the 1986 reform, the (P)NDC government had made a start on institutionalizing the teaching of culture in schools by launching what it called the Curriculum Enrichment Programme. The program, in the words of the Cultural Studies Division, was designed "to in-culcate Cultural Education, community work and Physical Education into our children. The C.E.P. really brought cultural awareness in our children. They are taught to be proud of their country, to appreciate and value our culture and to feel to contribute towards the improvement of their culture. The C.E.P. brought a wave of Cultural Rennaisance [sic] into our schools" (Ghana n.d., 2). Professor Esi Sutherland-Addy, undersecretary of Education and Culture in 1987, said that when the CEP was established in 1983–84, it was an afterschool program. Much was left up to the teacher's initiative, and teachers were not trained. Rather than a syllabus, the government provided suggestions. One suggestion, for instance, was to replace the bells used to signal class changes with drums.[16] Obuobi Atiemo Akuffo (or Teacher Okyen, as most people called him), a member of the Akropong royal family and a drummer who taught at Akropong Demonstration School, remembered the CEP being instituted later, in 1989. With the help of his uncles, he created the poetic words and allusions in the new school drum texts, and all the schools in Akuapem North and South districts came to his school to learn how to signal the change of classes (interview, 21 Sept. 1998). However, Professor Sutherland-Addy told me that teachers did not teach the CEP because it was not an examination subject, so the Ministry of Education decided that culture needed to become a school subject. The (P)NDC government credited itself with putting cultural studies on "the school time-table as a subject [in 1986]. Hitherto, culture was only considered as drumming and dancing and [an] extra-curricular activity" (Ghana n.d., 2). Teachers in Akuapem schools remembered 1988 as a time when music and dance became a compulsory subject; before that, if it was taught, it was because of an individual teacher's interest. Obviously, in the experience of teachers at the local level, these reforms overlapped and were difficult to distinguish. Through the 1986 educational reform, the focus on schools for cultural interventions became institutionalized and under the guidance of the Ministry of Education, rather than the Arts Council, which by this time had been renamed the National Commission of Culture.[17]

The cultural studies curriculum, ideologically, was essentially no different from the Arts Council's program of activities. It too presented the cultural traditions of different ethnic groups within a framework of national unity. According to Afua Ampene, one of the writers of the new textbooks, cultural studies was instituted as a separate subject from Ghanaian languages so that students would be able to learn about the cultures of the different ethnic groups in Ghana, rather than just learning about the customs of Twi-speaking peoples in Twi language class or of Ewe-speaking peoples in Ewe language class (interview, 12 June 1999). The Ministry of Education and Culture formally stated the goal of cultural education in the 1986 reform this way: "Every Ghanaian needs a sense of cultural identity and dignity. Ghana has a Cultural heritage of individual ethnic cultures and promoting a unified Ghanaian culture will ensure a sense of national identity and make the nation stronger and more unified" (Ghana 1988b, 3).

But for all the structural similarities between the cultural studies syllabus and textbooks and the Arts Council's performances in bringing different ethnic traditions together in a single national space, the new school subject brought a new definition of culture: culture as not just drumming and dancing but as the way of life of a people that would go much deeper into the intimate domain of Ghanaian social experience. The cultural studies subject was to integrate "Social Systems, Drama, Drumming and Dancing, Religion and Music" (Ghana 1988a, 5). Social systems included "simple customary practice such as greetings, manners and etiquettes, our costumes, games, folklore, folksongs and traditional occupations"; and religious and moral education included the study of Christianity, Islam, and traditional religion (5). The subject became more advanced at the junior secondary school level, where students learned about the life-cycle ceremonies, verbal art, and dances and musical ensembles of different ethnic groups, as well as the religious beliefs and practices of the three main religions of Ghana. Students in the third year of junior secondary school, for example, were to study the marriage rites of the Ewe, in "some communities in the Northern and Upper Regions of Ghana," and among the Akan (Ghana 1989a, 21). Thus, the (P)NDC government aimed "to ensure the structuring of the total schooling environment . . . such that an authentic

Ghanaian message as well as pride in the Ghanaian cultural heritage is easily transmitted to the student" (Ghana 1991, 8). To that end it embedded
culture as a school subject within the curriculum rather than as an extracurricular, performance-related activity.

Although the 1986 educational reform enabled the government to expand its cultural programming, those same reforms seem to have affected
Ghanaians' structure of feeling. Rather than expressing pride in their
country, in everyday conversations, Ghanaians tend to contrast their nation to other countries they see as more socially and economically advanced in self-critical ways. Just as the Ghanaian economy is increasingly
dependent on outside flows, both the import-export market and loans, so
too do Ghanaians seem oriented toward capitalizing on global flows. These
days a majority of students and teachers give government cultural programming only a lukewarm reception at best. Some of those who felt
"burning love" for their cultural traditions during the 1960s and 1970s, like
Teacher Darko, maintain embers of that sentiment, and they are the most
loyal participants in government cultural programming today, serving as
judges for cultural competitions or teachers of Ghanaian languages.

Many people in Akuapem are not pleased with the 1986 educational reform, to which they attribute the poor quality of the schools and a general
deterioration of the educational system.[18] The subject of vocational studies, in particular, has not received the kind of equipment and teachers
needed to prepare students for a trade like tailoring, car mechanics, or hairdressing that they can engage in after junior secondary school without un-
dertaking a full apprenticeship. What immediately drew the ire of Christians, though, was the mandatory cultural studies subject. According to
Professor Sutherland-Addy, Christians wanted religion to be its own separate subject and not mixed in with topics like customs and music. Ms. Ampene told me that Christians complained about the study of traditional religion in the course, which by their account was "making students become
fetish priests" (interview, 12 June 1999). Under pressure from Christians,
the government in 1996 (but not implemented in Akuapem until 1998–
99), split up cultural studies at the basic school level into three subjects:
Ghanaian languages, which would include lessons on customs—ceremonies, festivals, chieftaincy, traditional professions—and verbal arts; religious and moral education, which would study the three religions of
Ghana; and music and dance, which would cover the performing arts of
different ethnic groups (Ghana 1998, 1996). Ms. Ampene commented
that the only difference between the old cultural studies program and the
reformed system was that the students might not get "the sense of belong-

ing" and being "part of the community" because, as the new syllabus for Ghanaian languages put it, they would only study "the cultural and historical heritage of their linguistic group" (Ghana 1998, iii).

When I began my major period of fieldwork in 1998, I was initially concerned that my research topic had disappeared into thin air. When I visited the thirteen primary and junior secondary schools in the Akropong/Abiriw circuit and asked to observe a lesson of either the old subject of cultural studies or the new one of music and dance, I found that none of the schools regularly taught either, although they were willing to put on a special performance for me. The reform that introduced cultural studies has thus been stymied by state and public ambivalence about the role and meaning of culture. Since neither music and dance nor cultural studies are tested in national examinations, unlike most other subjects, the absence of cultural studies within the schoolday can be left to slip by unnoticed. As before the reform, its teaching depends on a teacher's or principal's interest and expertise. The only place in the school curriculum that students are likely to be taught an explicitly marked culture is in Ghanaian languages, a subject that is nationally examined but where the emphasis, as in the teaching of English, is on grammar and literacy. Furthermore, the study of Ghanaian languages had been made voluntary in secondary schools in 1996. The teachers are aware that textbooks for cultural studies exist, but I encountered only two who had access to a copy, and the textbooks are completely out of the financial reach of students. The teaching of culture exists only on paper and not in students' experience of the regular schoolday. As a result, this study does not focus on the curriculum and its textbooks except as an example of state ideology about culture—culture as a way of life of a people—that entered the debate recently but does not seem to be on its way to becoming hegemonic.

Even as the (P)NDC government worked to disseminate a more encompassing definition of culture, it continued to promote culture as drumming and dancing. In 1987 it created a cultural studies unit within the Ghana Education Service to "monitor, supervise, and conduct research into the teaching of culture in our schools and colleges" (Ghana n.d., 2). The new unit, made up of three men at the national office with additional personnel at the regional and district levels, began organizing school festivals and competitions like the ones the Arts Council had organized, in which schools competed with one another at the district, regional, and national levels in various performance categories. The first national meet, the Elementary Schools National Cultural Festival, was held in 1988, followed by a second in 1989 (but cultural officers said they had organized school festivals at the district and regional levels since 1985). According to teachers and cultural officers, in the beginning few schools participated, and neither students nor school staff showed much interest, but that has slowly changed. At first national festivals were held only for the primary schools; national festivals for secondary schools were instituted in 1995 and for kindergartens in 1999.

In 1996 the drama category, which had been performed in a Ghanaian language, was replaced by that of dance-drama, in which, like the members of the Ghana Dance Ensemble, students use dance alone to tell a story. As Stephen Sedofu, cultural studies officer for the Eastern Region Commission on Culture, Institute of African Studies graduate, and occasional judge for school cultural competitions, explained (and as the Arts Council had long before appreciated), at a national event dance-drama allows the storyline to be comprehensible to an audience that is (to use his word) "heterogenous" (interview, 23 Mar. 1999). Since 1996 the school competitions have featured student performances and productions in six different genres: poetry recital, in which students recite poetry in a Ghanaian language; drum language, in which students imitate the tonality of recited phrases on the drums; dance-drama, in which students act out a story through dance, without words; choral music; sight reading, in which students are given a written piece of music to sing; and vocational skills, in which artwork, crafts, and other materials produced by students are displayed. Schools are least likely to put forward contestants in the genres of musical sight reading and vocational skills. The performance genres take place on a school stage or in the center of a school courtyard, with the vocational skills (if any) on exhibit in nearby classrooms. All the performances of a single genre follow one another, school by school, until they are done, so that, depending on the number of schools performing, the competition lasts between six hours and three days.

Each genre is judged by two or three judges, who, to escape charges of bias, are unaffiliated with any of the schools. They are usually from either the immediate area or a nearby town, because of travel costs. Although it does not seem to be an absolute requirement, most judges have studied to degree level either vocational studies (for the arts and crafts exhibit), music (for the choral music and sight-reading competitions), or Ghanaian languages (for the poetry recital, drum language, and dance-drama competitions). At the circuit and district competitions in 1997, 1999, and 2002, the judges either taught secondary school or worked in a supervisory capacity for the district educational office. The regional and national contests similarly draw on people at these levels, but they are able to bring in additional experts to help them. The organizers of the Eastern regional competition, for example, invited a few officials from the regional Center of National Culture, located in Koforidua, and the national competition brought in several faculty members from the School of Performing Arts and the College of Education in Winneba. Although chiefs are usually invited to the competitions and one or two may come with their entourages to serve as honored guests or give a welcoming speech to the crowd, they are not invited as judges or experts in culture. Instead, continuing the tradition of the Arts Council, expertise in culture resides in those who have positions in and training from state institutions. Because of the high educational criteria needed to be considered an expert, the overwhelming majority of judges are male. Most judges serve repeatedly in this capacity, traveling to different circuit competitions during the month or so that they are organized and returning year after year. Judges take their role seriously, listening and watching carefully before filling in the score sheets, and when they announce the final results, they often give advice on what could be improved. Across all genres, performances are judged according to three sets of criteria. The greatest emphasis is placed on technical excellence (the tonal correctness of the drumming, the clarity of enunciation in the poetry recital). Adherence to rules (such as time limits or the number of participants) contributes to the total score, as does the performance's "authenticity" or conformity to that year's theme.[19] The festivals are fiercely competitive, with teachers and students questioning the judges' fairness and remembering the results from previous years.

The competition begins at the circuit level (in the case of the primary and junior secondary schools) or the district level (in the case of the secondary schools); the winners in each genre progress to the regional contests and, depending on their success at that level, to the national meet. Much of the organization of the competition in general depends on the work and dedication of the district and regional cultural officers, and not all district and regional competitions take place. Although the Eastern regional cultural competitions are not well run, the cultural officer in the Ghana Education Service for Akuapem North district, Mr. Devoh, is particularly energetic and organized. For the secondary school competition that I observed in 1999, Mr. Devoh first held a workshop for teachers at all twelve of the secondary schools and teacher training colleges in early February 1999 and then visited each of the schools individually throughout February and March. The district competition was held at the end of March; some schools had three weeks of practice, and others began practicing three days before. The regional competition was held in the middle of April and the national one at the beginning of May, over the school holidays.

Under the (P)NDC government, the bureaucracy, personnel, and organization in cultural programming grew. Cultural programming became more focused on schools, and a unit within the Ghana Education Service was created to organize those cultural interventions. The innovations of the (P)NDC government lay in its attempts to create national cohesion and ethnic tolerance through the new form of the dance-drama and the cultural studies syllabus, in which students learned about the customs and verbal arts of ethnic and language groups other than their own. The (P)NDC government presented itself as being both revolutionary and an heir to Nkrumah's cultural policies (Ben Abdallah and Novicki 1987), and the leaders were in many ways correct to stress both the continuity and discontinuity. Their innovations were a refinement of the practices and the ideology of the Arts Council of creating national cultural forms for national unity. They also sought to expand the definition of culture from "drumming and dancing" to "a way of life," in order to engage people at a deeper level. However, because of criticisms from religious groups, the (P)NDC government's reforms were not entirely successful. Their implementation has depended a great deal on teachers' and students' understandings of culture, which I describe more fully in the next two chapters.

Conclusion

In the fifty-year history outlined here, culture became increasingly associated with the state and experts linked to it, such as members of the Ghana Dance Ensemble, bureaucrats in the Arts Council, and cultural officers in the Ghana Education Service. Over time culture came to be seen as a national asset and property, which could be transmitted by the state through its schools and other institutions. This process was most apparent with the Ghana Dance Ensemble, which set a new performance standard by combining musical and dancing traditions associated with specific ethnic groups to present "national" displays. Schoolchildren putting on similar displays thus needed assistance from Ghana Dance Ensemble dancers to perform ethnic dances not their own. It is also evident in the identity of the judges of school cultural competitions during the 1990s, whose expertise comes from their education and position within state institutions.

The state chose to highlight only a narrow swath of the richness of cultural experience, that which was most amenable to the display of the nation: drumming and dancing. What is the effect of this small selection of cultural practices being called cultural? As drumming and dancing, culture becomes purely aesthetic, stripped of spiritual connotations. Simultaneously, culture becomes depoliticized—at least for those (such as most children) unaware of the history of colonialism and the politics of the contemporary government. The politics is in the staging: through the state-sponsored buffet of culture, the government makes the statement that different ethnic groups coexist side by side within a national space. Performing arts also take place most comfortably outside the normal schedule of the school, in Saturday-night or afterschool entertainments, and in annual national and school celebrations such as Independence Day or open house and prize-giving day. Furthermore, drumming and dancing were more available to schoolchildren and teachers than other, less public forms of cultural practices. Those arts thus became a route by which some educated people could participate in and show their enthusiasm for culture, although some took other avenues, such as language study and the documentation of local festivals. Drumming and dancing competitions served some students' interest in looking "smart" and performing in public. What is unclear, though, is how many students also felt national sentiment as such (Bendix 1992). Drumming and dancing became the way the nation appropriated cultural traditions and engaged many of its citizens, particularly schoolchildren, in naturalizing both that appropriation and this selected meaning of culture at the level of bodily, habitual experience and the subjectivity of the person.

In order for this activity to become natural and hegemonic, the government's project needed to articulate with the personal mission of other groups, particularly teachers and students, because of the focus on schools as a site for intervention. Although the Young Pioneer movement was generally not criticized publicly by teachers because of the dangers involved, they found methods of subtle resistance such as nonparticipation to protest its activities or the government behind it (see Scott 1985). At the same time, particularly in the years just after independence, private intellectual concerns and initiatives concatenated with the Arts Council activities, so that each seemed to be stimulating the other. As the desires and projects of the state and some educated people came together, the state, teachers, and students were involved in a reinforcing feedback loop in generating a particular conception of the cultural. The case of Ghana is thus different from that of Tanzania, where Askew (2002) concludes that the presentation of culture proved ineffectual in legitimizing the state precisely because it was a top-down project. Ghana presents a more complicated case; here teachers and students, for a brief historical moment, found that government cultural programming allowed their own feelings and identities to find full expression.

That moment in which the state's definition of culture became hegemonic did not survive the political upheaval of the late 1970s and early 1980s. The (P)NDC government sought structural adjustment programs to stabilize its power. Those neoliberal economic and educational reforms allowed the state to expand its presence in the realm of the cultural, and the new definition of culture it promoted, as a way of life, reflected the attempt to incorporate even more intimate domains of Ghanaians' lives. For Ghanaians, however, the restructuring of the economy wrought by these reforms adjusted their structure of feeling as well. Increasingly enchanted by global flows of people and resources and disenchanted with the promise of the nation, many Ghanaians are ambivalent about the role and importance of culture in their personal lives and their country.

Chapters 1 and 2 have drawn on archives and personal accounts to show how the Basel missionaries, African Christians, and the state rendered culture an object of discourse and reification. The state attempted to reintegrate the definition of culture that legitimated its own authority—that of drumming and dancing—back into the habitual practices of its citizens by engaging schoolchildren in cultural programming and making schools sites for the transmission of culture. The remainder of the book will be an ethnographic study of the teaching of cultural traditions in classrooms and through school competitions in the current context of ambivalence and neoliberalism, in which the state's claims about culture are only one of a sizable array. The next two chapters explore the limits on the state's hegemony precisely because culture and schools were used to carry out that project.

How Culture Is Reclaimed by Its Citizens

PART 2

3

IN THE NATIONAL school cultural competition held in Cape Coast in May 1999, the drummer representing the Eastern Region used the opportunity to praise his paramount chief, or ɔmanhene, to the assembled secondary school students, teachers, government officials, and judges. Because Ghanaian languages are tonal, a set of drums, one with a low tone and one with a high tone, can be used to "talk" relatively formulaic phrases. But unlike the drum texts used in the chiefly courts, the majority of drumming riffs in school competitions are not formulaic, and drummers or their speech mediators (akyeame) recite each phrase aloud so that their drum text is comprehensible to the audience and judges. This drummer chose to praise and recite the appellations of the paramount chief of New Juaben (encompassing Koforidua and its environs) as if he was drumming within the chief's court. Here are his opening "lines":

The Location of Culture

*The Politician,
the Chief, or the Teacher?*

Introduction:

Ayan a merebɛyan yi mebɛyan de afa
    Dasebre Nana Oti Boateng a ɔyɛ
    ɔmanhene wɔ Dwaben Foforom. Ne
    din ne n'abodin na mede brɛ mo yi
    nti monyɛ aso ntie.

Drummed text:

Dasebre Nana Oti Boateng,
Dwaben Adua Ampofo Antwi,
    Konkorihene.
Akete-ɔnam-brɛmpɔn asum agum popa
    w'anim ma yɛnkɔ ɛ.

Ɔkyekye akuro brempɔn a ɔde ne
    man nam.

Introduction:

The drum language that I will drum is
    about Dasabre Nana Oti Boateng,
    paramount chief of New Juaben. It
    is his name and appellations that I
    will bring you, so pay attention.

Drummed text:

Dasabre Nana Oti Boateng,
Juaben Adu-Ampofo, Konkori chief.

The small man who walks majestically,
    who has pushed mightily, wipe your
    brow and let's go.
Great founder of towns who keeps
    his nation sharp [on its toes for
    defense].

Ayɔko Sakyi Ampoma Nana Yokoni,
ɔsansa fa ade a ɔde kyerɛ

Aberewa Ampem, ɔhyeadwerɛ Nana
Asumegyani
Adakwa Yiadom Brempɔn.
Ɔsagyefo kasabaako a otwaa asuo
barima,
Akuamoa Nana fi Dwaben Dɛeboase.

Ɔsɛsɛ Tretu Akomea a ɔko foro
kwasafo brebuo
Na ɔresiane a osi no ɔsɔreɛ so.

Ɔten Boafo Kɔhweakwae a ohu dɔm
sereɛ.

Ayɔko Sakyi Ampoma Nana Yokoni, if
the hawk catches something, it
shows it.

Aberewa Ampem who burns *adwere*,[1]
Nana Asumegyani

Adakwa Yiadom Brempɔn.
Savior from war who does what he says,
who banishes strong men.

The grandchild of Akuamoa from
Dwaben Dɛeboase.

Ɔsɛsɛ Tretu Akomea who goes to
climb the nest of the community.
And if he comes down, as soon as he
touches the ground, he rises up [an
amazing thing].

Ɔten Boafo Kɔhweakwae who, on
seeing the enemy, smiles.

He went on in this vein to the finish.

Unfortunately for him, although the judges recognized his technical skill, they were put off by his choice of text. As they said in their public comment, "For the theme, we expected the citations to be drummed to reflect the theme of the festival. Here is a clear example cited. There is a master drummer from Eastern Region, good by all standards. But when we went back to look at the theme [for the competition], then we detected his text didn't have any bearing on the general theme, 'Culture: Gateway to the Nation's Prosperity.' Organizers, take note, and create texts reflecting the theme."[2] The judges gave a clear signal to teachers and students that performances during the school cultural competitions should be geared toward addressing the importance of culture to the nation of Ghana, not toward praising individual chiefs.

Their stance reflected the position of the new political elites in postcolonial African states, who have always seen traditional elites like chiefs as competitors for political power. From the start political leaders, whether Mobutu in Zaire or Nkrumah in Ghana, tried to appropriate the practices and attributes of traditional chiefs in order to simultaneously subvert and incorporate their political power (De Boeck 1996). Kwame Nkrumah chose Okyeame Boafo Akuffo, one of the sons of the paramount chief F. W. K. Akuffo of Akuapem, to be his *ɔkyeame*, traditional poet and speech mediator. Okyeame Akuffo prefaced all Nkrumah's speeches, even in parliament, with awe-inspiring chiefly appellations, such as "Osagyefo"

(Savior in battle) and "Kantamanto" (One who does not break his oath), the latter used traditionally to praise the chief of Aburi (Pobee 1976). Furthermore, although Nkrumah was an Nzema from the Western Region, in these paeans of praise, Okyeame Akuffo endowed the First Prime Minister with ancestors from all over southeastern Ghana, especially from the eight traditional Akan states (Yankah 1985). These cultural accouterments were not only symbolic of the independence of one of the first black African nations; they were also statements about the power of the central government over traditional chiefs and kingdoms. Historically, then, the postcolonial government of Ghana has attempted to appropriate the cultural symbols of royalty in traditional kingdoms, in order to flaunt its own power, cement its legitimacy, and create a national identity over and above allegiances to traditional chiefs and kingdom- or town-based identities. As Thomas Turino (2000) argues in his study of music and nationalism in Zimbabwe, nationalism involves balancing the threats to the nation inherent in both a global cosmopolitanism and a localism. Distinctly local cultural practices allow the nation to differentiate itself on the world stage within an overall framework of similarity; but they may also threaten the nation's existence, should local groups desire to create their own nation. Cultural intervention has been an important mechanism for states, including Ghana, to demonstrate the power and presence of the state vis-à-vis other, possibly competing political allegiances.

Chiefs have been just as active in this process, attempting as best they can to use their alliances with the state and political parties to increase their own power and status (Dunn and Robertson 1973). With the right connections to politicians and civil servants, for example, chiefs learned they could bring government services like electricity, piped water, and educational facilities to their towns or kingdoms. Increasingly, the men and women the elders select as chiefs and queen mothers are educated and attached to urban, governmental networks that allow them to facilitate flows of resources from outside, what the political scientist Jean-François Bayart (1993) terms "the politics of extraversion." The chief of Amanokrom, for instance, was a government statistician and is currently an economic consultant; the queen mother of Akuapem, Nana Dokua I, was a nurse. Although the domains of chieftaincy and state remain distinct ideologically, the actors involved are increasingly becoming the same as new and traditional elites become assimilated to one another, a process that involves both points of tension and points of convergence (Bayart 1993). Culture has become a key signifier in the mutual assimilation of these elites and the legitimation of political power in Ghana.

Who has the power to define culture? To whom does culture belong—

traditional kingdoms represented by chiefs or the nation as represented by politicians? In Ghana the government's educational and cultural policies are aimed at making culture a national property associated with the state. State policies and curricula make cultural practices more organized and systematized and thus more open to state control and intervention (Scott 1998). In the process they attempt to eliminate alternative notions about the meaning of culture. However, the state cannot gain complete hegemony over this slippery signifier. Because the state reaches into intimate domains, such as the performing arts, to seek legitimacy, citizens can draw on the dense meanings of those same practices to subvert the power of the state (Herzfeld 1997). Although the state seeks hegemony, "the instability of these symbols demonstrates once again that no hegemony is ever total" (Guss 2000, 16). Both chiefs and churches are also engaged in defining the meaning of culture and identifying the proper locations for its use and practice. Discourses are ways of thinking that may overlap and reinforce each other but that may also close off other possible ways of thinking. The proliferation of these cultural discourses accounts for the fierce debate taking place in this postcolonial state.

Furthermore, the state contributes to the polyphony because it does not speak in one voice. As we saw in chapter 2, by the late 1990s the government in its embrace of neoliberalism began to drop the definition of culture as drumming and dancing and to articulate two other discourses— culture for development and culture as the way of life of a people. Thus, as scholars have noted in other instances, the state's own strategies shift and its policies change; its policies are "not necessarily coherent" (Rockwell 1994, 173; Vaughn 1997). Furthermore, implementing those shifting policies depends on state actors such as teachers who are variably invested in the goals of those policies. Schools form a policy-rich site, serving as a receptor for the many top-down directives issued by the Ministry of Education over several generations of people, governments, and ideologies. Policies become sedimented in schools, often in uneven layers, because some policies are picked up by teachers and others are not. Although a new discourse may mandate a change in a particular activity or subject, it can and often does run into resistance from teachers and students accustomed to doing things in a certain way from an older discourse. The cultural project in schools thus produces contradictory messages because of the swirl of cultural discourses available both from the present and the past.

Many of the state's discourses arise directly from the academic sphere. In Ghana, as in Nigeria (Amuwo 2002; Jega 1995), the flagship university, the University of Ghana, is closely connected to the government. Historically, its graduates have entered government employment. Students of the School of Performing Arts have become cultural officers in district and regional education offices, employees of the Arts Council, and teachers in schools. University professors and government ministers travel in the same social circles; they are members of the same families, live in urban areas, and attend the same churches and parties (see Cohen 1981). Furthermore, their positions are interchangeable, and many professors enjoy a stint of a few years in a government ministry, influencing state policy on cultural programming from the inside, before moving back to the university and seeking to influence it from the position of scholarly expertise (Arhin 1981; Institute of African Studies 1989). The IAS alone supplied three top officials in the (P)NDC government: Mohammed Ben Abdallah, a drama scholar, and Kwame Arhin, a historian, each of whom served as Minister of Culture (1982–94, 1998–99, respectively); and Esi Sutherland-Addy, a drama scholar, who as deputy secretary of Education presided over the reforms of the 1980s. When the New Patriotic Party came to power in 2000, Kwesi Yankah, a folklorist and linguist, and George Hagan, a historian, were put on the board of the National Commission of Culture. Whether inside or outside government, scholars promote their views of culture at a national level, to government ministries and to teachers' organizations (Arhin 1981; Nketia 1997), while their students articulate that vision at a local level, within district and regional education offices and schools. But even though the actors in both institutions are sometimes the same people, this does not mean that the relationship between them is always amicable: students and faculty can be some of the strongest critics of the government-in-power and as members of the elite can be crucial in supporting opposition parties.

It is within a hotly debated arena that government educational policies make their unsteady way. Although a state may seem to be producing authoritative discourses or defining the field of acceptable discourse through its policies, a state discourse may simply become part of a heated mix. "The cacophony . . . continually threatens to deafen state attempts at harmony" (Askew 2000, 161). The debate about the location and meaning of culture results in the government's lack of control over how the cultural curriculum is actually implemented in schools by teachers and students. Because teachers and students undermine, contest, and support the government's cultural project in schools according to their own understandings of the location of culture, the cultural curriculum as produced in schools is rarely ideologically univocal. Rather, it reflects the ideological negotiation over culture that is happening more generally in Ghana. The cultural curriculum forms a site in which Ghanaians negotiate the meaning of culture in a postcolonial state, and while it is a site that government policy has created, it is not simply a site where government ideologies about culture are produced. Following others who study educational policy and curriculum anthropologically (Anderson-Levitt 2003; Guthrie 1985; Hornberger 1988), I am interested in showing how social actors transform the meaning of top-down educational projects as they put them into practice. For that reason, although the political contest between chiefs and politicians helps us understand the intensity of the debate about culture in Ghana, they themselves will slip into the background. Rather, this chapter will concern itself with how teachers and students appropriate the spaces opened up by top-down educational reforms to influence the ideological debate about the meaning and location of culture within a postcolonial African state.

One reason I focus on discourses, rather than actors, in the paragraphs above and in this chapter as a whole is that these discourses are rhetorical positions or stances that are taken up by actors at different moments, just as the chief of Amanokrom wears the suit of an economist in his private life during the week and the *kente* cloth and sandals of a chief during festivals and ceremonies. A teacher may articulate a government discourse at a durbar or in a letter to the newspaper and a popular discourse in a conversation with me. The different meanings of culture form a repertoire available to many Ghanaians, who don the discursive stance appropriate to the context. Ghanaians play these ideas off one another and are aware of opposing discourses. Operating on the principle of a show of unity and indirection of speech in public situations, especially in areas of conflict, they cut and splice, patching different discourses together. The words may be the same, but the cluster of ideas shifts as people seek to synthesize opposing ideas or use one discourse to argue its opposite. There is constant jockeying for persuasive positions as Ghanaians struggle to make sense of dichotomies they feel as real, between traditional kingdoms and a modern nation, between tradition and progress, even as everyday life troubles those dichotomies.

This chapter examines how three government and two popular discourses about culture are produced by teachers, students, government ministers, and district education officers, and transmitted through cultural programming in schools. Some of the discourses will be familiar from the previous chapter, but this chapter complicates the discussion of hegemony by exploring the multivocality of the cultural curriculum. Although the state sponsors cultural programming in schools, the teaching and performance of culture in schools ends up producing more contradictory messages than the state intends.

Polishing and Beautification: Culture for Development
(Government Discourse I)

A television ad for Vaseline shea butter begins with a view of *kente* cloth, saying "traditional" and then "natural" as the picture changes to liquid being poured from a calabash. Women are dancing in colorful *kente* cloth, and a voice intones: "Shea butter. To keep skin healthy and shiny." The women are shown applying the shea butter onto their smooth and shiny arms. The last frame features a bottle of shea butter and a woman's face as the voice says, "Vaseline shea butter: Tradition with progress." This ad, which I first saw in October 1998, reflects the commercial uses of tradition, rather than government rhetoric, but the state is actively involved in the marketing of "Ghana," both for tourism and for business investment. The use of "tradition with progress" is expected to create a beautiful image of Ghana: shiny, black, and smooth. But the tradition is in need, like shea butter, of "refinement," a common euphemism for the process of modifying tradition. A primary school teacher and devout Christian from Akropong, Beatrice Offei, echoed these sentiments. She said that at first "our culture was dirty." In the past people put leaves, charcoal, and red sand on their bodies. But now they wear cloth and nice beads. "Yɛrepolishing. . . . Yɛre-revising. . . . Culture asesa ayɛ biribi fɛfɛfɛ" (We are revising it. . . . We are polishing it. . . . Culture has changed to become something beautiful; interview, 28 July 1999). In other words, Ghanaian culture as practiced in the past was barbaric and unpleasant to view, but it has now become presentable and beautiful through "revision" and "polishing." Clothing, dress, and presentation are often used as the metaphors or images of this progress: culture becomes a product.

For both the government and ordinary people, this metaphor of polishing is a way to accommodate a Christian discourse that highlights the negative aspects of culture to a popular view of culture as tradition that should be handed down from generation to generation. This discourse of refinement makes culture subject to evaluation, in which only some aspects should be preserved and the rest discarded. The government perspective has been aided by academics at the Institute of African Studies at the University of Ghana who have argued, using newer anthropological concepts, that culture is not static but is instead "dynamic," changing with the times and incorporating the new.

The National Commission on Culture agreed. "Culture is a growing phenomenon," it said in a 1991 document, "The Cultural Policy of Ghana." The writer continued: "This is established by our concept of Sankofa [go back for it], which established linkages with the positive aspects of our past and the present. The concept does not imply a blind return to customs and traditions of the past" (Ghana 1991, 2–3). Cultural studies officers in the Ghana Education Service promote this idea at festivals and public events. At the regional secondary school competition in Kumase in 1997, Nana Sakyi, director of the national Cultural Studies Unit, told students and teachers, "Culture is dynamic" and Ghanaians must "refine" what they have received and what they will pass on.

The refinement process raises the question of what will be polished and on what basis. Speakers tended to emphasize the functional qualities of cultural practices they thought were worth keeping. Mr. Devoh, the cultural studies officer for Akuapem North district, was excited that the guest of honor at the district secondary school competition at Nsawam, in Akuapem South, had talked about the positive and negative aspects of Ghanaian culture, and he made arrangements to find a speaker who would be willing to speak on that topic for the competition he was organizing in Akuapem North. The speaker he invited focused on the scientific rationale for certain cultural practices, such as shaking hands when greeting.[3] The Minister of the Eastern Region, Patience Adow, was reported as saying in a speech read on her behalf at the secondary school competition in Koforidua in 1997 that "in the past some of the taboos had scientific basis and cited for example that environmental degradation was checked by restricting entry into forest reserves along rivers and shrines while teenage pregnancy and family planning were taken care of by customs such as [girls' puberty rites like] 'Bragoro' in Akan or 'Dipo' in Krobo" (*Daily Graphic*, 28 July 1997, 14). She thus highlighted cultural practices that accorded with the current emphases of the government's development policies: environmentalism, family planning, and teenage pregnancy. By describing the scientific or functional aspects of certain cultural practices, speakers at government events, including cultural competitions, argue that these practices are necessary for the nation's development. Turino (2000) labels a similar discourse in Zimbabwe "modernist reformism," which "typically objectifies, recontextualizes, and alters indigenous *forms* for emblematic purposes in light of cosmopolitan dispositions" such as development or scientific rationality (16). In this discourse the reification of culture and the emphasis on cultural dynamism are in tension with each other.

Putting a new twist on the romantic-nationalist view that vernacular culture and language are crucial for the nation's welfare, the government stresses that indigenous culture is necessary for national economic development. Ghana's leaders have wholeheartedly adopted the World Bank's slogan "culture for development." But they do not mean by this the bank's pragmatic approach, after years of disappointing progress, that development projects should take local cultural practices into account. Theirs is instead the romantic-nationalist idea that culture is intrinsically valuable to the national well-being. In 1998–99 Malaysia and Indonesia were constantly cited for attaining middle-income status—which was Ghana's goal for the year 2020—an achievement attributed to those countries' promotion of their own language and culture.[4] Mr. Devoh told the teachers at one secondary school in Akropong that "the nation cannot rest on borrowed culture," and there was a need for "indigenous culture." But what he did not say and is less than clear is how development would be accomplished through the promotion of indigenous culture; it is more of a vague slogan than a philosophy guiding action or policy, unlike state decentralization or market liberalization.

Still, it is easy to see one way in which culture could be used for development. Elsewhere in Africa, neoliberal economic reforms have led to the growing marketing of "traditional culture" for the purpose of tourism (Ebron 2002). Ghana is also working to promote tourism, and tourism is an increasingly important source of foreign exchange,[5] but the cultural curriculum in schools is not primarily oriented toward preparing students to work in the tourism industry, as is done, for instance, in Hawaii (Kaomea 2000). This may change of course if tourism grows enough to warrant it. Tourism as an industry is highly localized, affecting some areas much more than others. While officials in the Akuapem North district were working to promote tourism by developing tourist brochures and maps in the late 1990s, I did not see much evidence of their success, either then or when I returned in 2002.

What the slogan "culture for development" primarily accomplishes in non-tourist areas of Ghana is to justify the state's role in heritage management and promotion. The discourse of development itself provides legitimacy for the nation-state, allowing it to make the claim that it is working in the best interests of the people (Chatterjee 1999). The expansion of cultural programming in the 1980s and 1990s has allowed the state to be more visible at a local level. In general the state in Ghana maintains its visibility through the events and ceremonies it sponsors. Beyond their immediate effect of drawing local crowds and participants, news of these events is reported in the government media, to reach a far greater number of people across the nation. "Culture for development" gives the state a platform on which to sponsor functions for cultural activities, which then increases its visibility at a local level when those functions are organized through schools.

As a social language "freighted with the valences of power, position, and privilege" (Holland et al. 1998, 191), the discourse of "culture for development" is associated with an elite closely tied to the state in urban centers like Accra and Kumase and in the university, which has consistently promoted the importance of cultural traditions for the nation. It has not fully replaced an older government discourse, that of culture as "a way of life of a people" which continues to coexist alongside it. The discourse of "culture for development," perhaps because it only dates from the 1980s, does not seem as sedimented or ingrained as that of culture as the way of life of a people whose history goes back, at least within academic circles, to the 1960s. Through the conflation of "a people" with citizens of the nation of Ghana rather than members of a traditional kingdom or ethnicity, the discourse of culture as the way of life of a people, like that of culture for development, justifies the nationalization of cultural practices and therefore their appropriation by the state.

Not Just Drumming and Dancing: The Way of Life of a People (Government Discourse II)

The definition of culture as a way of life of a people closely corresponds to definitions anthropologists promoted in the 1930s and 1940s but have since discarded. This functionalist discourse renders culture both national and secular, and characteristically sets out a list of cultural practices to show that culture is not just the worship of traditional gods, but encompasses all that Ghanaians do, including some behavior acceptable to Christians, such as dress and language. The following poem, "The Nation's Future Depends on Culture" (Ɔman yi daakye gyina amammrɛ so), is typical:

Ɔman yi daakye gyina amammrɛ so.	This nation's future depends on culture.
Amammrɛ yɛ ahyɛnso	Culture is the identifying mark
Ma ɔman tease-man biara.	Of every living nation.
Sɛnea yesiesie yɛn ho	The way we dress,
Gyidi a yekura ne ɔsom ko a yɛsom,	The beliefs we hold and the type of religion we practice,
Awaregye, afahyɛ, ne ayiyɛ	Marriage, festivals, and funerals,
Dwuma a yedi no ɔman yi mu,	Occupations in this nation,
Ago' horoɔ ne ɛdo asa,	The different entertainments and accompanying dances,
Ne nyinaa nkabom ne amammrɛ.	All together make culture.[6]

Another characteristic of this discourse is the assertion that culture, as the totality of cultural practices of a people, becomes their identifying mark, differentiating them from other national identities. At the Eastern regional cultural competition for secondary schools in April 1999 that I at-tended, the guest of honor, the acting regional director of education, Su-san Kennedy, put it this way: "Culture is the sum total or embodiment of the way of life of the people or the nation. This way of life distinguishes the Ghanaian from maybe the British or the Nigerian. It gives a nation its identity. Culture, for that matter, is agriculture, sculpture, arts, gover-nance, philosophy, religion, clothing, food, songs, dance, architecture; in fact, the entire behavior of a people" (17 Apr. 1999). In short, Ghana is different from other countries because of the way that its people live. The level of generalization here—agriculture, sculpture, dance—is important because if Mrs. Kennedy or Abigail Mintaah, who recited the poem quoted above, had named specific agricultural, festive, or culinary practices, some Ghanaians would no doubt feel excluded. While the existence of a na-tional entity is taken as a given, the actual content of that national being is the subject of constant negotiation and dispute (Handler 1988). Of the three state discourses, this one aims to delve the most deeply into the lived experience of Ghanaians, but the vagueness about the actual practices be-ing discussed—necessary in order to unify Ghanaians as a single people—renders it somewhat superficial.

Although this definition of culture began to be propounded by academ-ics at the University of Ghana at Legon, and especially at the Institute of African Studies, in the 1960s, it took some time for that academic dis-course to become government policy. Not until 1991, during the tenure of Ben Abdallah as Minister of Culture, was this vision of "culture as a way of life of a people" officially articulated. The key passage, as set out by the National Commission on Culture in "The Cultural Policy of Ghana," reads: "Our culture is the totality of the way of life evolved by our people through experience and reflection in their attempts to fashion a harmo-nious co-existence between them and their environment: material and non-material. This, as a continuing process, gives order and meaning to social, political, economic, aesthetic and religious norms and modes of or-ganisation which distinguishes us from other people" (Ghana 1991, 2).[7] Similar to other national ideologies that highlight cultural differences (Mosse 1964), "The Cultural Policy of Ghana" proposes that culture is the product of adaptation to a particular environment, and that as environ-mental and climatic conditions change, so too do cultures.

The current cultural studies syllabus promotes the "culture as a way of life" discourse with expositions on life-cycle rituals (birth, puberty, mar-riage, and funeral rites), language (proverbs, stories, greetings, etc.), per-formance arts, religions, occupations, and some aspects of material culture.

But that syllabus is rarely taught in schools, not only because of the lack of books for either teachers or students, but also out of respect for Christian sentiment (chapter 2). After I found on my visits to the thirteen primary and junior secondary schools that many seemed to be teaching this subject solely for my benefit, I chose to observe three schools—two primary and one junior secondary—over the whole weekly schedule of classes to find if the teaching of culture was part of the routine. I never saw a cultural studies lesson. Students in these and other schools confirmed my observations. Asked when they had been taught about culture, students recalled previous years when they had performed in cultural competitions, not classroom lessons. "Culture" for them referred to the competitions, and those competitions highlighted the discourse of drumming and dancing, not culture as a way of life. Thus, there is a disconnect between the discourse of culture as a way of life and how the state's cultural program is played out in schools. Although culture as a way of life of a people is the official ideology of the cultural program in schools, that program took the form mainly of cultural competitions, and these promoted ethnic or regional identifications and the notion that culture was, in fact, just drumming and dancing. The government's rhetoric notwithstanding, the way schoolchildren experience the cultural enrichment program reinforces the notion that culture refers to performance arts like drumming and dancing.

Culture as (Ethnic) Drumming and Dancing (Government Discourse III)

The cultural competitions are the product of an older policy and ideology than the two we have discussed, dating to Nkrumah and the founding of the Arts Council. The aim, as we saw in chapter 2, was to build national unity by showcasing performing arts associated with different ethnicities and regions at national events like arts festivals. The competitions, which are the students' main experience of culture in school, are explicitly oriented toward creating "national" art forms out of ones that are associated with various ethnicities.

As an institution of higher education, the School of Performing Arts is seen as the arbiter of taste and instruction in these areas. It furnishes judges for school cultural competitions, particularly at the national competition, and their aesthetic of combining different kinds of ethnic dances for national purposes pushes school groups to present an ethnically diverse panoply of dances and musical forms, as in Tanzania (Askew 2002). At the workshop for teachers in all the secondary schools in the Akuapem North district in 1999, Mr. Devoh, the district cultural studies officer, speaking of the dance-drama performances, advised the teachers that people from the School of Performing Arts were going to come to judge and would want a variety of dances. During his workshop at Gyahene Secondary School, he told teachers that they could use any Ghanaian dance, like *kpanlogo* (a Gã dance), *agbaja* (an Ewe dance), or *kete* or *adowa* (Asante, Akyem, and Kwawu dances), but that by all means they should bring in more than one dance. Similarly, Margaret Rose Tetteh, serving as judge at the Akropong district primary and junior secondary school festival, stressed the importance of using a variety of dances during dance-drama, telling me that because the festival was for the nation of Ghana, the students should use different styles. These dances did not seem differentially valued, although dances from southern Ghana were generally more familiar to students and teachers in Akuapem. The School of Performing Arts' emphasis on variety is curious, to say the least, considering the avowed goal of national unity. It is an orientation that, ironically, seems to strengthen the ethnic and geographical association of performance traditions.

The ethnic, rather than national, association of cultural practices is obvious to an observer of the rehearsals for the competitions, where students and teachers wove together a variety of dances and chose issues of national importance specifically designed to garner the favor of the judges, as Mr. Devoh suggested. In the rehearsals for the dance-drama at Abɛ Secondary School, which I regularly attended, the teacher and students had difficulty deciding on a plot. Frank Boateng, the faculty sponsor, told me that they could not do something on *Trokosi*—a system of ritual slavery, which had been very much in the news at the time—as they had wanted because they did not know its style of drumming. They decided to present a program on street children, which was a much-discussed problem, he said; he had just viewed a TV show on the subject. Although he seemed to have picked the plot for the relevance of its theme as a national problem, the story of a northern girl going down to the big city to carry loads (called *kaya-yoo*) in the market gave them the opportunity to dance a variety of dances, including a northern dance, and this also was a consideration for Mr. Boateng and the students.

Rehearsals were held almost every night over three weeks in the teachers' lounge, a big room with many chairs where a space was cleared at the front for dancing. Students met at 8:30 p.m., after the end of study hall, a time when most of their fellow students had gone to sleep or were studying. At one of the early rehearsals, I asked one performer what the group was planning to present for the dance-drama, and, illustrating a concern for aesthetics over plot, she replied that they were linking dances from different areas into a single dance-drama. During that rehearsal, when the drummers started playing an *adowa* beat for a market scene in the capital, Mr. Boateng interrupted, saying that playing *adowa* contradicted what they wanted to portray. Several girls agreed with him. He continued, "If the [market] sellers are dancing *adowa*, then the impression is that they are Kwawu [an Akan group from elsewhere in the Eastern Region]." But the *kaya-yoo* girls who carried loads in the market, the focus of this scene, were in fact from the north, so it was wrong to have them dance *adowa*. One girl thought that the sellers should dance *kpanlogo*, a Gã dance, to represent the setting of the city of Accra. Others agreed. Mr. Boateng disagreed, saying, "This needs to cut across many cultural boundaries." They would have a narrator who talked about the Dagomba in the north, where they were in their "right cultural environment," he pointed out, and then the northerners went to the city and adopted city life. Reversing himself, he said that the sellers should perhaps dance *adowa* after all because they were from Kwawu. At a rehearsal three days later, Mr. Boateng commented that the drummers were not drumming *adowa* well, so they should drum *kpanlogo*, and the sellers could be Gã. *Kpanlogo* is what they ended up with in the district competition. Discussions during the rehearsals reflected the ethnic association of certain dances and revealed the tension between representing a multiethnic Ghana and performing artistic genres in which the student musicians and dancers were competent.

The dance-drama group at Gyahene Secondary School was given its storyline by an outside expert, Kofi Martin, a dancer trained at the School of Performing Arts, and it was constructed to showcase many different dances. Called "Unity," the dance-drama portrayed the arrival of different ethnic groups (Northern, Ewe, and Gã) at an Akan royal court, each dancing its characteristic dance (*bambaya, agbaja,* and *kpanlogo*), where a land dispute between them is resolved.[8] Although the requirements of the form forced students to learn and perform dances new and strange to them, the dance-dramas also heightened the association between a particular dance and an ethnic identity.

A similar association between ethnicity and genre occurred in two cultural studies lessons put on for my benefit in two primary schools. Students were called up to the front of the room to perform the dance associated with their ethnicity before the rest of the students. In one lesson at Kenkan Primary, the teacher told a girl, "You are a Gã. What special food is eaten?" After the girl had explained the different foods, the teacher then told her, "Come and dance for me," which the girl did. The teacher then asked for the name of an Asante dance. The response was *adowa*, and an Asante girl was told to come up and dance. While she danced, the children sang a song that went with it and thumped on their desktops. There was so much noise it hurt my ears. Children from other classes gathered around the windows and doors and had to be chased away by the teacher and students. A boy was dragged up to perform a northern dance, and he fled back to his seat after dancing a little bit. A girl danced an Ewe dance, and others in the audience danced with her in the aisles. There was much thumping of desks and vast excitement. This was similar in strategy and structure to what happened in a lesson at another primary school. Teachers relied on students' knowledge, using them as representatives of their ethnic traditions. Luckily for teachers in Akuapem, many different ethnic groups were represented in their classrooms. It is worth noting that both these classes occurred early in my stay, before I realized that cultural studies was not a routine part of the curriculum. All the singing and dancing and discussion were prompted by my presence, and it was perhaps in part the break from their usual schedule in school that caused the students to respond with such enthusiasm and high energy.

Since the 1970s the Arts Council (and its successor) and the School of Performing Arts have attempted to create a national culture by having students learn dances associated with ethnicities other than their own and weaving those dances together into a single performance. This ideology is still present in the structure of the cultural competitions, not only because some of the judges are from the School of Performing Arts, but also because even though governments have changed, the tradition of the school cultural competition contains within it the ideologies that established it. The structure of the competition, particularly at the national level, in which students represent regions and thus ethnicities, also heightens the association between ethnicity and specific music-dance genres. In the circumstances, the government officials' speeches stressing culture as "a Ghanaian way of life" are more than a little contradictory when the competition itself highlights performing arts and regional/ethnic identities, in competition within a national space.

"Culture Is Inheritance": Historical Knowledge and the Way of Life of the Ancestors (Popular Discourse I)

All three government discourses—culture for development, culture as a way of life, and culture as drumming and dancing—coexist in schools and cultural competitions, presenting different aesthetic and ideological ideals for students and teachers, and producing sometimes overlapping and sometimes contradictory messages about culture. However, all three discourses attempt to render culture a national product and thus justify the government's attempt to appropriate culture through the institution of schooling. In this section and the one that follows, we turn to two popular discourses that associate culture with the past and the ancestors, and more specifically, with the secret rituals of chiefs.

A popular positive view of culture sees it as historical, the practices and wisdom of the ancestors. Culture should be taught because the traditions and knowledge of past generations should be passed on to the next generation, as a responsibility and obligation, and to avoid the wrath of powerful ancestors.[9] Two poems illustrate this definition of "culture as inheritance." The first is a drum text from the Brong-Ahafo region:

Mpanyin se:	The elders say:
Tete wɔ bi ka.	The past has something to say.
Tete wɔ bi kyerɛ.	The past has something to teach.
Mpanyin se:	The elders say:
Tete asoɛe	The resting place on the journey of the olden days
Yɛnsoɛ hɔ	[We say] We don't rest there
Nanso	But
Ɛhɔ ara na yɛsoɛ.	It is precisely there that we rest on the journey.[10]

Note how the proverbial phrase, "*Tete asoɛe, yɛnsoɛ hɔ,*" or "in our journey, we don't stop at the old resting spot any more," which refers to changing practices over the passage of time, was changed subtly to mean its opposite.

This theme appeared over and over again in the poetry recital and drum language performances in the secondary school competitions in 1999. Here is the other example, "Ghana yɛ ɔman tease" (Ghana Is a Living Nation), which was recited by a girl representing Asamankese West district at the Eastern regional competition (16 Apr. 1999):

Yedu amanfo so a,	If we come to the oldest part of the town,
Yaanom na yɛkae.	It is the forefathers that we remember.
Ɛyɛ nsɛnnahɔ.	It is an accepted fact.
Tete asoɛe,	The travelers' resting place of long ago,
Wonsoɛ hɔ bio mpo a,	Even if you don't rest there again,
Wubu kɔmpɔ hwɛ hɔ.	You turn around to look there.

People ought to look back or to rest there again because the ancestors have wisdom to teach.

Furthermore, the current generation has an obligation to be a bridge between past and new generations. In 1997, at the Ashanti regional secondary school cultural competition in Kumase, the director of the national Cultural Studies Unit, Nana Sakyi, told the audience, "We are a link between the succeeding generations." An official in charge of dance at the regional Center for National Culture in Koforidua and judge at the Eastern regional cultural competition, Stephen Sedofu, told me that the objective of the competitions was to ensure that "cultural knowledge is passed down from generation to generation" (interview, 23 Mar. 1999). Although some government officials expressed this view as well, I count it as a popular discourse because I heard it articulated primarily in the school cultural competitions and among teachers in their classrooms.

When I asked teachers in Akropong and Abiriw why it was important to teach about culture in school, many responded with a sentiment about the need for continuity. As a teacher of Twi at Osuafo Junior Secondary School, Mr. Robertson, put it, "Daakye yɛn mpanyinfo bewu, na ɛsɛ sɛ yɛn mmofra behu, bɛtoa so, for continuity. . . . Yɛbɛkyerɛ wɔn sɛnea ɛbɛyɛ na ammamrɛ nnyera" (In the future our elders will die and it is necessary for our children to see, to continue, for continuity. . . . We will teach them so that culture won't be lost). In a lesson on folktales, or *Anansesɛm*, for his class 3 students, he began by saying in Twi that *Anansesɛm* were something people from long ago did and left to the next generation. We have to teach it to continue it, he told them, so our culture is not lost (*amammrɛ nnyera*). He then switched to English, quoting a beer commercial, "The tradition—," and the students joined him to say the rest, "goes on." Teachers were remarkably similar in their responses to my direct question about why culture should be taught in the schools: it was important for continuity's sake. Under this formulation, culture was seen as inheritance that was available to everyone.

But the other side of the coin meant that although students *could* learn the knowledge of the ancestors, they were positioned as currently lacking knowledge. Teachers tended to contrast past practices with present ones, in which the present was condemned as a deviation from and a pale shadow of the authentic practices of the past. One primary school teacher told me that naming ceremonies used to be performed in a different way, one that children today did not know: they needed to know "the real thing." The headmaster of a combined primary and junior secondary school told me that students should know the way it was before white people came. Girls used to learn these things during puberty rites (*bra goro*), but now that these were not performed, they did not know about the past. The quest for authenticity and the purity of the past "is oriented toward the recovery of an essence whose loss has been realized only through modernity, and whose recovery is feasible only through methods and sentiments created in modernity" (Bendix 1997, 8). Teachers felt that the loss of tradition was visible in students' lack of knowledge, and that schooling would replace other social institutions, like puberty rites, that had broken down. Nana Sakyi, director of the national Cultural Studies Unit, stated what many teachers left implicit: because cultural practices are not currently taught at home, it falls to the school to do so. In other words, although this discourse glorified ancestors and elders as knowing more than the youth of the present, it justified the teaching of culture in schools. Because tradition had broken down, teachers and the state needed to step in and ensure that "the tradition goes on."

The sentiment of nostalgia and loss had several implications for the cultural program in the schools. During several lessons on customs taught for my benefit, the teachers dwelt wholly on the past, saying nothing about the present. The lessons did not incorporate students' everyday knowledge, but rather presented an idealized view of the past. At Obikyere Primary School, the teacher gave his class 5 students a lesson on "traditional occupations," a topic in the cultural studies syllabus for primary schools (Ghana 1988a). After writing "Some Traditional Occupations" on the board, he asked students to name their father's occupation and put down their responses: teacher, farmer, doctor, trader, dressmaker, and driver. He checked off doctor and teacher, explaining to the students that traditional meant "in the olden days," and that he was asking "what our forefathers were doing" before the white people came. He then got some answers he accepted: farming, trading, fishing, and hunting. He tried again, asking what their grandfathers had done. The students came back with painter, baker, carpenter, and mason. But the teacher was after specific traditional occupations—potter and *kente* weaver. Clearly, although he thought he could elicit responses about tradition by asking about the children's male parents and grandparents, their answers did not correspond to his, or the cultural syllabus's, notions of traditional. If culture is defined as tradition, then, culture is not in the realm of experience of children or indeed that of their immediate ancestors, despite the expectations of the teacher. Instead, the syllabus, and by extension the teacher, became positioned as an authority on what constituted tradition.

In secondary schools, examinations help in this reconstitution of the teacher and syllabus as authorities on what is "pure and authentic." The Akan language teachers in the secondary schools and teacher training colleges that I observed were more diligent about teaching customs than their counterparts in the primary and junior secondary schools, in part because they were teaching to an exam that emphasized both the grammatical and the social aspects of Ghanaian languages. In the Akan language lessons that I observed at this level, teachers stressed the differences between the past and the present. I asked the Akan language teacher at Gyahene Secondary School why he emphasized the past in his classes, and he replied that he told the students to answer each and every exam question as if it was asking about the past, or they would not do well. As I explore further in chapter 5, culture as tradition helps to systematize cultural knowledge in the classroom, thereby turning it into school knowledge.

Even as the discourse of culture as tradition honors ancestors and elders, it replaces them with the institution of the school as the route by which young people will become knowledgeable about the customs of the past. Articulated by cultural studies officers and teachers at competitions and in classrooms, the discourse justifies the school's teaching of tradition. Although it does not directly justify the nation's appropriation of tradition, because schools are state institutions and teachers government employees, the discourse of culture as tradition does shift the location of expertise to teachers and syllabi developed by the Ministry of Education. Our second popular discourse, to which we now turn, completely denies the authority of teachers and schools to teach culture.

Culture as *Amammrɛ*, or the Customs of Traditional Kingdoms (Popular Discourse II)

The Twi word *amammrɛ* is usually glossed as "culture" in English. But it contains the word ɔman, or kingdom, and so *amammrɛ* connotes the practices of the traditional kingdom. At Horeb Secondary School in Akropong, the girls who had been involved in the cultural competition told me in a group discussion that they had originally wanted to do a dance-drama about puberty rites. One girl explained their reasoning, saying that it was "ammane a ɛwɔ kan tete mu no . . . amammrɛ a ɛwɔ yɛn Akuapem ɔman no mu" (a custom of the distant past . . . culture that is part of our Akuapem nation).[11] As this remark illustrates, the sense of culture as *amammrɛ* locates it within the realm of a traditional kingdom—of the "Akuapem nation" in this case—not the nation of Ghana as a whole. In southern Ghana "chiefdoms served as the surrogate of ethnicity," even though as political units, traditional kingdoms contained people of many different ethnicities (Lentz and Nugent 2000, 10). They, along with hometowns, constitute a salient identity and sense of belonging that had more pull historically but continue to resonate strongly for many Ghanaians.

Chiefs and the elders who advise them embody the power of the ɔman, or traditional kingdom. When I first told people in Akuapem about my project—I wanted to study culture in the schools—they laughed and asked why I was interested in exploring the subject in the schools. They advised me to go talk to the chiefs if I really wanted to learn about culture. Thus, a popular discourse in Akuapem locates cultural expertise with chiefs and denies its presence outside of chiefly rituals. This discourse associates culture closely with traditional religion and the traditional state.

Because of the influence of Christianity, many practices considered cultural—such as naming ceremonies and puberty rites—are not regularly performed in Akuapem. As a result, emphasis has been placed on chiefs as the "custodians of culture," a popular phrase. It is the chiefs alone who can perform the rites that will placate and please the spirits of the town. Kwame Ampene, a retired teacher of Twi and music, expressed this attitude most clearly to me: "The chiefs are custodians of our culture and the very embodiment of our customs and culture. They have retained our heritage from the ancestors. Ancestors founded the particular land, and they [the chiefs] have to see the land is properly maintained and ruled, and the taboos kept, festivals observed, and to see that development is going on" (interview, 3 Mar. 1999). Particularly because others are no longer participating in the rituals that will keep the spirits and ancestors happy, it has fallen to chiefs to ensure the prosperity and well-being of the people in their jurisdiction by performing the appropriate rites. While chiefs are sometimes reduced to a symbolic embodiment of both culture and their people, this discourse highlights the sacred significance of the rituals that chiefs perform.

The most powerful and sacred knowledge behind these rituals is considered secret. Just as chiefs are protected from the profane world by the mediation of their spokespersons (Yankah 1995), so too are powerful objects and events kept hidden and protected by indirection. Even individual elders know only certain parts of a ritual; few know the whole sequence of rites involved (Asiedu Yirenkyi, conversation, 26 Mar. 1999). A certain aura of fear surrounds the chiefs and their activities. Many Akuapem people not connected to royal families told me that they were too scared to go to the chief's court because they might make a mistake in etiquette. In the past offenses might result in fines, slavery, and even execution.

Some writers on cultural matters have noted the still-secret nature of this chiefly knowledge. In a popular book on the various festivals of Ghana, A. A. Opoku (1970) wrote in the preface that it was difficult to give acknowledgments "in a book dealing with what is sacred and to some extent, secret in our cultural heritage." In a review of two books about different Akan festivals, I. E. Boama (1954) wrote, "Two Twi festivals that every Akan should try to watch are Adae and Odwira. But there are many people who even if they have seen these festivals, they have seen only a part. For only insiders have permission to see the true activities. . . . If you are a child of a traditional state, buy these books to read, and once you know your nation's secrets, you won't avoid these festivals out of fear."[12] Cultural knowledge, at its deepest or most true, is thus considered hidden and not accessible to outsiders; and books like these that describe rituals for nonroyals violate the secrecy about certain historical and cultural matters that allows powerful elders and chiefs to manipulate important decisions regarding, for example, property rights. The content of the hidden knowledge does not matter as much as the privileged society (in this case, elders and chiefs) that the secrecy creates (Bellman 1984; Murphy 1980).

This discourse denies the legitimacy of teachers to teach culture to children and youth. Authentic culture becomes located in the secret ceremonies and historical lore of chiefs; the cultural program in the schools is dismissed as "not deep." The Twi teacher at Osuafo Junior Secondary School, Mr. Robertson, criticized the textbook *Cultural Studies for Junior Secondary Schools* (1989): "ɛmu nnɔ bebree wɔ ha" (it doesn't go into much depth in here), he complained.[13] During a lesson on festivals in another junior secondary school the week after Akropong celebrated the annual Odwira festival, it became clear that the students knew the festival had not been celebrated properly because of an important chief's death. The teacher, a young woman from Kwawu, was unaware of this death, which had been kept secret for several months. Thus, in contrast to the previous discourse, here cultural expertise was located not with teachers and syllabi, but with the students. The normal authority patterns between teachers and students was reversed, a phenomenon I discuss further in chapter 5.

This popular discourse thus helps legitimate chiefs and elders as the sources of authority on culture. In this view, culture resides in the secret, sacred domain of chiefs and not in a nationalized and secular state. Employees of the state, like teachers, cannot possibly teach culture to all citizens of the nation because they do not have access to those sacred, secret rituals except to the extent that they are affiliated with royal families.

Conclusion

Educational reforms and cultural policies are projects. They may not succeed, but this does not mean that nothing changes (Thomas 1994). Although school cultural performances produce a variety of sometimes conflicting messages, students, teachers, cultural studies officers, and government ministers are in fact negotiating key questions for a postcolonial African state: What is culture? Where is it located? To whom and to which institutions does culture belong?

As illustrated by the school cultural competition, the Ghanaian state is built on intense local rivalries. Towns and kingdoms struggle for the prize and status of development—such as electrification or school buildings—within the nation, just as schools and their students vie for first prize through the sequence of cultural competitions from the district to the national level. The state and chiefs are mutually dependent and work to assimilate one another, a process that has had a long history in Ghana, dating from the consolidation of British colonial rule during the late nineteenth and early twentieth centuries. School cultural competitions clearly reflect this process. Staged by the government, these events are designed to appropriate culture for national ends, whether that of identifying the nation on the world stage, developing the nation, or representing the nation through performance. But this is not the full story, for students and teachers may be bent on appropriating the stage set by the government to articulate alternative notions of culture. Those who participate in nationalist rituals do not necessarily feel nationalist sentiment but may instead use those national spaces to address local concerns (Bendix 1992). Recall how the drummer from New Juaben in the Eastern Region used a traditional form of drum language in a national forum to praise his paramount chief.

The state's cultural programming in schools, both the curriculum and the competitions, reflects a broader political struggle in Ghana. The representation of culture in schools is a contested process. Appropriating the chiefs' cultural authority is a principal route by which the state seeks to incorporate and undercut their power. But the effort has not so far been successful, for the chiefs in their turn attempt to shore up their power, sometimes by acknowledging the state's authority for their own ends (using their connections, for example, to bring development to their dominion), but sometimes by asserting their exclusive authority in the cultural domain by dint of their access to secret rites and rituals.

Furthermore, the chiefs are not the only challengers to the state's interpretation of culture. Through charismatic Christianity, Christianity in general is being reinvigorated in southern Ghana, and it too has begun to contest the meaning of culture. Because of this movement's growing power in Akuapem, I will examine it in more depth than this chapter allows. The church has long functioned as an oppositional force in Ghana's political scene (Pobee 1977). As secondary school students bring together a Christian discourse and the government discourse of development, these future elites promote a Christian nationalism and set the stage for a different kind of elite fusion with the state.

IT WAS FASCINATING to watch Mr. Devoh, the cultural studies officer in the Akuapem North district education office, as he was organizing the secondary school cultural competition in 1999 (fig. 2). As he made the rounds seeking to persuade teachers to participate in the competition, he often had occasion to defend the schools' cultural program as compatible with Christianity. At the workshop at Horeb Secondary School, he recounted how he had once told a fellow church member that he was a cultural officer and the church member had expressed surprise at his occupation because he viewed Mr. Devoh as a devout Christian. Mr. Devoh, as the local representative and advocate of the government's cultural policy, tried to persuade teachers of the morality and importance of the cultural program by pointing to his own example as "a devout Christian." He presented himself as an embodiment of how participation in a national cultural educational program could be part of a Christian life, and he invited teachers to join him in this endeavor.[1]

Modernity Divided

Christianity and the Cultural Program in the Schools

His qualifications for the position of district cultural studies officer actually bolstered his identity as a Christian. He had been named to the office because of his expertise in choral music. Some cultural studies officers have been trained by the School of Performing Arts as musicians, drummers, and dancers; others are former music and Akan language teachers who have been promoted into educational administration. Mr. Devoh, a man in his fifties, was a former music teacher who, like many other Ghanaian teachers and professionals, had moved to Nigeria during the economic hard times of the 1970s and 1980s. He was choirmaster in his church, the Evangelical Presbyterian Church of Ghana, and had become a Christian as a boy in order to sing in the choir. He was willing to help local schools with the choral music section of the competition, but did not feel he had enough expertise in the other genres to be of technical assistance there.

Figure 2. Mr. Devoh, the district cultural studies officer, helping to set up the drums for the Akropong circuit competition, June 2002

Why did Mr. Devoh feel it necessary to persuade teachers that Christian faith and the nationalist cultural program were compatible? Culture is a salient symbol for both Christian and nationalist discourses in Ghana. Since the Enlightenment, modernity has been defined in opposition to traditional culture. But modernizing nationalists in fact often use cultural traditions to stress continuities with the past and to demonstrate their nation's uniqueness. Modernity feeds off culture and the past in multiple ways.

So what does it mean to be modern? Some anthropologists hold that alternative forms of modernity have arisen outside the West (Barber 2000; Rofel 1999). Others argue that the notion of alternative modernities renders the term "modernity" too diffuse and vague, that in the end it comes to mean only what is contemporary (Knauft 2003). Rather than understanding modernity as unitary—a homogenous entity arising in the West—or as plural—a plethora of modernities—I see modernity as similar to colonialism. Just as colonialism was riven by the competing interests of missionaries, settlers, government officials, and commercial interests (Stoler and Cooper 1997), so too is modernity made up of different social orders that are sometimes aligned and sometimes in tension with one another (Appadurai 1996). For Friedman (2003), modernity is a configuration of several social orders, including individualism, capitalism, and the nation-state. These social orders create slightly different imaginaries of what it means to be modern, which sometimes concatenate with one another and sometimes do not, leading to the fracturing of modernity from within. These social orders create different models of how individuals should act, which do not necessarily overlap, creating tensions for those who seek to embody the good and gain the respect of their associates (see Abu-Lughod 1986). How do Ghanaians handle the contradictions posed by these different visions of modernity and opposing stances toward culture?

This question becomes all the more salient when a single context is simultaneously producing different kinds of modern people. A primary site for the production of modernity—schools—has been largely overlooked in anthropological research on modernity (but see Ahearn 2001; Stambach 2000). In Ghana the schools, though now managed by the state, traditionally served as the site for producing Christian identities. Although Max Weber (1958)—in his brilliant, if flawed, argument—shows how Protestant belief contributed to the growth of capitalism, Friedman (2003) does not include religion among the processes central to modernity, treating it instead as a form of tradition. While I do not want to make global claims about the role of religion in modernity, Christianity played a critical part in the development of capitalism, the nation-state, and individualism in Ghana (chapter 1), and thus I would argue that Christianity is integral to the notion of modernity in this case.

The historical association of schools with Christianity and teachers' and students' identities as Christians, reinvigorated with the growth of charismatic Christianity, make it difficult for the government of Ghana to use schools to create a national culture. Because schools are simultaneously the sites for the production of nationalist and Christian selves, students, teachers, and educational administrators are especially affected by the stresses caused by the internal divisions of modernity. The devout among them, students and teachers alike, find problematic the teaching of cultural traditions in classrooms as mandated by the 1986 educational reforms. In their struggle to resolve the tensions between government policy and their personal Christian beliefs, they rework the state initiatives through their imaginations and everyday practice to arrive at their own definition of culture—one that is often at odds with the state's. In this chapter I will first lay out the ideological underpinnings of charismatic Christianity and then illustrate how it affects classroom interactions about the cultural. Finally, I will turn to a group of students who, like Mr. Devoh, attempted to align Christian and nationalist discourses of modernity and to devise a performance for the school competitions that was compatible with both.

Boxing; or, "Temptations Are Everywhere before Us"

On a Sunday morning in February 1999, the minister of the new Peace Presbyterian Church, which met in the largest classroom in Presbyterian Primary School in Akropong, gave a sermon about the devil, or *ɔbonsam*. He likened the confrontation between the devil and Jesus Christ to a soccer match, in which one wears either a white or a red jersey. He also linked the events of a recent boxing match between Ghanaian Ike Quartey and American De La Hoya to an encounter between the devil and a Christian: Ike fell back, regathered strength, and came back to fight, just as the devil will surely return after a Christian fights him off. "Temptations wɔ yɛn anim baabiara. Ɛba, wo bo befuw, na ɛbɛsan aba" (Temptations are everywhere before us. They will come, you will get angry, and then they will come back again). The minister's sermon expressed a central image of the Christian's relationship to the devil. It is conceived to be a violent confrontation between two opposing parties, one that needs to be continually refought by individual Christians. In fact, it is this struggle with the devil that marks one as a Christian.

The metaphor of battle between Christianity and the devil has a long history in Ghana. From the early nineteenth century to the present, the missionaries who brought Christianity to Akuapem, Kwawu, and Ashanti conceived their mission as a war with forces of darkness, represented by "heathen" ways and "fetish" priests. This was as true of the Presbyterian Scottish missionaries as it was of their Basel predecessors. (The Presbyterian Church, as earlier noted, continues to be the strongest church in Akuapem.) To this day believers narrate Christianity's history in Ghana as a symbolic struggle against the forces of darkness.

In a study on the image of the devil among Ewe Presbyterians, Birgit Meyer (1999b) examined how, following in the tradition of Bremen missionaries, they equate traditional gods and spirits with demons and the devil. Likewise, in Akuapem, although the Basel missionaries rejected traditional religion as fraudulent and thus impotent, African Christians continued to believe in the power of these gods and spirits. However, rather than conceiving of these gods as having the power to give both life and death, Christians in Akuapem demonized them as capable of only working evil in the world. That the power of the devil has remained a core belief of Ghanaian Christians speaks to the fact that Christianity has been appropriated and Africanized to reflect local concerns and beliefs, but in ways that causes Christians to passionately reject traditional gods and all that is associated with them—what Ghanaian Christians mark as the cultural.

Mainstream Presbyterianism, however, did not directly address its congregations' need to combat and deal effectively with evil forces. In the 1960s and 1970s, an increasing number of "new wave" Pentecostal and charismatic churches appeared across Africa, attracting members from orthodox mission churches by offering special means for countering the forces of the devil, such as prayer groups, healings, and deliverance from evil spirits.[2] Not only have charismatic churches become more popular, but the orthodox churches have themselves become more charismatic in their attempt to address their congregations' concerns about the workings of demonic forces in their lives (Stuiver 1995). The Presbyterian Church in Ghana was changed slowly from within; mainstream congregations formed bible study and prayer groups and other charismatic movements in the hope of preventing a loss of membership to the new churches.[3]

In Akuapem these trends are clearly visible. Although Pentecostals and Presbyterians emphasize their differences, they seem to share many similar beliefs and understandings. The most quoted parts of the Bible, in conversations and in sermons in churches of both denominations in Akropong, deal with the difference between idol worship and the worship of God. The charismatic revival of Presbyterianism is shown in the activities of the new Grace Presbyterian Church, which was started in 1997 by teachers at Abɛ Secondary School. It has a popular Saturday afternoon deliverance service to which people, but mainly women of all ages and young men, flock, not only from Akropong but also from neighboring towns and the capital, Accra. In this service, as the name indicates, through Christian prayer and exhortation, worshipers are delivered of the evil spirits that are possessing them and working evil in their lives. Meyer, in her study of Ewe charismatic churches (1999b), argues that the women possessed by the spirit in the deliverance sessions moved in exactly the same ways as priestesses of the spirit did during traditional possession dances. The service thus makes room for some elements of traditional religion, such as possessing spirits to manifest themselves, but within a Christian framework that simultaneously demonizes them and shows them to be less powerful than the Christian God. The deliverance sessions allow participants to experience the power of the satanic at the same time as it is denounced.

Saturday deliverance services are held in Grace's newly constructed chapel, a simple but large affair with bare cement block walls, a cement floor, and a roof made of aluminum sheeting. People sit on wooden benches, and the hall tends to become packed quite quickly. Many young people, dressed in their best, attend, and young women carry babies on their backs. Two or three men with "spiritual gifts" granted them by the Holy Spirit walk up and down the aisles pointing out people who have "something against you," as one deliverer put it—financial problems, physical pains, infertility, marital difficulties, and general worries about the future. Those identified then step forward to be delivered of the spirit afflicting them. This happens very rapidly, so that perhaps sixty people are temporarily delivered during the entire three-hour service. During the deliverance, some people become openly possessed, shaking, falling on the floor, or walking around and shouting. The flailing felt dangerous to me in the crowded space, where it is hard to make room for the possessed person's wild motions. If a possessed woman has a baby on her back, a woman sitting nearby will quickly retrieve it before the mother throws herself to the floor. The men in charge of deliverance violently confront the spirit by shaking the possessed person, insulting the spirit, and calling on the name of Jesus. "Come out," yelled the deliverer in English to the spirit possessing a young man, at one service I observed. "I will pull you out in the name of Jesus. I pull you out of the system. Bɛfa kɔ [Take it and go]. Pack and go." The spirit will also shout insults and threats to both the exorcist and the person he or she is possessing, "Kwasea! Me nso mekum wo!" (Fool! I will kill you!) The violent battle between God and Satan, between Christianity and traditional spirits, is reenacted in a ritual that at once reveals the superior power of God over the traditional gods and demonstrates the continuing influences of those forces on people's lives.

In Ghana charismatic Christianity objectifies "tradition" as a past wrapped up in ancestral and devil worship. Many charismatic Christians believe that every Christian has a past that affects his or her present condition because it exposed that person to demonic influence. Curses directed at ancestors affect their Christian descendants, and demons are believed to inhabit places and objects with which one may unwittingly come in contact. Charismatic Christians do their best to avoid rituals like festivals and funerals, which traditionally have served as occasions for those living elsewhere to come home and reaffirm ties to their families and hometowns dependent on their income. At a deliverance service at Grace Presbyterian Church that focused on the importance of a person's making good choices in life, participants were asked to "pray that you will abhor all ungodly practices—in the society (ungodly traditions), in marriage (e.g., widowhood rites, naming ceremonies), at work places (bribes, fraud etc.), all other such practices irrespective of the form, shade and colour it takes" and to "reject all forms of curses that have been imposed on you either by yourself or by another person or an institution through a bad choice" (printed service notes, 20 Feb. 1999; parenthetical glosses in the original). Not surprisingly, Christians in Akropong, especially those influenced by charismatic movements, take care to avoid contact with evil spirits. For instance, a teacher and friend, who had taken her son to numerous prayer camps to be cured of his drug (marijuana) habit, stayed home when her neighbors and relatives celebrated festivals like Odwira. Beatrice said that children should not go to festivals because the spirits might bother them afterward. Because of the "illness" in her family, she stayed away (conversation, 19 Oct. 1998). She felt that the spirits could bring only bad consequences. She also avoided funerals, even the one for a traditional priest, or *ɔkɔmfo,* who was her father's kinsman. She told me how, during that funeral, when many traditional priests came to honor their colleague, she was sitting near the main road in Akropong and saw a female *ɔkɔmfo* far off in the distance, and how, when she momentarily turned her head away, the next thing she knew the *ɔkɔmfo* was sitting beside her. The *ɔkɔmfo* asked Beatrice her name, and my friend did not want to tell her because she was afraid. After some pressure, Beatrice told the *ɔkɔmfo* her name was Akua, the name given to girls born on Wednesday, when she was really born on a Sunday. The *ɔkɔmfo* said that she had come to sit with Beatrice and give her something—either it was advice or it was yet to come. The *ɔkɔmfo* said she would return right away, but when she got up, Beatrice fled to her house. I asked what she was afraid of, and she said, "otumi ma wo kɔm na meyɛ kristoni nti" (because she could make you possessed and I am a Christian).[4] She said that she knew the *ɔkɔmfo* did not want to trouble her, and Beatrice tried to be respectful to the *ɔkɔmfo* despite her fear (conversation, 30 Mar. 1999).

Although the Basel missionaries made the avoidance of traditional rituals and festivals a condition of Christian conversion, charismatic Christianity has reinvigorated that separation at a time when Ghanaian church leaders such as Bishop Sarpong of the Roman Catholic Church and Reverend Dzobo of the Evangelical Presbyterian Church were beginning to consider ways to Africanize Christianity. Meyer (1999b) argues that these efforts at bringing together African religious practices and Christianity, driven by intellectual church leaders, are not acceptable to believers at the grassroots level, where the separation from traditional gods is vital to a Christian identity.

The fears of personal contact with the devil extend to protecting valued institutions, like schools, from demonic intrusion. Sometime before 1990 two murals had been painted on the walls of Presbyterian Junior Secondary School in Akropong, which was situated next to Grace Presbyterian Church; the church used the classrooms on Sundays for its children's services.[5] One painting showed a drummer on the talking drums (*ntumpan*),

Figure 3. Drummer on the talking drum, painting on the wall of Presbyterian Junior Secondary School, Akropong. The slogan means "Ghana, listen!"

with the drumming phrase "Ghana muntie" (Ghana, listen!) under it (fig. 3). The other depicted the famous moment when the ɔkɔmfo and wonder worker Okomfo Anokye brought the Golden Stool down from the skies, thereby inaugurating the Asante empire and giving it its spiritual power. One day I heard a rumor that some people in Grace Presbyterian Church wanted to paint over the Okomfo Anokye painting.

I went to talk to the headmaster of the school to hear the story. He said that someone had had a dream indicating that evil spirits were in the painting and that this was the reason why the school was doing badly. The headmaster himself considered the painting harmless, even as he confessed that he did not have spiritual gifts to see what those with vision granted by the Holy Spirit could see. And he personally thought the school was losing enrollment because it was on the edge of town and because as a newer school, it had relatively few alumni from whom to raise funds. But he had to take the feelings at Grace Presbyterian Church into consideration, he said. The church was wealthy and could possibly help the school financially. Besides, the school was under the church, so he would have to do what it said. He would agree to paint over the picture if they painted the whole outside of the school (conversation, 18 June 1999). By the time I left in August 1999, rumor had it that the whole school block was to be given a new coat of paint. But when I returned three years later, in June 2002, the school was still unpainted and the murals remained intact. Devout Christians are alert to the possible presence of evil spirits and their negative effects on the success of individuals and institutions. Furthermore, the incident shows that as their churches grow in popularity and financial strength, their viewpoints may become more influential among people and schools that seek their patronage.[6]

At the same time as Christians have become more concerned about separating themselves from the past and "tradition," they have also incorporated elements associated with Ghanaian culture into their worship services. For instance, following in the steps of Ephraim Amu (chapter 1), many men and women now wear cloth, rather than suits and dresses, to church. More significantly, Pentecostal and independent churches use drums and music based on African rhythm in their services. This has slowly spread to Presbyterian churches in the form of the singing bands, women's fellowships, and bible study and prayer groups. In the 1980s dancing was allowed only during the offertory in Presbyterian churches in Akuapem, but it is now common at various points during the service. These reforms, however, are not seen "as Africanisation, but rather as the realisation of biblical directives (after all, the psalms approve of making music to the glory of the Lord) or as an expression of the Holy Spirit" (Meyer 1999b, 114).[7] Even as Christians continue to condemn the drumming and dancing performed during festivals and other ceremonies, they are reconfiguring these performance arts as an appropriate method for praising God. The church service itself is increasingly becoming a performance space for drama, music, and dance for talented artists, such as touring gospel choirs, but also for ordinary people, who enjoy the opportunity to sing and dance during the service.[8] Some traditional practices that the missionaries would have called "heathen" are being redefined as Christian.

The spiritual battle between Christianity and tradition sometimes caused actual physical conflict as well, and many of these conflicts turned on the churches' adoption of music and dance into their services. There is a one-month ban on drumming and noisemaking in anticipation of the traditional annual Homɔwɔ festival in Accra. Charismatics refuse to obey a divinity other than the Christian God and tend to ignore the ban, and in 1999 gangs, sometimes affiliated with the Gã traditional council and sometimes self-appointed, invaded the churches and appropriated musical instruments and the collection plates (*Daily Graphic*, 31 May 1999, 1, 3; 1 June 1999, 29). Conflicts of this kind between charismatic churches, which first used drums, and traditional councils apparently dated to the first charismatic churches in Ghana (*Mirror*, 29 May 1999). During a celebration marking the beginning of a six-week ban on noisemaking in August 1999, a period of silence before the celebration of the festival Odwira, the *ɔmanhene* (paramount chief) in Larteh warned Christians not to make noise by preaching in the streets or drumming in churches loudly or he would bring them to court as the owner of the streets. He was also annoyed by a young man who had been preaching provocatively and loudly outside his house. His *ɔkyeame*, Teacher Darko, told me that some Christians had been disregarding the prohibitions on noise for the past few years. From evidence in Akropong and from other studies done on charismatic movements in Ghana, the "devotion" or evangelism of Christians has been growing since the 1970s, with increased intolerance for manifestations of tradition, even as traditional performance arts have been reinterpreted as a joyful way of worshiping God in church, something that puts Christians in further tension with traditional authorities.

For Christians who are especially devout or influenced by charismatic movements—and even mainstream Christians have become more charismatic—"tradition" and "the past" have become a route by which gods can affect one's life, and they only affect it negatively. Family members' activities, participation in festivals, and images on walls all are potential sources of insecurity and ways in which people and institutions are prevented or "pulled down" from the prosperity, health, and happiness that are the birthright of all believers. For these Christians, God is the supreme being, more powerful than all other gods, but maintaining one's defenses against the ever-present devil involves constant vigilance, moral life choices, and prayer. Christianity has therefore been localized in Ghana, but in ways that heighten the dichotomy between "tradition" and "Christianity." Charismatic Christians incorporate traditional religious beliefs like spirit possession into their services in order to drive evil spirits out and redefine others like drumming as appropriate ways to praise God. The constant rejection of culture and spirits is one of the main identifying marks of a Christian, and people's own lives become the battlefield between the forces of good and evil.

Scholars of charismatic movements elsewhere in Africa stress their creation of a new symbolic order that is "a bricolage whose signs appropriate the power both of colonialism and of an objectified . . . 'tradition,' welding them into a transcendent synthesis" that speaks both to the necessities of daily life and to political configurations (Jean Comaroff 1985, 12; see also Gifford 1998; Marshall 1993; Ranger 1986). In the rest of this chapter, I will illustrate some of the political implications of this increasingly influential movement. Christian interpretations of tradition led teachers and students to criticize and rework the Ghanaian government's cultural studies program. Ultimately, teachers and students are engaging in aligning Christian and nationalist discourses and thus contributing to the growing importance of Christianity's role in the public sphere in Ghana.

Being Holy: Christianity, Educated Identities, and the Teaching of Culture in Schools

Christian concerns about traditional practices have an impact on how culture is presented in schools because many teachers follow in spirit the tradition of the Basel Mission, in which teachers were also catechists and evangelists (chapter 1). Educated identities are produced in specific cultural and historical contexts (Levinson and Holland 1996); in Ghana education is closely tied to Christianity, revitalized with the growth of charismatic Christianity.

In my discussion with boys at Abε Secondary School, one of the two elite boarding schools in Akuapem, one said, "Most of our teachers are pastors," and indeed, many of the teachers at Abε served as presbyters and founders of Grace Presbyterian Church. Church participation can allow a teacher who comes as a stranger to a town find a supportive community. Teachers, especially the older women, take seriously their role of being good Christians in the community: I accompanied two teachers from Kenkan Primary School when they visited a boy with a broken leg and prayed for his recovery. I also witnessed another teacher at the same school scold an old man about his drunkenness. The headmaster of one junior secondary school was the organist and choir director of the affiliated church. Students at the Presbyterian Training College are in charge of leading Sunday school services in the surrounding communities. Socialized to be devout Christians, many teachers seek to limit the power of spirits over their lives and maintain the holiness that gives them God's protection. Because these teachers believe that many of the practices described in the cultural studies textbook open the way for evil spirits to invade them and their students, they avoid the ones they think especially problematic or refigure them as Christian and morally instructive.

Despite government financial support and a new constitution that guarantees freedom of religion, schools continue to be religious institutions in their practices, rituals, and discipline. Currently, the government writes syllabi for subjects and pays teachers. But religious educational units control the placement of teachers, and schools in Akuapem have a close relationship with the nearest denominational church, especially when it comes to handling sensitive issues and raising extra funds. Prayers to the Christian God figure prominently in the assemblies that begin and end each schoolday. Wednesdays begin with a short worship service of a half hour to an hour, in which a teacher preaches a homily and the students sing hymns and give an offering. When I visited Kenkan Primary School on a Monday morning, the few students who admitted to not attending church over the weekend were hit three times on the back of their legs with a switch. As one student there told me, in school they learn "adesua ne Onyamesεm," study and the worship of God. A classroom in a Larteh junior secondary school has a mural of the Sermon of the Mount above the blackboard. Thus, although older people lamented the schools' lack of religiosity compared with the good old days, when the schools seemed firmly under the control of the church, in my secularist American eyes schools seemed to retain their historical role of transforming children into moral Christians, at least on the day-to-day level of school life.

The Christian orientation of schools also extends to keeping students away from traditional festivals, although people told me that this prohibition used to be enforced more strictly than it is today. When I visited a junior secondary school the Monday after the Odwira festival, at the morning assembly a teacher accused a class prefect of being out late (9 p.m.) during the Saturday night festivities, and the student argued that he had been sent on an errand to the place where his sister worked. The same teacher called out a group of boys and girls she had also seen that night, and as the students implicated their friends, the investigation grew; all those found in the wrong were beaten with a switch. Thus, the punishment taught the lesson that students should stay away from traditional festivals, not only because they are linked to the worship of traditional gods but also because they tempt one into immoral behavior like drinking and dancing in the street late at night.[9]

Although all the teachers I met identified themselves as Christians, they differed greatly in the overt expression of their faith. Some went to Sunday church services only a couple of times a month, while others had prominent roles within the church and attended midweek as well as Sunday services regularly. Those who called themselves more devout tended to make distinctions between themselves and those they considered Christian in name only, whom they suspected of participating in traditional religious activities as well. Because "the devout" were more vocal and seemed to be growing in strength, the teachers who were less so tended on the whole to be reticent and defensive about their differences.

The struggle to reconcile educational directives with personal religious beliefs led many teachers to depart from the official textbooks. For instance, in the religious and moral education course, primary and junior secondary school teachers were supposed to teach about the three main religions in Ghana—Christianity (the religion of 63 percent of Ghanaians), Islam (16 percent), and traditional religion (21 percent). Illustrating the standardizing impetus of education (chapter 5), the syllabus for that course makes the three religions both equal and comparable; each is presented as possessing divine power, a mode of prayer, specific beliefs, and a prophet or messenger: Okomfo Anokye for traditional religion, Jesus Christ for Christianity, and Mohammed for Islam. But teachers did not see the three religions as equal and often turned these lessons into a lecture on the superiority of Christianity.[10] Even if they discussed all three religions, they belittled traditional religion, describing it as the worship of natural objects like streams or trees or of divinities less powerful than the Christian God. Islam was often ignored, an indication that it was not seen as being in competition with Christianity, at least in this area of southern Ghana. During one class 5 session at Kenkan Primary School, the teacher, Mrs. Gyimah, after a short discussion in which she named the leaders of the three religions, asked, What do traditional religionists believe in? "We are Christians and believe in Jesus Christ," she said for clarification. A student answered: gods. But Mrs. Gyimah said that these were "lesser gods. In the Good Book, we are told we shouldn't believe in idols" or lesser gods. She repeated this in Twi. What do traditionalists worship? she asked. Acceptable answers were stones, river, trees, streams. Mrs. Gyimah said, "In the Good Book, does a tree or a stream have eyes? They don't have hearts or mouths. They [traditional religionists] bow down to lesser gods. But we believe in Jesus Christ." She then told the students the stories of God's creation of the world in seven days and the garden of Eden, from the first two chapters of the book of Genesis. Similarly, at Osuafo Junior Secondary School, in a lesson on libation during Twi language class, when the students mentioned that one prays to *nananom*, the ancestors, and *abosom*, gods, while the alcohol is poured on the ground, the teacher, Mr. Robertson, was quick to explain that the gods were "the lesser gods" (in English). Generally, teachers used religious and moral education as an opportunity to teach Christian beliefs and practices, on the assumption that all the students in the classroom were or should be Christians. And indeed, in the school records that I saw, all parents identified themselves and their children as Christians. Thus, in the hands of teachers, lessons that were supposed to compare the various faiths of Ghana neutrally were very much like what the students were taught in Sunday school.

For teachers who were particularly devout and considered traditional religion not simply to be fraudulent but associated with the devil, the content of the cultural studies subject posed real problems. One retired teacher told me that the subject covered a lot of material, and you had to be careful about what you were picking to teach. The way you should teach cultural studies should not be "deep" (in the sense of being spiritual or demonic). According to the syllabus, teachers were supposed to teach about customs and festivals that devout Christians avoided, such as naming ceremonies, puberty rites, and the Odwira festival. The least problematic topics to teach were names, greetings, and proverbs. Proverbs were seen as containing moral lessons and often mentioned the supreme deity (known in Twi variously as Onyankopɔn, Onyame, etc.), who has become con-

Figure 4. Libation being poured by Teacher Darko at Adae Butuw festival, Larteh, August 1999

flated with the Christian God. The most troubling topic for Christians was libation, a rite in which a person, generally a senior man, pours alcohol on the ground while praying out loud to the supreme deity, the Earth, the ancestors, spirits (*abosom*), and various other powerful beings, inviting them to come and partake (fig. 4). Libation is poured during rituals such as funerals and naming ceremonies, which some Christians refuse to attend because of the invocation of traditional gods. The teacher who taught the religious and moral education lesson described above, Mrs. Gyimah, told me that culture was "*akɔmfo nneɛma*," the doings of traditional priests. It was not good, she said, because it invoked the spirits. But the syllabus "is not of our own making—it is not our fault. Some parents don't see any good in it." She said that parents complain that evil spirits manifest themselves when drums are beaten so that their children become possessed (conversation, 14 Sept. 1998). As a result, state orders or not, the cultural studies subject is not regularly taught in schools in Akuapem.

During the few times that I saw teachers even touching on such matters in their classes, they were careful to take precautions. At Nhoma Primary School, the teacher, Mrs. Kissiedu, had taught her first-year students about Twi day-names for boys and girls, and she wanted the young children to role-play a naming ceremony in which a new baby receives his or her name. Mrs. Kissiedu first explained to the students, "Sɛ wuyi mpae a, wofrɛ asaman, abosom. Onyankopɔn yɛ kɛse sen abosom" (If you pour libation, you call charms, spirits. God is more powerful than spirits), then assigned various roles. A boy was given the role of family head and a bowl of water to use for the libation, but Mrs. Kissiedu told him urgently that he should take care not to pour water on the ground. She said in English to me, "We're not supposed to use water [i.e., pour anything at all] because of the spiritual [used in the sense of demonic] effect." But when the young children had difficulty enacting their parts, Mrs. Kissiedu took over as family head, pretending to pour water from the bowl as she prayed quite seriously and intently out loud to God and to the spirits. At the end of the lesson, when I asked her why she said that they were not supposed to pour the water, she replied that if you pour water, the ɔbosom, or god, might possess the children. I asked if that had ever happened, and Mrs. Kissiedu said that it happened to one girl, who ran away into the forest near Koforidua, and the parents had to go find her. If a student became possessed, she had to stop going to school, because the spirits could descend on her at any time. Schooling, associated with Christianity, and spirit possession were thus seen as paths—career tracks, almost—that were diametrically opposed. This teacher clearly respected the power of the spirits even as she sought to protect her students from them.

I encountered differing opinions about whether school cultural competitions opened routes for spirits to enter people. A seamstress told me that the school's festivals were "flat" (her word), while the town's festivals had the backing of spirits. When I commented that some people believed that spirits were also in what schools did, she conceded that they could "penetrate" (her word) there too. Some teachers who were very active in their churches likewise considered the school cultural competitions "entertainment" and thus without demonic influence. Because there are not many large indoor spaces in Akuapem, churches with large sanctuaries are popular places for meetings and other community activities. Although the Presbyterian Church in Adukrom refused to let the organizers of the 2002 primary and junior secondary school competition use its sanctuary on the grounds that the event was "fetishism," and a church in the regional capital of Koforidua had reportedly done the same that year, the Presbyterian churches in both Abiriw and Larteh allowed the kindergarten cultural competition to take place in their sanctuaries in 1999. Thus, the Christian public, teachers, and ministers do not all or always interpret school cultural activities as inviting the presence of spirits, although they may feel that special precautions are necessary to prevent their entry.

I was told stories about students who became possessed through performance, particularly girls who were playing the role of ɔkɔmfo, priestess.[11] One cultural studies officer said that in 1975, when he was attending the School of Ghana Languages at Ajumako,[12] a student in that role became possessed during a cultural performance; she went home for purification and was not troubled again (Amin interview, 26 Apr. 1999). When I told a young Gã woman and University of Ghana graduate I met during a trip to Brong-Ahafo about my project, she remembered that when she was in form 4 in secondary school in Juaben, in the Ashanti Region, she performed in a play called "The Black Hermit."[13] Although the story was a love story of travel and betrayal, when her school's drama troupe staged it, they added pieces about charms, witchcraft (juju), and Christianity to spice it up. During their tour the girl playing the role of "the fetish priestess" (her words) got possessed during the performance. Other performers felt dizzy, but my friend just felt weak. After the girl was possessed, the other students prayed over her for several hours and she recovered, but they stopped performing the play after this incident. Later the girl got hay fever, but the school and the girl did not tell her parents that the reason for her illness was the possession. "Spirits touch you through blood," my friend said, meaning that a person whose family has ancestral spirits or has a marking on his or her face is susceptible to spirit possession or influence. The spirits want you to serve them, she said, because they are losing people through schooling. Drums and libation were particularly dangerous: "They can get to you through drums." But singing and dancing were safe if they were done in a Christian ceremony, she said. When libation was poured in her presence, she prayed, reminding herself that she was "covered in the blood of Jesus" and so was protected by God (conversation, 15 Feb. 1999). Just as drumming and dancing have a double significance — used to praise God but also to invite the spirits — so too is blood both protective and dangerous for Christians, a highly powerful substance with multiple interpretations.

In Akropong adolescence is a time for increased participation in church and heightened identification as a Christian. Churches, with their youth choirs and activities, serve as a space for youth to gather and to meet marriage partners. Especially for girls, it is an acceptable reason to leave the house and the chores that always need doing. Whereas the Presbyterian congregations are relatively evenly balanced between elderly, middle-aged, and youthful participants, the Pentecostal church in Akropong was made up largely of young adults and adolescents, with only a few people over the age of thirty (mainly elderly women) attending. By respecting both young and old who have spiritual gifts, such as prophesying the future and discerning spiritual problems, the charismatic churches give young adults and adolescents authority that they do not otherwise have in a society where elders command respect.

An important religious organization for youth is also available in schools: the evangelical Scripture Union (SU). This organization was originally formed by university students to promote Bible reading and daily quiet time with God. It flourished during the 1960s, passed on when those first SU members graduated from university and began teaching in secondary schools and teacher training colleges. The SU focuses on members' "holiness" and separation from worldly things like fashion, alcohol, social dances, movies, smoking, and sexual immorality (Adubofuor 1994, 122–23). SU meetings are also characterized by Pentecostal speaking in tongues and possession of spectacular gifts given by the Holy Spirit, such as seeing the future or perceiving demonic influence in a painting on a school wall. As with other charismatic groups, confrontation with traditional religion is considered important. In the Volta Region in 1966, SU students supposedly persuaded traditional priests of the power of Christ, so that they gave up their profession and spiritual items (Adubofuor 1994, 167–69).

Many school authorities view student evangelism as disruptive (Adubofuor 1994, 215), because their own authority may be challenged by the claims of students to holiness. A former principal of the teacher training college in Akropong (1973–78) described how some teachers objected to the SU there (S. K. Aboa, conversation, 23 Oct. 1998). Although none of the junior secondary schools in Akropong had an SU, young adolescents (aged 12–15) were certainly drawn to charismatic Christianity. During a Wednesday morning worship service at Osuafo Junior Secondary School in Akropong, a girl in form 1 (the seventh year of schooling) began screaming "wiase, wiase!" (world, world!), a common possession shout in deliverance services, to the surprise and consternation of the teachers and the other students. After a moment of shock, a male teacher quickly took her out of the room. Some students considered her possessed by "Onyankopɔn," God, but most thought it was "ɔbonsam," the devil; a teacher told me she was possessed by "an evil spirit." As this incident shows, it is not necessarily easy to recognize the difference between possession by the Holy Spirit and possession by a traditional spirit. In a discussion among the male teachers on the veranda later that morning, I was surprised to hear some of them disapproving of the incident, saying that students should devote their time to study and not to prayer. Apparently, some first form students were holding prayer meetings on their own; others were rising at five in the morning to attend adult religious services. One male teacher in his thirties said that the Holy Spirit did not take anyone who was not "mature," using the English word: with the gift of the Holy Spirit, you can see the future or some secret about someone, which is not proper for children to know because they might misuse the information. Yet, he added, unsure, perhaps thinking of the upcoming millennium, the Bible says that when the end of the world is near, children will prophesy and old men will have dreams. Young people's claims to holiness and spiritual gifts make adults, including Christian teachers, uncomfortable because it gives youth a platform from which to challenge adults' authority.

At Abɛ Secondary School, SU meetings were led by students, usually male, even though about two-thirds of the perhaps 200 student attendees were girls.[14] Although they had a faculty sponsor, the meetings were clearly in the students' hands except when Mrs. Mensah felt she had something specific to tell them. The worship meeting was characterized by exuberant singing and dancing and loud, emotional praying. One day the sermon took as its starting point the story of the failed burning of Shadrach, Meshach, and Abednego by Nebuchadnezzar (Daniel 3:16–26), and much was made of how the three "did not bow down to graven images." After the sermon there was a long time of standing and praying. The boy who had given the sermon kept saying that God was near, was "moving," and we might be able to touch the hem of His garment and have our lives changed forever. Some girls near me were shrieking and sobbing and screaming; one boy was breathing as if he was crying. Some of the boys walked up and down the aisles to find anyone who needed support, but it did not seem to be for deliverance purposes. We were told to keep standing while praying. We held our arms raised, palms up, to receive the blessings. At another SU meeting, Mrs. Mensah expounded on the subject of the body as a holy vessel, a talk that was quite explicit about controlling one's sexuality. She told the students they were each "a born-again child of God" and so had "become special." Each was a "prophetic child." They were "special people for the Lord." She read passages from Revelations and Corinthians about the body being God's temple and sacred space, paid for with the blood of Jesus. She also recounted how Samson lost his power because of his love for the pagan woman Delilah. Samson was a prophetic child, she said, his birth foretold by God. If the body ceases to be God's vessel, then God withdraws power from you and you may not even know it. Maintaining holiness meant avoiding "pagan," immoral influences and people who cause "the prophetic child" to lose God's protection and favor.

When cultural matters come up in the classroom, as they inevitably do, some Christian students may challenge what they perceive as an attack on their holiness and ability to receive God's gifts. Some will go so far as to criticize the teacher, albeit in mild and oblique ways out of respect for the teacher's authority. The course in Akan language, for example, which is currently an elective for secondary school students, includes lessons on customs, proverbs, and libation, as well as grammar and reading. A former Akan language teacher at Abɛ Secondary School (1992–94) said that the students used to challenge him by telling him that what he was teaching was "fetish" (Larbi interview, 23 Mar. 1999). During a lesson on libation I observed at Abɛ Secondary School, a male student questioned the lesson obliquely by declaring, "Me papa yɛ kristoni" (My father is a Christian). The teacher, Mr. Danquah, responded to the student's criticism about the un-Christian nature of the lesson by stressing the difference between participating in cultural activities and studying culture as an object of school knowledge, a distinction that I explore further in chapter 5.

Other students respond to tensions caused by the school cultural program by refiguring it as amenable to a Christian project of moral edification. I will turn now to a group of students from Abɛ Secondary School who sought to present Christian identities despite their participation in the dance-drama section of the cultural competitions. In the process they articulated a discourse that wed the government's program of creating a national culture to a Christian project of persuading others to behave morally.

Development Morality Plays: Christianity in the Public Sphere

On a Saturday afternoon in March 1999, in Abɛ Secondary School's common room, I gathered together a group of eleven girls who had performed a dance-drama in the secondary school cultural competition the month before. Many of them were also members of the school's Scripture Union. Because the students came from all over southern Ghana, the discussion, like many of their informal conversations with one another, was in English. In the course of the extended conversation, Naomi spoke of how she and a schoolmate had dealt with the pressure from fellow SU members to desist from performing "culture":

> I remember one boy who was an SU executive. And he was a drama member. . . . They nearly drummed him out of SU because he was going to play the part of the chief in a play here. And there had to be some cultural dances in it. And these people called him and were telling him that he can't be in SU and then come here, and then act like a chief, where people would come and dance all around him. [They said:] He should come here and pray, this and that. But he understood

himself and was able to prove them wrong. And he went ahead. And he even encouraged me—I was also there—that I shouldn't listen to what they would be
telling me. We recently had to act a play, we acted a play, and it got to the point
that there had to be a fetish priest, a shrine in the play, for someone to go there for
this kind of *juju* [charms related to witchcraft]. When we got there, people were
saying, "Oh no, people will start talking about us," because we criticized others
that they shouldn't act or do cultural, this kind of fetish things. It's not good. . . .
They said, "Oh no, this one, we are believers and we can pray." I said, "Okay, if we
are believers, if we are dancing and playing the drums here, it is the same thing.
We can also pray to God and go ahead and do it." And the people liked it. Someone had to dress like someone who was possessed by a demon. We did it all right.
And there was this cultural and everything—drums. But they said that because it
was in SU, they accepted it, that God is with us. And if it is dance-drama too,
God is with us here [Other girls agree: Yes], and if we do it, it is the same thing, so
I don't see why people should try to distinguish between those two things [an SU
drama and a cultural dance-drama].

Given the degree to which a Christian discourse has polarized interpretations of culture in Ghana, students and teachers feel considerable pressure
to avoid school cultural competitions. My discussion with these girls
showed that they felt compelled to maintain identities as "good Christians" even as they participated in activities that were viewed by their
peers as dangerous to Christianity.

Discourses of modernity do not simply ventriloquize through individuals. Instead, say Dorothy Holland and her coauthors (1998), people orchestrate discourses, such as nationalism and Christianity, that emerge from
different sites of identification. Holland et al. are here building on the work
of Mikhail Bakhtin and his notion of dialogism (or intertextuality; see
Todorov 1984). Bakhtin's argument was that utterances are infused with
others' words and are articulated in relation to a response, whether imagined or not. He examined the orchestrating of different conflicting voices
in a literary work, such as the novel, in which different points of view are
brought into dialogue with one another. For people, he saw a process in
which authoritative discourses become internally persuasive discourses,
which are then elaborated and developed through interaction with new
contexts. "Our ideological development is just such an intense struggle
within us for hegemony among various available verbal and ideological
points of view, approaches, directions, and values" (Bakhtin 1984, 346).
Holland et al. (1998) also draw on Bakhtin's notion of orchestration in the
novel to conceptualize a process in which "the self authors itself, and is
made knowable, in the words of others" (173). In this section I examine how

students and teachers in Akuapem orchestrate the competing discourses of modernity through their performances during the cultural competition. In the process they show that Christians can appropriate government-sponsored cultural competitions for their own ends. As Naomi said, they want to persuade fellow SU members that a cultural dance-drama performed during a school cultural competition is similar to a Christian drama performed by the Scripture Union. They thus attempt to unify the internal divisions of modernity.

As is typical in a world where anyone who deviates even a little is the most harshly rebuked by the orthodox, it was Scripture Union members who were most criticized by fellow SU members, because, Naomi explained, "people believe that, once you belong to the SU, you must be solely holy, like you shouldn't participate in anything. You should just dedicate yourself to God." Although I use the girls' remarks in this section, the boys from the same school also discussed, less freely, the SU pressure to keep holy and how cultural drumming and dancing were seen as "some fetish something, some bad thing," as one boy said. For SU members, participation in cultural activities meant potentially making enemies and losing the support of a group that had given them a sense of community in the school. SU pressure had its greatest impact when the students were at the bottom of the school hierarchy, in the first form. By their last year, form 3 (the twelfth year of schooling), as most of the vocal girls in the discussion group were, students had formed stances toward these authoritative discourses about why they should be able to participate in "cultural dancing." As Naomi said, "But I wanted to do it and I made them understand that I know my stance as a Christian and if I am doing it, I am not doing it to possess something to come and destroy what they are doing." By reformulating the authoritative discourses of Christianity, these students sought to author themselves (as Holland et al. 1998 put it) as Christians despite and perhaps through their participation in school cultural competitions.

Given their beliefs, students took seriously the need to protect themselves from the evil spirits they might be invoking with their drumming and dancing. One argument that supported their participation was that God was omnipotent, and prayer would protect them from spirit incursions. Patience said,

> So when I came to this school, even just this dance I was performing, a certain SU member called me, preaching to me that I should take care, so that I don't fall. And I was a very good Christian when I was in JSS [junior secondary school]; everybody, including my headmaster, everybody saw that I was a good Christian. So when I am dancing, I know what I'm doing. What I'm doing, I pray to God

that even if there are demons which will enter into me, God should prevent them and even I know this school is also a mixed [coeducational] school and through this performance, the boys can even worry you about [sex],[15] so I prayed to God before I did it.

When these students defied the pressure of fellow SU members, they relied on the tool of prayer to justify their participation in cultural activities. They did not disagree with their fellow SU members about the dangers of drumming; they simply felt that God was more powerful than the evil spirits and would protect them.

As with performers in the Yoruba popular theater tradition (Barber 2000), students also rationalized their participation by claiming their play was sending a moral message that would change people's lives and behavior. The dance-drama of Abɛ Secondary School illustrated a way of becoming modern. It told the story of a village girl from the north who was attracted by a friend with flashy consumer items (handbag, shoes, Western dress, etc.) to the big city, where she was able to survive only by working as a *kaya-yoo* girl, carrying loads in the market. Sleeping in the street, she ended up getting involved with a cart-pusher and getting pregnant. The faculty adviser, Mr. Boateng, took the central message of the play to be the dangers of urban migration (chapter 3). But the girls saw the play as conveying a moral message:

> FATIMA: I think it is a privilege to be given a part [of the *kaya-yoo* girl] like that.
> OTHERS: Yes.
> FATIMA: So that you think, if you had the whole world, looking up to you, a single person, acting to correct something which is wrong, it's an advantage. Makes you feel like you're on top of the world or something like that. [Some girls giggle.]
> GRACE: I also think for me, I appreciate any part which is being given to me. . . . I want to do it so I know how these people [*kaya-yoo* girls] are being treated or like how they are being felt outside. So it is a privilege when you are being given a part to play in something. Maybe being pregnant, being as if, "Ah! So if I am student and being pregnant, teenage pregnancy [a girl: "*Eeesh!*"], what am I going to do?" So put yourself, your shoes into, "*Ei!* so I am pregnant." How will you feel that, "*Ei!*" you have lost all your goods. . . . So if you're being given that part to be a pregnant girl, maybe a teenage — this thing — pregnancy, behave as if it is real. You are feeling it. So you know, so the people will say, "*Ei!* Look how she is suffering. Then I won't go into this sexual, this thing, so I will be pregnant, because I know it is not good." So if you are being given that part, then you need to put it on, so that, "Yes, this one, it is real," and people will get the message out so they will stay away from certain things.

Although the girls saw both the condition of *kaya-yoo* girls and pregnancy as moral messages to portray, they treated the issue of pregnancy and sexual relations as having more resonance and relevance for themselves and their audience.

The new dance-drama form is particularly amenable to appropriation by Christians. Before 1995 students used to enact a ceremony or festival, or "portray the actual culture of a people," as one judge from the regional Center for National Culture said (Sedofu interview, 23 Mar. 1999). These plays would involve un-Christian practices like libation and other customs. Another judge, from the Eastern Region Ghana Education Service, said about cultural competitions that "some people don't allow their children to get into these [un-Christian] things." A dance-drama about teenage pregnancy was acceptable, he said, but something portraying spirit possession "contradicted" Christianity, and so presbyters and church officials did not like it. He said a little later that the dance-dramas show "practical" lessons about teenage pregnancy and drug abuse, and "these things will educate young people" (Amin interview, 26 Apr. 1999). At the workshop at Gyahene Secondary School, Mr. Devoh argued, "Some people think these customs are outmoded or satanic but there is something in it that has nothing to do with religion," and he advocated doing a dance-drama on national social ills like puberty rites, teenage pregnancy, or street children as presentations that would not offend Christian sensibilities. Public service announcements that will improve young people on behalf of the moral and economic state of the nation, what I call "development morality plays," are acceptable to Christians in a way that reenactments of cultural practices on stage are not.

These sorts of development morality plays are certainly popular. Schooling and sexuality were popular topics in the circuit festivals for primary and junior secondary schools in Akropong and Adukrom in 1997, as well as among the secondary schools in the cultural competition in 1999. The suggested theme for 2003 was "Preserving Our Environment through Our Culture," and the majority of schools in Akuapem adopted that theme, although one junior secondary school in Akropong focused on teenage pregnancy instead (see appendix A). The moral points usually concerned sexual immorality (for girls) and drug and alcohol use (for boys). Sometimes the scenes of sexual dancing, drinking, and drug use were incorporated into dance-dramas on other themes. For instance, in a dance-drama titled "Kindness Brings Riches," presented by the student representing the Greater Accra region at the national secondary school festival in 1999, two good and obedient brothers avoid the temptation of drinking with their peers. When a group of "bad" boys beat up an old man, the good brothers take him home to their parents, and he ends up making their poor family wealthy. The presentations of immoral behavior in dance-dramas were heavily influenced by the media, especially Ghanaian-produced movies that were shown on TV, which often have a Christian, moralistic message (Meyer 1999a). There is reason to suppose that, in the case of some students at least, the desire to portray immoral behavior did not come solely from a Christian impulse to present a moral lesson. These themes allowed students to act in dangerous ways—to play the part of a pregnant teenager or a boy driven mad by drugs and alcohol—in a safe, public context, in a socially sanctioned way, just as charismatic Christians exhibited possession by evil spirits in a Christian church in order to demonstrate the power of a Christian God. In both deliverance services and cultural competitions, the frisson of brushing against the demonic and immoral adds to the excitement and is a necessary foil for the ultimately Christian message to be convincing.

The moral message justified the participation of Christian students and teachers, but also made their participation problematic because they had to portray immoral behavior in public. The girls were not concerned about being identified with a northern *kaya-yoo* girl because of the distance between their class position and hers, but they were worried about being seen as sexually active. In their theories of performance, students felt that acting might very well become doing: although playing the role of an immoral character might make the actor behave more morally, it might also encourage the actor to participate in sinful activities. This process is almost equated to possession by an evil spirit, coming onto one unawares and without being able to control it.

> DIANA: To add to it [the previous remark], it changes your whole life because the moment you act it, especially when you act it so well, people begin to look at you, "Is that your real character? Is that how you really are?" So even if that is not how you are, you don't like people to say, "Oh, this girl, she played her own character. That is how she is." It checks you. You do things, you like to do things right, so nobody will say, you acted that way because that is how you are.
>
> MILLICENT: I will also say, sometimes, too, it really has influence on you. You are acting that part, you always, anytime, you become so, that character you acted becomes part of you. You acted—you like girls, you were chasing girls here and there. Anytime, you know that you—this boy—can do it, anytime they give you this part to act. And when you go out, it is easy for you to take girls.
>
> ANOTHER: Yes.
>
> MILLICENT: So it has influence on you.
>
> PATIENCE: If you are being given a bad part, you should pray before you act, so the Lord will protect you in what you are going to act, so that you don't fall victim.

When I asked for an example of a role influencing a person's character (Did this ever happen to you? To someone you know?), they described how a boy and a girl had started dating after playing the roles of lovers in a play. Patience even said that she had been given "bad" roles in junior secondary school because of her reputation as a strong Christian. Her headmaster explained to her that if her role changed her behavior it would be seen more clearly than in other students. And perhaps her Christian faith would also provide her with better protection from the bad influence of her role.

Early in the conversation, Millicent had described her response to SU criticism: "I will also say, I am an SU member, right, but I don't care about what they say. . . . I'm acting. . . . But I told them, I am portraying a message out, for them to know that this is bad. So when I'm doing it and I am finished, it doesn't mean it is part of me, you see. So I urge you, so when you're singing it, you should also prove to them, that is your talent and it doesn't mean you get spoiled or something, okay?" But by the end of the discussion, it was clear that though the students defended their participation to SU members, they were concerned that they might very well "get spoiled," and that the behavior they portrayed on stage might influence their reputation or their own character. Although students did not mention spirit possession in connection with these fears but worried only that acting would make them familiar with certain immoral activities, within charismatic Christian discourse immoral behavior opens one up to the influence of traditional spirits or may even be caused by those same spirits. Thus, although some Christians felt that the portrayal of teenage pregnancy and drug abuse was not antithetical to their religious beliefs in the way that the enactment of libation or spirit possession would be, for these Abe girls, local theories of performance and concerns with the Christian unitary self meant that acting the role of a pregnant girl also put their Christian identity at risk.

Conclusion

The dance-dramas were more subject to becoming "development morality lessons" than other performance arts of the cultural competition. The themes of the dance-drama allow Christians to address their moral concerns about social vices at the same time as they participate in government programs they perceive to have been scripted by non-Christians. Student performers attempted to reconcile the internal divisions of modernity that competed in the public sphere by portraying themselves as artistically talented and morally virtuous in a dance-drama about urban migration. As Christian teachers, students, and educational officers sought to appropriate the school cultural competitions for Christian purposes, they ended up marrying the goals of national development and Christianity, in which teenage pregnancy was the central problem of urban migration. In the dance-drama performances, Christian morality and national development went hand in hand.

Schools in Akuapem serve as sites for the production of modernity, not only because of their connection to the state but also because of their long-standing association with Christianity. Thus, it is important to look at students and teachers when examining the stresses of becoming modern. Participating in performances and lessons produced by the discourse of cultural nationalism, students and teachers, particularly at Abɛ Secondary, the most elite school in the immediate area, worked to enact themselves as holy and Christian. In the process they combined the competing idioms of nationalism and charismatic Christianity into a new discourse, in which they authored themselves as Christians benefiting the moral state of the nation. In their dance-drama performances and commentary on those performances, they contributed to the infusion of charismatic discourses in the public sphere and state spaces occurring at other levels in Ghana (Meyer 1999a). As a result, state spaces like school cultural competitions in fact end up as sites where a variety of cultural discourses — and hybrid discourses — are articulated.

At the same time, because performances are inherently polyphonic (Carlson 1990), the contradictions internal to modernity are not resolved by the highly charged work that these students are doing. In the final scene of Abɛ Secondary School's dance-drama, the kaya-yoo girl carries a heavy load of groceries on her head for an elite woman in the Accra market, stumbling across the stage as she carries one baby on her back and clutches her belly where another baby is growing. This scene can be read as a portrayal of class differences between southern secondary school students and northern migrants, a horror story about a national problem of urban migration and poverty for the promise of consumer goods, a warning about the dangers of sex with strangers, or a presentation of some of the dances and musical forms that make up the nation of Ghana. The audience can praise the main actress for being talented or criticize her for portraying her own character. Although students attempt to fix the meaning of these performances for themselves and their audiences, the tensions within the performance, and modernity itself, are not resolved. Rather, because school cultural competitions are sites where modernity is being actively negotiated, interpreting students' performances cannot be anything but slippery and unsettled.

5

"ABOFRA bɔ nwaw a, na ɔmmɔ ɔkyekyere" (A child can break the snail's shell but not the shell of the tortoise), Ghanaians like to say. One primary school teacher provided the exegesis to this proverb, one of the most frequently taught to younger students in Akan classes in Akuapem: "Abofra ntumi nka mpanyin-sɛm" (A child cannot speak the way elders do). Other proverbs taught in classrooms similarly highlighted the differences between elders and children and dwelt espe-

---
Folk Culture

as School Knowledge

The Contradictions of Teaching

Culture in Schools

---

cially on the limited strength of children compared with adults. Why were proverbs that fo-cused on children so popular in school cultural lessons?

Culture in Akuapem is asso-ciated with the secret knowl-edge and rituals of elders and chiefs and is generally not available to children and nonroyals. The secret knowl-edge and closed rituals are less important for their actual content than for the way they allow elders to manipulate decisions regarding material and symbolic inheritance.[1] Elders are not simply elderly people; they are certain older men and women who have gained positions of rit-ual and political authority in their families and thus in their towns. As William Murphy (1980) says of Kpelle se-cret societies in Liberia, "while young men do become old men, not all old men become lineage elders" and "few be-come powerful elders in the community" (202). Similarly, youth are not simply young adults; they are men and women of any age who are in a position of subordination and dependence on powerful people. Rather than think-ing about youth and elders as a specific age group or co-hort, Deborah Durham (2000) proposes paying attention to when the concept of youth and elderhood is used in specific social situations, as when children's status gets highlighted in proverbs taught in classrooms.

Schools, however, operate under a different logic. As John Meyer and his colleagues have argued (1992), mass education is a distinctive product of the Western, modernist project, organized around a conception of the nation-state moving toward greater progress. With the universalization of the concept of the nation, so too has the idea of mass education spread, with "its highly institutionalized structure, its explicit incorporation of all members of society, its dramatic stress on individual action, and its homogeneous and universalized rationalistic frame" (Boli et al. 1985, 149). The projects of the nation-state and mass education have become inseparable in Africa; providing education is one of the major functions and sources of legitimacy of most national governments there. Childhood and a student identity are considered synonymous (Ariès 1962). Conceptually, the modern project of transmitting knowledge via schools aims at a general, common, and basic training of all children so that they will be good citizens and producers.

From an anthropological perspective, both schools and the gerontocratic system are cultural orders, underpinned by particular conceptions of the world and in which participants act in context-specific ways. Culture encompasses all that humans do and imagine, so schools, like all institutions and contexts, continually engage in fashioning social identities and ways of being in the world, both explicitly and through the rituals and practices of the hidden curriculum. The means by which one gains knowledge is deeply intertwined with the social relationships and social identities available in a particular social order (Lave and Wenger 1991), and so students may learn different modes of interacting and participating in school from the ones they learn in their homes or communities (Heath 1983; Philips 1983). Seeing schools as cultural institutions with distinctive modes of operating helps one understand why teaching an explicitly marked "culture" associated with another cultural order becomes so problematic.

From an Akuapem perspective, there is a contradiction in making schools the vehicle for transmitting cultural knowledge, a subject that is associated with the elders, to young people. The logic of the school goes against the more selective local transmission of culture, in which only those who have gained a ritual-political position learn particular rituals and history. This chapter examines the transformations that occur when a cultural form of knowledge, embedded in a certain kind of social organization, with a distinctive epistemology and cosmological order, is communicated in schools, institutions intimately connected to the modern nation-state. The incorporation of cultural knowledge into schools involves three transformations in the meaning, communicative form, and content of that knowledge and in local hierarchical relationships between young people, teachers, and elders:

1. As cultural knowledge is taught in schools, it is translated from one epistemology into another and abstracted from its embeddedness in a par-

ticular social context to be fitted into another. Everyday, vernacular knowledge about cultural practices is codified and systematized as it is transformed into school knowledge, which takes the form of lists and definitions, written or spoken in English—*facts*—for the purpose of examining students and determining their future school careers. Thus, although students draw on their existing knowledge of local cultural practices in classroom lessons, the schools transform and recontextualize that knowledge.

2. The construction of cultural practices as school knowledge creates new experts on culture, namely, teachers and the writers of curricula or textbooks. However, because teachers cannot fully resolve the contradictions of trying to teach a body of knowledge held closely by elders—culture in the local sense—the school teaching of culture ironically ends up re-legitimating elders as the keepers of the most authentic cultural knowledge.

3. In Akuapem the teachers' failure to transform traditional knowledge into school knowledge led to a shift in their relations with their students. As teachers showed themselves to be less than expert in cultural matters, students, young children as well as adolescents, came to have more authority than usual, a situation that, though occasionally seen in the classroom, was most clearly exposed in the rehearsals for the cultural competitions. Teachers and other adults tried to deal with this problematic situation by maintaining order, limiting participation, and controlling the creative content of the performances. The intrusion of schools into matters of culture caused tensions between teachers and students, and among students: battles over authority were fought through the language of competence and knowledge.

In making these claims, I am not suggesting that there is a "great divide" between schooling and traditional culture, as has been claimed for literacy and orality (Ong 1982), a clear demarcation based on mental processes and ways of seeing the world specific to each. Certainly, students and teachers move fluidly between school and nonschool domains and are able to shift their modes of operating and speaking as they move from one domain to another. At the same time people in Akuapem do make a conceptual distinction between culture as taught in the schools and the cultural knowledge possessed by elders, and that distinction helps explain why teachers teach culture in school in the ways that they do. Critical scholars of literacy have examined how the meaning of literacy is based on its practice in specific institutions (Street 1993, 1984). Following these scholars, I am interested in the meanings Akuapem people attach to these two forms of cultural knowledge, and how those meanings influence social practice, at the level of classroom lessons and rehearsals for cultural competitions.

Relations between institutions like schools and gerontocratic hierarchies have long preoccupied scholars of Africa. They have tended to consider education, like urbanization (Ferguson 1999), a vehicle of modernization. According to this teleology, school knowledge has diminished the value of traditional expertise and, by empowering youth and women, has led to social change and the loss of traditional practices. Drawing on previous studies that saw local socialization practices as integrating society (Ford 1997; Raum 1940), anthropologists in the 1960s and 1970s viewed traditional educational methods as controlled by elders and as socializing youth to accept hierarchical structures in which they had little power (Grindal 1972; Leis 1972; Peshkin 1972; Read 1987 [1968]). Schools represented a competing cultural system and therefore a threat to African societies. They gave youth new skills and opportunities for high status, and with them, the authority to challenge elders. "It is routinely assumed that 'modern' culture is defined by the disruptive creativity of 'youth' in collective opposition to old authorities and old ways" (Gable 2000, 201). Some more recent studies have been less dismissive of the elders, holding that modern, Western schools are being incorporated into local systems of knowledge-production and social stratification as elders seek to bring schools under their authority and control (Bledsoe 1990; Bloch 1993; Stambach 1996). These scholars argue that schools have served as a new resource for acquiring traditional goals and statuses, which those in power are best able to exploit.

In Akuapem, with a long history of local interest in Western education, incorporating schools into local systems of social stratification ironically depends on their symbolic meaning as modern and on their operation as a separate sphere from local communities. Many people in Akuapem understand schools to be a separate, subordinate domain whose sole purpose is preparing youth for salaried work and adulthood. The schools there do indeed isolate youth from elders, encouraging young people to form their own peer groups and to assume greater authority, even if only over one another. In this, Akuapem is no different from schools in the West that serve as sites of peer interaction and the development of nonfamilial, lateral connections (Eckert 1989; Foley 1990; Reed-Danahay 1996). To the extent that the local schools isolate young people, teach knowledge that is useful mainly within school contexts, and operate on the principle of preparing young people for future adulthood, they are compatible with local gerontocratic relations.

Nevertheless, the close association of culture with elders' knowledge complicates the ability of schools to simultaneously uphold the power of elders over young people and give students the broad, common knowledge they need as future citizens. Thus, as teachers produce cultural knowledge in schools, they change the meanings of that knowledge. This chapter will unravel the complex, multilayered dynamics of the politics of knowledge and pedagogy as a vernacular knowledge is turned into a codified knowledge taught in schools.

Learning the Knowledge of the Elders

As we walked down the main street of Larteh one day in February 1999, the retired secondary school teacher everyone called Teacher Darko told me that in 1957 he had wanted to do his senior thesis at Presbyterian Training College on the history of his hometown and had come to Larteh to talk to one elder. But the elder had said to him he would not tell him anything unless he brought drinks, and by the time Teacher Darko got around to returning, the elder had died. Another elder would also not tell him anything, and Teacher Darko, then a young man, made so bold as to rebuke him, saying, "If you don't tell, then how will the children learn?" Why wouldn't they say anything? I asked Teacher Darko in Twi. "Wosuro," he said. They are afraid. What were they afraid of? I asked. Teacher Darko, now himself an elder (as an *ɔkyeame*), said that they were afraid they would reveal something secret, and the *ɔbosom* (spirit) would punish them. Here, we see two different logics in conflict. Teacher Darko, training to become a teacher, felt that it was important for children to learn what their elders knew, and that teachers should be the link for transmitting this knowledge, whereas the elder's first concern was to keep his relationship to the spirits and ancestors in good standing, which required that he not pass along his knowledge to anyone who simply asked; he did not feel any obligation to make sure that children learned it. The importance and sacredness of the knowledge that the elder possessed were revealed not by sharing it, but by the need for indirection and secrecy.

A poem recited at the Eastern regional cultural competition for secondary schools presented the image Teacher Darko had hoped for—elders were teachers who rendered their knowledge accessible to young children—as if it reflected the actual situation:

Wunni panyin a due ampa.	If you don't have an elder, I am truly sorry.
Mmerewatia ne nkwakorawa yi	These old, old women and men,
Wɔne nkwadaa na edi afoofi.	It is they who stay home with the children.
Wɔyɛ akyerɛkyerɛfoɔ pa.	They are good teachers.
Wɔkyerɛ kasa pa ne mpanyinsɛm	They teach proper language and elders' matters [history]
Tete mmofra nimdeɛ kwan so.	And educate children to be knowledgeable.[2]

The poem suggests that one learns the knowledge of history and proper speech, the kind of knowledge most closely associated with culture, at the knee of one's elders, by being formally taught as a child in a school-like fashion. But most adults I spoke to talked about acquiring this knowledge piecemeal by watching and listening and as a process that continues throughout one's life. In Akuapem old women were considered experts at genealogy, and people learned their family history in the discussions, dominated by old women, that took place at funerals (S. K. Aboa, conversation, 29 Jan. 1999). A middle-aged woman told me that one never stopped learning Twi because at a funeral or other event, an old woman would sometimes use a word for a common object, like a chair, that she had never heard before. Sometimes using this exclusive language was seen as arrogant or showing off one's erudition. It also served to keep younger, middle-aged adults out of the discussion and made the information being communicated accessible only to certain participants. Learning this kind of knowledge therefore depended on spending time with older family members when matters of history and genealogy were being discussed.

Sacred knowledge is considered even more secret than family history. Asiedu Yirenkyi, a professor at the Institute of African Studies at Legon and native of Akropong, talked to me about his research on rituals. It took him ten years of attending local festivals to gain the elders' trust. He had also gained access to a sacred grove in a town in Akuapem and was surprised to discover that most of the ten elders who were allowed into the sacred grove did not know the full particulars of the three-day rite celebrated there; each man knew only what happened on one or two days. He imputed the insistence on secrecy to the violent history of the slave trade, which produced chaos and mistrust of strangers (see Ferme 2001; Shaw 2002). In those days people had typically entrusted sacred knowledge to the household member who was the least likely to be noticed, he observed. Some people who describe sacred rituals do not know what really happens, he said, and others are told what obfuscations to say publicly (conversation, 26 Mar. 1999). As Professor Yirenkyi's story shows, however much one is admitted to the inner circle, there are always more secrets and mysteries to be learned. Even at the highest levels, perhaps only one or two people know the entire body of ritual; the knowledge is held collectively, so that only a few know all of it. In Akuapem, as elsewhere in Ghana, sacred and historical information—what was considered cultural—was secret, the domain of a few, privileged people.[3] Precisely because this kind of knowledge was not accessible to everyone, it was not accessible to me, and I only learned that such a fund of secret knowledge existed obliquely, through others' comments.

Generating Distinction: The Structural Context of Schooling

The historian Robert Addo-Fening used his academic knowledge to frame his own childhood experience in Akyem Abuakwa in the 1940s: "When they sent somebody to school, the expectation was that he would be different from the ordinary run of people, so your father sends you to school, he wants to see you dressed, wearing a tie and shoes, to be like the missionaries, to be like the teachers and so on. So people thought that agriculture and manual labor generally were below the dignity of anybody who had gone to school. . . . They thought that an educated person must not do this kind of thing" (interview, 27 Sept. 1998).

The 1986 education reform encouraged schools in Ghana, especially the junior secondary schools, to become more practical and vocational, with the expectation that most Ghanaians would finish school at the end of junior secondary school. With nine years of schooling, educators thought, graduates would be able to provide for themselves through their own entrepreneurship. Historically, however, all attempts to make Ghanaian education practical have floundered because of the social meaning that attaches to education (P. Foster 1965), as Professor Addo-Fening's account makes abundantly clear, and the latest set of educational reforms has not been any more successful in this regard. Although the subjects taught in primary and junior secondary schools seem eminently practical (see table 2), they are taught in a way that has little application to students' everyday life.

Schools in Akuapem rely on the rote method of learning: a lesson is a game of word reproduction, a litany to be learned and endlessly repeated. In the United States and Europe, this method of transforming knowledge into facts to be regurgitated is usually the resort of teachers attempting to control students in a situation where they feel powerless (McNeil 1986; Willis 1981). In Ghana teachers clearly do feel demoralized. Common complaints are poor pay, lack of respect from parents and students, inadequate pensions, lack of influence on educational policy, lack of housing, and lack of textbooks for students. Many young teachers come into the teaching profession because, in an economy in which it can be difficult to find salaried employment, they perceive it to be a guaranteed and secure, if not necessarily well-remunerated, position. Ambitious young teachers, particularly young men, often pursue more risky ventures for financial success and status simultaneously, like entering the U.S. visa lottery or preparing for university exams. Many teachers supplement their salaries by pursuing other activities on the side, especially tutoring but also including farming, selling baked goods, and running a small shop. Their demoralization has resulted in teachers' "deliberately skipping classes for days or even

Table 2   Primary and junior secondary school curricula, 1998–99

Primary school		Junior secondary school	
Subject	Hours per week	Subject	Hours per week
Math	5.0	Math	5.0
English	4.0–5.0	English	5.0
Ghanaian languages	2.5–3.5	Ghanaian languages	3.0
Environmental skills[a]	2.5	Environmental skills[a]	2.0
Science	2.5	General science	2.0
Religious and moral education	1.5	Agricultural science	2.0
Music and dance	1.0	Technical skills and technical drawing	1.0
		Selected vocational skill[b]	1.0
		Religious and moral education	0.5
		Music and dance	0.5

[a]This course combines the older subjects of social studies and life skills. It covers much more than the name suggests: geography, history, and hygiene, as well as care for the environment.
[b]Each school could offer one of ten courses: catering, leatherwork, pottery, sewing/needlework, basketry, bead making, calabash art, graphics, picture making, and sculpture. Only the first four were taught in the Akuapem schools.

weeks on end, refusal to prepare lesson notes, drunkenness, laziness at teaching and carelessness of the well-being of their pupils," charged one *Mirror* reader in a letter to the newspaper (19 Dec. 1998, 2). But it is worth noting that the letter-writer's concern was with teachers *not* teaching, by skipping school or not preparing lesson plans, rather than with *how* teachers teach. From my classroom observations and discussions with teachers, teaching in the manner described below is a sign of good teaching and dedication on the part of the teacher, not the response of a demoralized profession. This pedagogical strategy arises from the historical and social context of schooling in Ghana, in which education has always been associated with the creation of a relatively small urban and white-collar elite whose distinction arose in part because of the disdain for practical subjects that schooling currently purports to teach.

One of the most important mechanisms determining one's admission to that class in Ghana has been progress to the highest and most restricted educational level. Driven by expectations of the next level, schools accordingly emphasize the academic much more than the vocational.[4] Currently, junior secondary students in Akuapem consider themselves unsuccessful if they do not go on to secondary school; and those in secondary school hope to go to university. But despite these dreams of higher education, very few junior secondary school graduates are able to continue their schooling, and even fewer secondary school students go on to university. This owes in good part to the fact that many students, especially in rural areas of Ghana, fail the exams.[5] But many of those who do well also "fail" because of a lack of available university slots.[6] In this situation of scarcity, exams have become the most important way of winnowing out students. Classroom lessons are oriented to helping students memorize facts that will help them pass exams.[7] English is also given increased weight because all the tests in both the Basic Education Certificate Examination (BECE) at the end of junior secondary school and the Secondary School Certificate Examination (SSCE) at the end of secondary school are in that language (except for the Ghanaian languages exam, of course).[8] Despite government reforms to make schools more practical and more oriented to the needs of students who will not go on to secondary school, teachers continue to teach to the national exams that determine whether students enter the next educational tier.

Townspeople and parents are very much aware that schools are not equal in this endeavor. Rural schools in Ghana, particularly, suffer from a lack of teachers and a poor quality of education.[9] Private schools have sprung up in places where parents can afford the higher fees, primarily in cities, but also in Akuapem, and greater emphasis is placed on English in these schools.[10] In Akropong some public junior secondary schools are thought to be better than others because of their relatively high pass rates on the BECE. Since many students wish to attend them, those schools have instituted entrance exams (in math and English) so they can pick the cream of the primary school crop. Because school finances outside of teachers' salaries depend solely on student fees, large student populations provide more resources to schools with good reputations.

Secondary schools vary even more sharply in the quality of education than the primary and junior secondary schools. Some of them, particularly the ones that used to teach to the sixth form under the system in place before the 1986 educational reform, have resources such as equipped science laboratories, books, and well-trained teachers. An editorial in the *Mirror* asserted that "it is a fact that most of the senior secondary schools in the rural areas only go by the name and do not in any way come near what a senior secondary school should be" (31 July 1999, 2). Every year graduating junior secondary students pick five secondary schools that they want to attend. The prestigious secondary schools, many clustered in the urban areas of Cape Coast, Accra, and Kumase, always receive many more applications than they can possibly accept.[11] In a few hectic weeks in January, as secondary schools pick their first-year class, parents cajole and beg head-masters to put their children on the acceptance list, drawing on personal connections and their financial resources to persuade them. Prestigious secondary schools can ask for astronomical educational and boarding fees. Those schools are out of the reach of the majority of Akuapem families, which are sometimes hard put just to pay for their children's schooling through the lower grades.

The result of this restricted educational market is that urban students from families of some means end up going to the most prestigious second-ary schools—including the best that the countryside has to offer (see Weis 1979). The headmaster of Begoro Secondary School, located in a rural area of the Eastern Region, told me that very few of the local students were able to meet the state's minimal entrance requirements, and that in order to fill the school in January 1999, he had had to launch an appeal for students on TV; 80 percent of his first-year students that year came from urban areas. In Akuapem, of the three secondary schools I studied, the two boarding schools, Abɛ and Gyahene, were considered better than the day school, Horeb, and except for a few local students with chiefly connections, their student bodies came from nearby urban areas such as Accra, Tema, and Ko-foridua. Horeb Secondary School, which was started by a prayer group in 1978 and taken over by the government in 1990, is housed in a church an-nex; it has far fewer resources than the other two schools and is populated by far more students from Akuapem.[12] This dynamic has been recurrent in Ghanaian educational history. During colonial times the small number of secondary schools created a small elite; then, as the number of secondary schools increased, distinctions between them became the new measure of elite status. The same process is likely to happen with higher education. A number of private institutions, primarily religious institutions, have begun establishing universities because there is such a gap between demand and availability. Unfortunately, most are strapped for money and struggling to survive.

In principle schools are supposed to provide equal access to students; all should have an equal opportunity to attain the dream of prosperity and high status. Furthermore, governments, including the Ghanaian govern-ment, have adopted the modernist vision of mass education: one that pro-vides the basic set of skills all citizens should have in order to contribute to the progress of society and one in which literacy, math, and science figure prominently (Meyer et al. 1992).[13] But in practice schooling functions as a significant gatekeeper of status and economic differentiation. It does so not because the skills and knowledge it provides—literacy, math, and science—are necessarily useful in the employment that is exchangeable for the school certificate, but because of the symbolic value of school knowledge. For instance, because English is the language of government and international business one might argue that fluency in English is an important criterion for being able to find employment in those areas. However, the symbolic meaning of knowledge cannot be separated from its practical value. English fluency serves as a status marker in Ghana. A woman with whom I had grown friendly because I often passed by her small shop in Abiriw asked me one day to teach her English. This request surprised me because we occasionally conversed in English. In the discussion that followed, she told me that she was ashamed to speak English because people laughed at her attempts, and that people do not respect those who do not speak English well. Math, the other subject that occupies as large a share of the school schedule as English, is taught very differently from the ways that people calculate in their households and the marketplace, so that while it might be useful in employment within a bureaucracy, it is probably not useful for those who will leave school at the end of junior secondary school. What primarily distinguishes school knowledge from the practical knowledge of everyday life is not its content, but its form. That form is abstract and systematized, articulated in words, mainly—but not necessarily—in English. On a local level, schooling in Ghana is associated not with the mass education project of citizenship, but with the creation of a Westernized and wealthy urban elite who can serve as brokers between the state or international resources and local areas.

The Theoretical and the Practical: Systematizing Everyday Knowledge

Teachers differentiate between two kinds of school knowledge. One kind is sometimes called theory and sometimes science. The reference is to the teaching of explanations, definitions, functions, and names of items. The other kind of school knowledge, "the practical," concerns the application of the theoretical and scientific. The term refers to students working with their hands with various sorts of physical materials and putting the concepts and names into practice or performance. Teaching students the names of different stitches and their appropriate uses in a lesson on sewing is theoretical; actually using the stitches to make a handkerchief is practical, according to this emic understanding that differentiates between the presentation of codified knowledge and its performance.

Although for most teachers the ideal lesson combines theory and practice, in the everyday curriculum teachers tended to emphasize the theoretical and ignore the practical. An art teacher at one of the boarding schools in Akuapem, Mr. Philip, told me that in the ideal, 40 percent of a lesson in visual arts and textiles would be devoted to theory, and 60 percent to the practical. But he was unable to maintain that ideal balance because materials were too expensive; the school had to buy the dyes and fibers directly from a commercial outfit that imported them from abroad. The lack of resources made teaching the practical difficult, if not impossible. In teaching a subject like woodworking, for instance, a teacher might provide a list of tools and their functions (the theoretical), but because schools did not have any of the tools, the teacher could not show students how to use them (the practical). Theory also hid gaps in the teacher's knowledge, because the teachers themselves copied their notes from a textbook or another source. The theoretical, not the practical, was tested on the all-important examinations.

At times the focus on theory was presented as a virtue, making up for a missing aspect in the surrounding community. Kobina Asare, an art teacher, explained the distinction more succinctly: "Wusua tete de no, εyε na sε woba sukuu a, wɔbεkyerε. . . . Wo papa bεkyerε wo, nanso bi wɔ hɔ wom a wunnim a, woba sukuu a, wobehu" (If you study the things of the past, you study the practical aspects but if you go to school, they will teach the scientific way of doing those things. . . . Your father teaches you, but some terms are there that if you don't know, if you go to school, you will learn them).[14] Mr. Asare felt that families provided mainly practical knowledge, with some scientific knowledge in the form of names and terms sprinkled in, but the main place to acquire scientific knowledge was in school. Like Mr. Asare, Mr. Philip emphasized the importance of theory in providing the scientific background for art, giving students a knowledge of the chemicals involved, the strength of fibers, and the physics of color and light. One teacher responded to my question about why culture should be taught in the schools by saying that in the community, students could watch a festival or ritual, but they did not understand what was happening. School provided explicit explanations and terms for cultural activities. Thus, when teachers touched on culture or other kinds of vernacular knowledge in their lessons, they highlighted the theoretical aspects.

Classroom teaching—and the pattern became increasingly clear and strong at higher levels of schooling—consisted of teachers leading a discussion, typically by first directing questions to students to test their knowledge. The discussion would result in various lists and definitions being put on the blackboard. Then the teacher would give the class a set of "notes," writing out sentences and paragraphs on the topic on the blackboard; these often duplicated the points covered in the previous discussion. Students would copy these notes into their notebooks for future reference; they would serve as the basis of exercises and questions in school tests and national exams. Sometimes, for homework or classwork, the teacher would write questions on the blackboard, based on the notes, and students would write the answers in their notebooks. This teaching strategy is to some extent a response to the lack of textbooks; when textbooks were pulled out of the closets, five or more students would share one book, huddled around a table, reading upside-down, sideways, or over someone's shoulder. Notetaking is a laborious process. Notebooks are often the material objects around which lessons revolve: after students hurry to copy notes down from the blackboard, the notebooks are usually collected to be graded by the teacher, who often has stacks of them on his or her table. They are then returned to the students for correction. Notes are therefore one of the most important mechanisms for turning vernacular knowledge into school knowledge.[15]

Let us see what this looks like in a classroom lesson on grilling foods, a subject that illustrates this principle especially well because it is an eminently practical topic. Grilling was a common method of preparing food in Akuapem; women and adolescents sold snack foods, many of which were grilled, on the streets and in the markets. In a second-year class at Osuafo Junior Secondary School (eighth year of schooling), students copied down the following notes for an Environmental Skills class, required for all students:

> Grilling. It is a dry method of cooking food over an open fire on a grill. It can be done on a coalpot or swish stove. It can be widely used for cooking food like fish, kebab, and yam. Advantages:
>   1. It is a quick method of cooking.
>   2. They are easily digestible.
>   3. Nutrients are not wasted.
>   4. They are tasty and appetizing.

The students would normally have gone on to copy down the disadvantages but this particular class ended before they could do so; instead, they had to copy the notes for disadvantages from the other second-year class. In the next class period, two days later, Mrs. Bampo began by writing "Grilling" on the blackboard, but before launching into a discussion, she asked for one or two rules on baking, reviewing a previous lesson. That out of the way, Mrs. Bampo said the word "grilling" and made students repeat it twice in unison. "You can grill on a swish oven, coalpot, or gas grill.

Grilling is over an open fire. What are the advantages?" Some hands went up, but there was a lot of talking in the classroom, and Mrs. Bampo herself seemed bored. She wrote on the blackboard, "It is a dry method of cooking food over an open fire with a grill."

Mrs. Bampo then gave the class examples of things that could be grilled, plantain, kebab, yam, and again asked for advantages. Justice answered that it was a "quick method of cooking." Solomon added that it was "easily digestible." Students seemed to be reading from their notes. Opare said, "The nutrients are not—" "What is in your mouth?" Mrs. Bampo interrupted, thinking he was chewing gum. "Nutrients are not wasted," he completed. Dinah repeated the final advantage, "They are tasty and appetizing."

"What are the disadvantages?" Mrs. Bampo asked. A boy said, "It wastes fuel." Christina said, "It needs attention." "Why?" Mrs. Bampo asked. "Abigail, tell me something." Abigail had not raised her hand; she stood but could not find anything to say. "You think," Mrs. Bampo chided her. "It's something we do in our house always, so don't act as if it is strange [to you]." She gave the Twi word for grilling: *toto*. Abigail said that it was hard "to prevent it from burning."

"Are there other disadvantages?" Mrs. Bampo asked. Dankwa was called on; he also had not put his hand up and did not know what to say. "Tell me something," Mrs. Bampo said. Then she gave up and asked for "someone to help," and he sat down with relief.

Danso said, "It is an expensive method of cooking." There was laughter near where Alice was sitting, and Alice was called on. "Why is it expensive?" Mrs. Bampo asked. Darko said, "It needs fuel," and Alice sat down.

Mrs. Bampo ended the lesson with the assignment of a short exercise: "1. Explain the term grilling. 2. Write down two different kinds of food that can be grilled. 3. Why is grilling an expensive type of cooking? 4. Write down one disadvantage of grilling."

Grilling foods is familiar to students, yet somehow they had trouble expressing their knowledge within this format. Students, particularly the boys, merely mouthed the words already given by Mrs. Bampo to describe that method of cooking. Abigail was able to give a disadvantage of grilling from her own experience once she heard the Twi term *toto*, but Alice was unable to think of an answer, and without Mrs. Bampo's words, she was silent. This system of teaching makes teachers and the notes they provide the primary source of information, and other ways of knowing from observation and experience are largely closed off.

Similarly, in a class at Nhoma Primary School, on a cold, misty morning, Mrs. Kwapong was teaching her fifth-year students about food production in a science class. She herself was quite knowledgeable about farming, and so were some of the students, especially those from Akropong whose parents had farms in the vicinity. The process of transforming this vernacular knowledge into notes made it strange; furthermore, students found it difficult to describe everyday items and terms in English. After listing various local food crops, Mrs. Kwapong asked students to describe how these food crops, one by one, were planted and grown.

"How do we get cassava for planting?" Mrs. Kwapong asked.

Patience said, "A cassava stalk."

"Cassava sticks or stems," said Mrs. Kwapong. "Cassava has seeds but you don't use the seeds for planting. What do you do to the stick before you plant?"

Godfried, a small boy who regularly helped his father to farm and who was sitting near me at the back of the room, knew and stood up but could not find the right words. "Cut it in smalls," he finally said. "Cut what?" Mrs. Kwapong asked, trying to get him to talk in full sentences and descriptively. "The stem," he said.

"You haven't seen one before?" Mrs. Kwapong asked the whole class. She was chiding, not questioning them, trying to provoke them into response. Some people seemed to know but could not describe it.

Joyce, whose family did not have a farm, said, "Then you dig a hole."

Mrs. Kwapong began to write a list on the blackboard: "1. Cut the cassava stick into pieces. 2. Dig a hole."

Faustina, one of the students who did have access to a farm, said, "Put the cassava stick into the hole."

Mrs. Kwapong asked if they put all of the stick into the hole.

"Put half," Godfried muttered to himself. Faustina remained standing, apparently thinking that, Mrs. Kwapong had directed her question about putting the whole stick of cassava in the ground specifically to her and so she could not sit down until she answered. There was silence. Finally Ampoma was called on, and I could not hear her answer. Mrs. Kwapong wrote on the blackboard: "3. Put the end of the piece into the hole."

Frustrated, Mrs. Kwapong demonstrated with the teacher's cane in her hand — one puts in just one end of the stalk and her other hand showed how far to put it in.

A girl said, "Cover it with soil."

Mrs. Kwapong moved on to go through the same process with plantain and cocoyam, and then said, "We are left with yam."

Godfried said, "You cut the head of the yam." "Head of the yam" is a literal translation of the Twi term *bayere ti*. Seeking the English technical term, Mrs. Kwapong asked, "Is it the rhizome, sucker, or what?" Asante repeated, "You use the head."

There was an interruption from outside the classroom, and Mrs. Kwapong left the room briefly. Godfried told Asante, who had his hand up, "Maka" (I have said it). Asante shot back, "Wonkae" (You haven't said it).

Mrs. Kwapong returned, and Ampoma and Patience had their hands up. Patience said, "Use the head of the yam." Clearly, the students were committed to this answer.

Mrs. Kwapong told them it was the part that one cuts to eat. "It is the tuber." She asked them to say it in unison two times. They did so, pronouncing it "tüber." Patience, Ampoma, and Lydia had their hands up, and one of them said that the next step was to "dig a hole."

"Woka borɔfo a, wose dɛn?" (How do you say it in English?), Godfried asked his seatmate. Mrs. Kwapong looked in her science book. After not getting a response, Mrs. Kwapong wrote on the blackboard, "1. Make a mound." She then explained the process of making the mound in Twi. "Then what do you do?" After getting no response from the students, she answered, "Cut part of the tuber." She wrote on the board: "2. Put a piece of the tuber into the mound and cover it with soil."

Many students were writing this down. "Leave it in the mound," said Mrs. Kwapong, "and the shoot will come out. For yam, when the shoot comes out, it needs a stick so it can climb. For the rest [the other vegetables], there is no stick. It is a climbing plant; give it a pole." She drew a pretty picture of yam on the blackboard.

This way of teaching simple everyday things like grilling and growing cassava and yam, although purporting to draw on students' knowledge, makes them feel confused and uncertain about activities that many of them have probably seen and done themselves; teachers accuse students of not thinking and not observing. In upper primary school, giving these lessons in English contributes to making school knowledge strange. At some level all subject lessons—besides Twi—in the upper primary school become lessons in English. In higher grades, although students have gained some competence in English, the terms that are used in their lessons are relatively formal. For instance, in an art lesson on signs and mottos at Abɛ Secondary School, students used the words "hoisted," rather than "raised," and "erected," rather than "placed." A boy struggled to show a mastery of the language by using the word "advertization." Moreover, the students' vocabulary tended to be limited to what was presented in the lessons, with the same English words provided by the teacher in the notes circulating over and over in the reviews of lessons and classroom exercises.

To sum up, this teaching method highlights definitions of terms, examples of a kind of item, steps in a process, descriptions of uses and functions, and lists of advantages and disadvantages. These elements become progressively more important as one goes higher up the education ladder.[16] Everything, even the most abstract concepts, gets reduced to the repetition of words, both in written and in oral form. Words are endlessly circulated in the school classroom. Students have to mimic this vocabulary to excel, and students (and teachers) can hide any lack of understanding of their meaning behind an exact recitation of words. Meaning is less important than the ability to flawlessly parrot the words. It is difficult to believe that very many students would turn to their notes for help on grilling plantain or planting cassava; they learn those skills from relatives in the actual performance of those tasks.

Although schools in Akuapem make everyday knowledge abstract and systematized, a fair amount of practical housework and labor happens as part of the everyday school routine, a historical legacy of missionary schooling, when students worked on school farms and as servants in teachers' households (chapter 1). In primary and junior secondary schools, students begin and end each schoolday by sweeping the classrooms and weeding the courtyard and flower beds; in the boarding secondary schools, these chores are done on Saturdays. During the schoolday, students run the kind of errands for teachers that they are required to perform at home, such as buying food, transporting items, fetching water, and cleaning basins and buckets. Primary school students spend the bulk of their time at the end and beginning of each term, perhaps totaling as much as ten or so weeks of their forty-week year, maintaining the school's grounds and buildings. But the classroom lessons curiously ignore the practical knowledge that students have.

Classroom schoolwork recontextualizes students' vernacular knowledge in a system that places a high premium on articulating and systematizing knowledge through words. According to Aurolyn Luykx (1999), "A defining feature of students' labor [as schoolwork] is its importance as an exchange value rather than a use value," meaning that students will exchange their schoolwork for an academic credential, which they can then exchange for a job (205). All the same there is also a use value in schoolwork: "the production of schoolwork is in a sense a foil for the production of student-subjects" (Luykx 1999, 207). Through schoolwork students produce themselves as particular kinds of subjects, with a particular kind of relationship to knowledge. Students in Akuapem schools are learning to articulate and reproduce school knowledge, a knowledge useful primarily in its circulation from the blackboard to notes to exercises to the examination paper. The focus on the reproduction and circulation of words within this closed space renders the knowledge safe and appropriate for young people, without posing a threat to the more deeply respected knowledge of the chiefs and elders.

Libation as Literature: Culture Becomes School Knowledge

How do teachers handle the contradictions of teaching a secret and sometimes sacred knowledge—marked as cultural—to young people in school? Teachers used a variety of methods depending on the depth of their knowledge, their interest in the topic, and their social position.

One method was to transform cultural knowledge into the logocentric school form of knowledge, as is done with other forms of vernacular knowledge like grilling plantain and planting food crops. The Akan language teachers at both Abɛ and Gyahene secondary schools sought to convince their students that culture was a worthy subject of school knowledge. As one might expect, neither teacher ventured into the practical in these lessons. Both taught solely "theoretical" lessons of the usual kind: holding discussions with students, putting notes on the blackboard for the students to copy, and systematizing their subjects (culture in this case) into lists of definitions and advantages and disadvantages. Mr. Danquah, at Abɛ, was a gentle man in his sixties who was always dressed neatly in a political suit— a short-sleeved, buttoned-down shirt that hangs over matching trousers, promoted by Nkrumah as an adaptation of a Western suit to an African context. In his lesson on libation (nsagu) for a first form class (tenth year of schooling), Mr. Danquah divided a libation text into three sections: calling (ɔfrɛ), news (amaneɛbɔ), and curses (nnome). He then gave the students a sample libation text to copy from the blackboard, along with four lists that had grown out of the class's discussion over the course of the lesson: the foods and drinks that could be used to pour libation; the objects needed for pouring libation; the places where one pours libation; and the order in which higher powers are mentioned during libation. Likewise, in a lesson on funerals for a third form class (twelfth and final year of schooling), Mr. Danquah created lists of the different kinds of inauspicious deaths for which funerals are not performed; the people involved in a funeral; items needed during a funeral; different kinds of funeral cloths; and the purposes (functions) of alcohol at funerals. Perhaps aware of the missing element of the "practical" in his classes, Mr. Danquah said during the lesson on libation that one day he would give a demonstration of libation-pouring, wearing his cloth. (I am not sure he kept this promise; I did not myself see such a lesson.) The theoretical focus of his lessons supported the secondary school teachers' argument that culture was an object of study and an appropriate school subject.

This form of pedagogy also protected them from Christian criticisms. During the lesson on libation, I watched Mr. Danquah fend off criticism from a student about the un-Christian aspects of culture by saying that customs should be studied and evaluated. The Akan language teacher at Gyahene, Mr. Opare, also in his sixties, had become head of his extended family (*abusuapanyin*) several years earlier, but as a Jehovah's Witness, he refused to pour libation. As a result, he told me, several people in his family had died since he became *abusuapanyin*, even though an older relative poured libation in his stead. I was surprised, therefore, that he taught about libation in his classes. Like Mr. Danquah, in his justification of this lesson to students, he stressed its "literature aspects," as he said to his students. "Apae te sɛ anwinsɛm" (Libation is like poetry), he told them. Unsurprisingly, he did not perform libation in front of his students, nor did he ask one of his students to do so. By treating libation as a text like poetry, he managed to bracket off its sacred significance and power and thus render it safe for his own and his students' Christian beliefs.

If teachers are to retain their authority over students, cultural knowledge has to become school knowledge, or an object of study, delineated by definitions, lists of elements, functions, advantages and disadvantages, and so forth, as is done with other kinds of vernacular knowledge in school. Thus, as cultural knowledge becomes incorporated into the institution of the school, it assumes a different meaning and power, becoming factual knowledge to be memorized and reproduced in exams. Through classroom lessons students are able to appreciate and understand "libation as literature," but do not learn to pour libation themselves. They thus take on the position of an urban, educated elite like the graduate of Achimota school (chapter 2), able to appreciate a reified tradition in an abstract way but unable to participate in it.

A second method teachers used to resolve their felt contradictions was to teach students cultural knowledge appropriate to or associated with their childhood station. The lessons that I saw most often taught were greetings (*nkyia*), child-naming ceremonies (*abadinto*), and names and appellations (*edin ne mmran*; see appendix B). Libation (*nsagu*) can be added to this list, but that rite did not involve children; the lessons I observed on libation were mainly for secondary school students. Other lessons taught to children, but less frequently, were Ananse stories and games. As noted earlier, the proverbs that were most often taught seemed meant specifically to remind children of their status vis-à-vis adults (recall the proverb with which this chapter began, about a child being too weak to break the shell of a tortoise). It has been said that as people of lower status gain access to prestigious occupations, those occupations lose their prestige (Bourdieu and Passeron 1990). Here we see an analogous but slightly different process in operation, in which as youth gain access to cultural knowledge through schools, a hierarchy and differentiation within that body of knowledge appears. Akuapem people considered the "deepest" historical and ritual knowledge to be held by elders and the cultural knowledge that youth gained in school appropriate to young people (child-naming ceremonies, greetings, Ananse stories). Thus, by teaching cultural knowledge associated with children, the school continues to legitimate the power of elders relative to young people.

In order for the state to become involved in the transmission of cultural knowledge, the location of cultural expertise has to shift away from, or at least expand beyond, elders to teachers or other state bureaucrats. The state put one mechanism for attaining such expertise at teachers' disposal in 1989: *Cultural Studies for Junior-Secondary Schools*, a series of textbooks for classroom use. But textbooks are scarce in Akuapem schools; teachers are lucky to have a copy of their own, much less one for every pupil. A more accessible mechanism for acquiring expertise, for new teachers at least, is the teacher training institution.

Teachers vary widely in their command of knowledge about culture. To be certified for primary and junior secondary schools, teachers must attend only a general course in college, whereas a secondary school teacher has to go on to receive a specialist diploma or a university degree. In a country where educational opportunities are restricted, especially for women, earning a degree can sometimes take years. As a result, many secondary school teachers are older—in their forties and fifties—and more likely to be male than their primary and junior secondary colleagues. In Akuapem the Akan language teachers in the secondary schools were eager to promote Akan literacy and felt competent in their subject. Both Akan language and Akan customs were regularly taught in secondary schools, but to dwindling numbers of students, who see greater social value in learning French instead.[17] Thus, while there are expert and passionate Akan language teachers at the secondary school level, many are teaching subjects other than their specialty owing to a lack of student interest.

Because of their age, interest, and educational training, these Akan language teachers have been more easily able to position themselves as knowledgeable experts in traditional culture. Some have attained ritual roles within their families, as we saw in the case of Mr. Opare. Some older teachers, like Mr. Danquah, were even able to present themselves to their students as the equivalent of elders, with as complete a knowledge of the past and "deep" Twi language as they possessed. One of Mr. Danquah's favorite strategies was to contrast today's practices negatively with the past, a strategy that gave him authority because of his age. In his lesson about funerals, he said, "Seesei, asɛe. Ɛyɛ party" (Now, it has been corrupted. It is a party) and "Ayi nyɛ awerɛhow bio" (Funerals are not sad anymore). He emphasized to his students how people had once fasted during funerals and how food was only served to those who had traveled, not to all guests as is currently done. To demonstrate his expertise, he gave students Akan words that they had never or rarely heard, as elders were wont to do. In the lesson on libation, a student said that a "glass" (using the English word) was needed for libation to be performed. Mr. Danquah asked for the Akan word for "glass." A girl from Akropong replied, "kɔnkɔnkɔ," which Mr. Danquah corrected to "kɔnkɔ." The students responded with surprise: *"Eh!"* and *"Ehsh!"* He also gave another name for Asaase Yaa, a spirit of the earth mentioned in libation prayers, that the students had never heard before. A boy asked what the name meant, and Mr. Danquah gave him a ready answer. So successful was Mr. Danquah's strategy of maintaining authority by taking on the role of an elder who had knowledge of the authentic ways and purer language of the past that many colleagues and students honored him by calling him "ɔpanyin," or elder. This was one teacher whose expertise and personal experience of the past allowed him to bridge the divide between school knowledge and elders' knowledge.

But many teachers, especially at the lower levels, did not feel comfortable or competent in teaching about culture. Some, as we saw, were devout Christians who avoided going to festivals, considering them dangerous to their faith (chapter 4); by not attending such cultural events they missed the best opportunity to learn about them. Other teachers were strangers to the local community, such as the young Kwawu teacher teaching about the Akuapem festival of Odwira (chapter 3). Although a few of them were teaching in their hometown, even they were "outsiders" to the extent that they had traveled for their education and from teaching post to teaching post throughout southern Ghana; several had not lived very long in their hometowns. Some teachers told me that they preferred not to teach in their hometowns to avoid financial and social pressure from their families. Many teachers, especially in the primary and junior secondary schools, were young. Consequently, their incorporation into ritual and political positions such as *abusuapanyin* will happen, if it happens at all, well down the road. For these reasons most teachers know little about the traditions of the town where they are teaching. Similar to schooling during the Mexican revolution, teachers "lacked the training and resources necessary to effect the transformation assigned to them" (Vaughn 1997, 191). Because the teachers in Akuapem have the reputation for not knowing very much about culture, local people continue to honor elders as the only legitimate source of knowledge about the past.

So far as I could tell, few teachers felt qualified to say much about culture. When I visited one junior secondary school in Akropong and said that I would like to see a cultural studies lesson, the teachers around the table said that it was not being taught. They then tried to get a recent Presbyterian Training College graduate, a young man, to do it. "You can teach them *ketekete*" (you can teach them a little), teased a young woman. The headmaster tried to persuade him: "You did this at PTC." There was lots of laughter among the teachers, the young man included. The young man protested, trying to extricate himself from the situation. I agreed to attend a vocational studies lesson instead to avoid embarrassing him further. This situation was not unusual. As noted earlier, this subject was not taught regularly in any of the thirteen primary and junior secondary schools in the circuit. Thus, teachers pursued a third strategy for dealing with the contradictions of teaching a subject that was inaccessible to them as "youth," strangers, or Christians: to not teach the subject at all.

The following description of a cultural studies lesson on traditional funerals comes from my visits to schools where teachers decided—unlike those at the junior secondary school above—to put on a lesson for my benefit. All told, I observed forty-three of these specially designed lessons in the primary and junior secondary schools of the Akropong-Abiriw circuit (table B.2). The majority of the lessons were taught from a theoretical angle, like most other classroom lessons. But teachers incorporated the practical dimension to a far greater extent than they did in their regular classroom lessons. Because of their own lack of knowledge, some of these teachers relied on their students for information, which resulted in different kinds of tensions and possibilities from what one would normally expect in a classroom. A few lessons in fact were taught solely through performance or demonstration; and little more than a quarter of them came close to achieving the combination of the theoretical and the practical that Akuapem teachers considered ideal. Thus, cultural lessons differed substantially from the usual run of lessons by relying far more on the enactment of knowledge than on the codified presentation of lists, definitions, and facts.

The degree of the teachers' participation and authority in these classes, especially during demonstrations and performances, depended on both their own knowledge and the ages of their students. Sometimes the students, especially older ones, drew on their personal observations of funerals and festivals to reenact them in the classroom; at other times students were dependent on direct prompting and direction from teachers standing on the sidelines; at still others the teachers themselves performed. At one end of the extreme was the Akan language teacher in one of the junior secondary schools; she was not from Akuapem, nor was Akan her first language. An Ewe speaker, with an uncertain grasp of her subject, she relied heavily on *Akanfo Amammrɛ* (Akan Culture), a book that she carried to the classroom. Rather than teaching a lesson based on notes and word-reproduction, this teacher asked students to enact a funeral and thus created an opportunity for them to show off their knowledge. The students, especially the boys, took on the task with great gusto as the teacher sat in the back of the room and glanced through her book. A boy who was assigned the role of the organizer of the funeral (*ayipasohene*) gave a confident little speech, standing at the front of the room. Then, to the sound of laughter and giggles, another boy made his way to the front of the room to pour libation. He adjusted the cloth tied over his school uniform so that it was around his upper chest, rather than over his shoulder, a sign of respect for the spirits about to be addressed. Another boy went forward to be the speech mediator (*ɔkyeame*) for the libation-pouring, but the teacher told him, "Ɛnyɛ hwee" (don't bother), and he retreated to stand at the back of the room. The boy pouring libation did not have the usual props of a calabash or bottle, but he prayed with full confidence, using his cupped hands. Because there was no *ɔkyeame* responding to the prayer, other students seated in their chairs took on that role, responding at the end of each phrase, "Wɛ! Wɛ!" The students giggled at themselves. Next the boys beat on their desks to represent the drumming, and the girls pretended to weep. Then they all rose, swept up a table representing the corpse, and marched down the corridor of the school wailing and making a commotion, bringing other students out of their classrooms. Although the boy heeded the teacher's comment that no *ɔkyeame* was needed, the students felt the lack of response that an *ɔkyeame* normally gives during the libation-pouring, and they took on that role, moving from observers to participants. Yet they were embarrassed, giggling and laughing. In following their sense of what was appropriate, they created a disruption in the school routine, bringing students out of their classroom to see what was going on.

This brings us to the third argument made at the beginning of this chapter. The attempt to teach culture in school does indeed change pedagogical and authority relations between teachers and students when teachers are unable to turn cultural knowledge into school knowledge. Because few teachers are expert in this domain, they rely on their students' knowledge far more than they do in other lessons. For this reason, they are more likely to shift from the note-taking pedagogy generally seen in classrooms to a performative mode of pedagogy when they teach about culture and find themselves in a situation where the students often take command and decide what is appropriate. As will be explored in greater depth in the next chapter, which focuses on the rehearsals for the cultural competitions, cultural performances allow students to gain greater authority, over one another and in relation to their teachers, than is normally possible in school classrooms.

CHAPTER **6**

FACED WITH the problem of teachers who, for one reason or another, were unwilling or unable to teach the nationally mandated course in cultural studies, most schools in Akuapem responded by not offering it at all. But participating in the annual school cultural competitions was an entirely different matter.[1] On the whole, the directors and teachers of schools were happy to cooperate with this facet of the state's educational program. When I asked Mr. Robertson if Osuafo Junior Secondary School was planning to participate in the 2002 competitions, he replied, "By all means, we will do something because we don't want to isolate ourselves." Teachers recognized the competitions as an opportunity for the school to be visible on a local level.

"Do You Know How to Drum?"

Youth, Knowledge, and the State

In a junior secondary school with a poor reputation, the new headmaster had worked hard to prepare his students for the 2002 event and was upset with the judges when the school did not win more first-place positions because he had hoped to showcase the improved quality of the school under his leadership. His passion was not unusual. Emotions ran high among teachers and students about the fairness of the judges because they wanted their school to win in the competition and thus gain honor and a good reputation.

School cultural competitions, as one of the sites through which the government attempts to organize and reach its subjects, operate according to the political mechanisms occurring generally in Ghana. The national government and local political bodies vie with one another for legitimacy, and groups and individuals can gain a name locally against their rivals by taking advantage of government resources and government-sponsored opportunities for visibility. To review briefly how the competitions are judged, performances in six artistic genres (poetry recital, dance-drama, drum language, choral music, musical sight reading, and arts and crafts) are evaluated by a specific set of criteria. The bulk of the points are awarded for aesthetic quality and technical skill, but the judges also take into account adherence to the competition rules about length of time and number of performers, and whether the entry is consistent with the year's national theme. Teachers and educational administrators from surrounding areas who are considered expert in a certain field are chosen as judges: specialists in Ghanaian languages (for poetry recital, dance-drama, and drum language), music (for choral music and musical sight reading), or vocational studies (for arts and crafts).

It is primarily through these competitions, rather than school curricula, that young people participate in the state's effort to maintain and promote a national culture. In Ghana the state pursues two models simultaneously, sometimes merging into one, to shape the way young people participate in the nation. One model is that of a state giving all children an education so that they can become productive, patriotic citizens. The other model is that of a clientelist, patron state, in which in return for the investment in education by students and their families, the state will give them good jobs in the civil service. The cultural education project as a whole, particularly the cultural studies curriculum, operates under the ideology of citizenship, rather than that of clientelism: each citizen should have access to the nation's cultural heritage. But the competitions are structured in a way that gives only a select few access to performance and honors, so that they are essentially clientelist in nature.

In both models of the state's relationship to young people, access is controlled by agents of the state, such as teachers and cultural officers, and young people are viewed as having little knowledge or agency. In the citizenship model teachers are responsible for giving all young people of the nation the knowledge they need to be productive citizens as adults. In the clientelist model teachers, like other agents of the state, are the distributors of the state's rewards and resources. The perception that young people can only be in the position of recipients is fortified by the local logic that elders alone possess and embody cultural knowledge.

The operating model by which the state relates to its citizens is particularly salient for young people in Africa today. For scholars of Africa, they are "a lost generation" that has not been able to attain the promises of modernity that the generations of the 1960s and 1970s attained so easily, at least in retrospect: the exchange of schooling for civil service employment (Cruise O'Brien 1996; Sharp 2002). "Education produces inequality and privilege . . . but it has in recent years failed to deliver enough in terms of privilege" (Cruise O'Brien 1996, 65). State decay elsewhere in Africa has meant the failure of the clientelist state. As a result young people in many parts of the continent are increasingly marginalized, with small chance of becoming "somebody" or at least becoming economically independent of their families. The result is the emergence of disaffected groups that loom as a potent political force, ready to take part in a "politics from below" (Mbembe 1992) or in rebel movements, as in Sierra Leone (Richards 1996). In Ghana, the structural reforms of the late 1980s, guided by the World Bank, led to an expansion of the state (Hutchful 2002). Consequently, even though there has been an erosion of the educational exchange, so that numbers of young people flock to urban areas to engage in semi-skilled work, trading, and hawking, the promise of schooling has not proved completely illusory for the current generation. Secondary school students, in particular, continue to dedicate themselves to their studies in the hope that they will be one of the lucky few who get to continue to university or teacher training college. Thus, young people still willingly participate in state institutions like schools that afford them at least some chance of gaining access to state patronage.

However, in rehearsals for the school cultural competitions, both the clientelist and the citizenship model of education began to break down. Very different learning styles emerged, which contrasted sharply with classroom lessons in which teachers more easily served as authority figures. In rehearsals, students drew on indigenous models of learning to "pick up" dancing and drumming techniques from their peers through observation and imitation. They wanted to share their knowledge with others, so that many more of their schoolmates could participate; teachers wanted to limit participation so that an already competent few could become more practiced. Thus conflicts between teachers and students arose during rehearsals, and students began to create a mode of participation based on solidarity that challenged both citizenship and clientelist models.

Although learning is central to cultural transmission and reproduction, anthropologists outside of the subfield of anthropology and education have tended to ignore how people acquire various skills, knowledge, and ideas, even as they point to the importance of knowledge in maintaining and negotiating social relations (Levinson 1999; Pelissier 1991). In part this is because anthropologists have associated learning almost exclusively with children, rather than looking at it as a long-term process that continues throughout the life span as people move between different social contexts. Furthermore, they have generally focused on adult forms as representative of cultural production, despite the recent surge in research on youth culture. Yet as anthropologists of education have shown, learning is central to issues of power, agency, and identity.

Learning is not simply the acquisition of skills and knowledge, but requires becoming a participant in a social space (Lave and Wenger 1991). One does not simply learn to weave; rather, one becomes a weaver. Learning is therefore a process of identification and belonging, in which one imitates and impersonates those whom one wishes to be among (Cantwell 1999). Inherent in social spaces are power dynamics. Access to learning reflects the social hierarchies of the communities that learners seek to become members of. Since knowledge in a particular community is always produced in relations between people who are differently positioned, by age, gender, and family (among other things), conflict is inherent to learning (Lave 1993). In short, learning encodes authority relations as well as expertise and identity. It is in learning contexts and modes of participation that challenges to the relationship between state and young people can be observed.

Children as learners are active participants in shaping their education (Modell 1994). In the last chapter I examined the strategies that teachers relied on to maintain their authority when they taught a form of knowledge associated with elders. This chapter examines how students attempted to assert their cultural expertise as they practiced for the annual competitions. In the process they tried to devise performances that allowed their peers to join in and to share the putative rewards of participating in state processes.

"I Watch and I See": Learning to Drum and Dance

As Professor A. Mawɛre-Opoku, late teacher of dance at the University of Ghana, kept reminding me, the Twi word *sua*, normally translated as "to learn" or "to study," originally meant "to imitate." "To *sua* is to watch something, listen to something and pick it up, try to imitate the sound, imitate what you see, imitate the habit," he told me passionately (interview, 29 Oct. 1998). For the active side of the process, Ghanaians use the word *kyerɛ*, which means both "to teach" and "to show" or "to demonstrate." The Twi words for learning and teaching emphasize imitation and performance, rather than verbal instruction or inner awareness, knowledge *how* to rather than knowledge *of*. Yet just as Twi appellations for the Supreme Deity such as Onyame and Onyankopɔn are now used to refer to the Christian God, so the words *sua* and *kyerɛ* are applied specifically to school learning and teaching.

This distinction became clear to me during discussions with students who participated in the cultural competitions. Rather than using *sua* to describe how they learned to drum and dance, the students repeatedly used the verbs *tie* (to listen), *hwε* (to watch), and, for the moment of learning, *hu* (to see). Rosemary, a student dancer in the Horeb school's dance-drama, made this explicit: "Mansua saw, nanso, obi saw a, na mehwε na mihu" (I did not study [*sua*] dancing, but if someone dances, I watch [*hwε*] and I see [how to do it] [*hu*]).[2] Gifty, another of the Horeb girl dancers, added a step to follow observation—private practice: "Ebi wɔ hɔ nso a, ahemfo yε biribi a, wugyina hɔ na wohwε ade na εno akyi, wopractici ne ade. Obi yε saa, na εyε fε, obi yε saa na εnyε fε nti woba fi na wose, 'Ebia metumi asaw' nti woyε saa na nkakrankakra na wo de wo nsa ato fam na wuhu" (Sometimes, if the chiefs do something, you stand there and watch and later, you practice. Someone did something beautiful and someone did something that wasn't, so you go home and say, "Maybe I can dance" so you do it and little by little and you put your hands down [as a sign of respect for the dignitaries present] and you see [know]).

The Horeb boys, all of whom were from Akropong, also said that they learned the techniques of *fɔntɔmfrɔm* drumming by watching and then practicing in private. They conceived of learning as imitating the performers and becoming "perfect." (Secondary school students, particularly the boys, tended to mix English and Twi in their everyday speech. They also often used Twi slang words whose exact meanings escaped even Afari Amoako, who helped me with the translations, although we understood the general gist of what they were saying.) Opoku said,

> Yetie, wuhu. Saa ade no, εnyε one day na wɔdebɔ fɔntɔmfrɔm. Sε yetie fɔntɔmfrɔm a, εnyε one day anaasε in a minute pε na wɔbεyε na woagyae. Wɔbεyε no continuous, enti wɔyε no nyinaa na yetie. Yetie how it goes, te sε yetie sεnea sound no ba ara, na yεn nso yεfollow. Enti sε mete sε na wɔbɔ no seε a, mefollow saa ara, pattern no. Next time, sε mekɔ [name of a place] na nkurofo nni hɔ a, me nso mekɔpractici sε me nso metee sεnea wɔbɔ no. Saa na mihuu bɔ. Saa na medesuaa sεnea wɔbɔ akyene fa.

> We listen, you see. That thing, they don't drum *fɔntɔmfrɔm* on one day only. If we hear *fɔntɔmfrɔm*, they don't do it for just a day or a minute and then stop. They do it continuously, so we listen throughout the time they are doing it. We listen to how it goes, like we listen to exactly how the sound goes, and we follow it. So if I hear that they are drumming it like that, I follow the rhythm exactly. Next time, if I go [to a place] and no one is there, I practice the way I heard them drum. That is how I saw how to drum. That is how I learned how to play the drums.[3]

Danquah emphasized that you can use wood or other objects to drum, and as time goes on, you become perfect. Opoku agreed, saying that one could become perfect playing on cocoa tins until one had the opportunity to play on actual drums. Learning to drum was conceived as imitation, *following* the expert drummers.[4] Although improvisation is part of the performances at the chief's court (*ahemfi*), where drummers are expected to create new honorifics or combine old ones in new ways, it was discounted or ignored in the comments of these drummers, who emphasized their imitation of experts in the process of becoming "perfect."

The main dance performed in Akuapem, *fɔntɔmfrɔm*, is considered one of the most difficult because the dancers have to end the dance at the exact moment when the drumming stops. A poetically charged artistic form used to communicate loyalty and unity, it is closely associated with the chief's court. Learning how to dance and drum thus depends in large part on access to contexts in which drumming and dancing happens — the households of traditional priests (*akɔmfo*) and chiefs and their retinues — and that access is open mainly to those born and raised in such households. Festivals, the other route to learning, have their limitations for would-be dancers and drummers. While some events are open to the public, others, particularly the practice sessions discussed below, are usually attended only by those who play important roles in the festivities themselves or live in chiefly households. The Horeb students seemed to have had access only to the most public performances, where children are typically allowed to stand on the outskirts, watching and listening. None appeared to have had the advantage of growing up in the households of the traditional elites, the only ones that contain adults competent in drumming and dancing who can provide direction to young people.[5]

Reynolds Addo, the drummer who represented Abε Secondary School in the district cultural competition, was from a royal family in Akropong. Whereas the students quoted above emphasized a process of watching the performance and then practicing in private at home, Reynolds Addo described how observation of the drumming sessions during festivals was interspersed with both private practice and instruction from elders, once they learned he was dedicated to learning how to drum. He told me:

> Akyenebɔ no de, εyε biribi a, sε wufi royal family mu a, wɔn a wɔwɔ hɔ, wobetumi akyerε wo. Enti bere a wɔbɔ nyinaa, na wɔtow wɔsɔw [na mehwε. Akyiri yi,] na enni hɔ a, wokɔfa dua bi na wodebɔ table so [he drums on the table], na wusua kakra kakra kakra. Sε wohu sε wowɔ interest wom a, εnna wɔbεfrε wo na wɔbεkyerε wo. Wo ankasa wutumi alearn on your own. Sε wonni hɔ a, na wusua kakra kakra kakra. There is a saying sε practice makes man perfect. Nti wo practice nyinaa a, woyεperfect paa.

As for drumming, it is something that, if you are from the royal family, those who are there can teach you. So all the time that they are drumming, and tossing it back and forth, [you watch and later], if it [a drum] isn't there, you can take a piece of wood, or use the table to drum [he drums on the table], and you learn little by little by little. If they see that you take an interest in it, then they will call you and teach you. You even can learn on your own. If they aren't there, then you learn little by little by little. There is a saying that practice makes a man perfect. So as you practice it all, then you are becoming perfect.[6]

The students' comments show that the way to become competent or "perfect" in drumming and dancing is to watch, practice at home in private on substitutes like tin cans or tables, and then—for those from royal families—to reveal one's talents in performance, after which adults will teach them.

My observations during festivals support these statements, but they also reveal a peer learning process that was not mentioned by these adolescents. Young people in royal households participate on the borders of musical events, learning from one another, arguing over the correct form, helping and watching more experienced musicians, and slowly moving on as they become more competent to more and more central roles. The students I spoke to did not highlight learning from their peers. But peers were important in the learning I observed.

Festivals and funerals provide the main opportunities to observe drumming and dancing, or in the case of young people from royal households, to try out their skills. On festival days in Akropong, whether the annual Odwira festival or the Adae festivals held twice every forty days, the drums of the *fɔntɔmfrɔm* ensemble are brought out from their storage places and set out in the courtyards of chiefs' households. Before a public event can start—and many start in the afternoon—contingents of chiefs gather in their various divisions in the chiefly houses, until they finally all gather in front of the paramount chief, or *ɔmanhene*. My host the queen mother was part of the Kronti division, so she first went to the court of the queen mother of that division (the Krontihemaa). When the full contingent associated with the Krontihemaa had gathered there, they moved on to the court of the chief of the Kronti division (the Krontihene), where they again waited for the chiefs associated with the Krontihene to assemble. Then, the train complete, they continued to the palace of the paramount chief and took their seats next to the chiefs from the other divisions. This process of assembly takes two or three hours, and the time of waiting and gathering allows young people to practice drumming and dancing. The youngest participate on the periphery of the event, dancing in semi-private or informal gatherings or taking on minor roles within the drumming ensemble, where they continue to watch and imitate as they move between the different kinds of instruments. As the audience becomes more important, older and more expert musicians and dancers take over.

For one Wednesday Adae (Awukudae) we gathered in the Krontihene's palace around nine in the morning. Drums were being beaten in the courtyard. My ten-year-old "brother" from the queen mother's household and I sat there along with various worthies and the female spokespersons, or *akyeame*, while the queen mothers passed through the outer courtyard to an inner room. The *akyeame* invited me to dance with them, and I did so, following their movements. As people wandered through, they too were invited to join in, and one teenage girl who accepted danced particularly beautifully. All the drummers were teenagers or young men, and they were surrounded by children of all ages, watching. This point when few chiefs had gathered was a practice time for young people; I, a complete novice, was invited to dance, and mistakes in performance did not matter much. Even so, one boy about seven or eight years old danced to the music in semi-privacy, hidden by the two long walls of a corridor, where the musicians could not see him. The teenage drummers were teaching each other, arguing about how a piece should go and correcting each other's mistakes. An old man sitting nearby shook his head occasionally while he listened to the music. Although he was indicating what sounded right and what did not, he did not venture an opinion on the quality of the performance, and the young people did not turn to him for advice. As more and more chiefs gathered, the younger drummers were replaced by more experienced ones, and the dancers who took center stage were older and of higher status.

The annual Odwira festival goes on for a full week. For the one during my second stay, in 1998, a group of men and boys aged ten to thirty gathered for a practice session around noontime on Friday in the Krontihemaa's courtyard. At first the youngest boys took on the least important roles in the ensemble, beating the gong-gong or bell (*dawuru*) at the back and the smaller drums. The role of *dawuru*-beater switched among various young boys. The oldest drummer, in his thirties, took the central drum. The two drums on either side of it rotated slightly — two boys in their late teens exchanged places. This was obviously practice for all. My ten-year-old brother was watching intently. Again, as time passed, the younger drummers gave way to more experienced ones.

On the previous Wednesday, when we arrived at the Krontihene's palace around one o'clock in the afternoon, and thus closer to the time when we would join the ɔmanhene, several men were playing on the drums, and people kept coming in to sit on the right-hand side of the courtyard. A few younger boys and teenagers occasionally played the drums in the back and also fetched drums, but the main drummers were old men. The boys competed for the honor of holding the fɔntɔmfrɔm drums—larger than their bodies—tipped at an angle so that they could be drummed by the older men. By the time we had gathered in front of the ɔmanhene, the drummers were all grown men, ranging in age from their thirties or forties to old age. Thus, during the two or three hours in which the chiefs were gathering, young boys and teenagers moved from full participation, to peripheral participation, to observation as the event shifted from more of a backstage, preparatory affair to a full performance in front of the ɔmanhene, where mistakes might be interpreted as a political insult.

Teacher Okyen, a teacher and drummer in his late thirties and a member of the royal family in Akropong, described how he had learned to drum during Adae festivities:

> I remember, when I was about [long pause, remembering] ten or eleven, I started playing this traditional drums. Yes. We were just going there, during the Adae, we were going to Krontihene's place, during the Adae, to help them play. At times, you will be there, you will be at the back there, you will go and help them hold the drums for them and that kind of thing. . . . So out of these things, I started learning properly. I have already told you that my family members are very good in those things. So, my father is also very good in it. He is very good in it. So whenever we went out and drum, after that, my father would just call me and say, "This is not the way that thing should have been done. It should have been done in this way." Then he would drum on the table for me, just to practice what actually he is also doing. So from there, I also go to some of my relatives and then ask them, "Is that how to drum? Is that the way to drum this?" They would just say, "No, do it in this way." Just with their hands, their fingers, on the table. And then I picked the whole thing up. (Interview, 21 Sept. 1998)

As both a teacher and a drummer, Teacher Okyen was sensitive to the difference between the way things were taught in school and the way he had learned to drum. His training as a teacher made him critical of the process of "picking up" and learning from peers:

> There are a lot of people in town who are very good, who have got the flair, but their problem is imparting the knowledge onto the new generation. You see, this is the [fɔntɔmfrɔm] ensemble; I am at the palace. I don't remember the day our leader called us and taught us that, "This is the way you are supposed to drum, this is the

way." So, we do it anyhow. But if you do it anyhow, then you just come and hit with the stick. But I don't think that is the right way of teaching. Call us that, "Today, you are going to learn how to drum. This is the way it should be done." Or, "This is the words that we are going to use in drumming." But they don't teach us that way. . . . Nobody taught us; nobody has been teaching us. Nobody has been teaching us. (Interview, 21 Sept. 1998)

In the few years he had taught drumming at Demonstration School in Akropong, he had followed, in his words, "a system" and had "a developed method of teaching." He considered the pedagogy he had developed superior to the way he had learned from the elders and the methods of his peers in the fͻntͻmfrͻm ensemble. As a result, he was trying to teach his drumming troupe in the Krontihene's court to become better teachers, by which he meant giving more verbal instructions and directions. How successful he would be in this endeavor is unclear. He commented that as a teacher in a school he had greater authority with his students than he has with his colleagues in the troupe, who do not always listen to him.

It is not necessarily that these drummers have difficulty imparting their knowledge, only that a strategy like theirs puts the onus of learning entirely on the learner. The learner watches closely and imitates the expert's actions in private. Direct, verbal instruction either does not happen or, according to Teacher Okyen and Reynolds Addo, is given after performance, after one has demonstrated sufficient interest and skill to be worthy of receiving further knowledge. But almost always the direction takes the form of modeling and action, not words: the experts tapped their fingers on the table so that the learner heard the rhythm. John Chernoff (1979) says of his drumming teachers, "In many ways, their adeptness at mimetic techniques made their teaching perhaps less ambiguous than it might have been had they used words, and in fact, whenever I found one of my teachers trying to explain what I had to do, I knew he was at the last resort of his teaching capabilities" (21). Whatever one's evaluation of the merits of each pedagogical strategy, teachers and students were fully aware of the difference between the way that teachers taught through explicit instruction and the way that people "picked up" drumming and dancing skills through observation and imitation.

Teachers and Expertise

Because teachers typically know little about traditional drumming and dancing and the cultural competitions require practical—not theoretical—knowledge, they could use neither the rote-learning strategies they relied on in their classroom lessons nor the more subtle pedagogy associated with elders to help students perfect their performances. As the student drummer from New Juaben who represented the Eastern Region at the national competition (chapter 3), put it, if he made a mistake in drumming at school, the teacher could tell it was a mistake but could not show him how to do it well. So if you are not perfect, he said, then you have to do it yourself. But at the palace where he was raised the elders or older people knew how to do it. So when you made a mistake, they would take the drumsticks and show you the right way to do it (conversation, 3 May 1999). This student felt that his teachers had some drum knowledge, but merely as spectators, recognizing when the drumming sounded wrong, not as performers, able to show him how to do it better.

The gaps in teachers' knowledge were exposed most clearly during the rehearsals for the drum-language competition. During practice sessions boys came forward to beat drum texts that the faculty organizer recited from memory or read from a book; the best would be selected to represent the school in the drum-language competition. Students tended to recognize mistakes that the faculty advisers missed. At Gyahene Secondary School, on a Saturday afternoon, Mr. Opare, the teacher-organizer, was teaching Amoako drum language, reciting poetry he had written in his notebook while Amoako drummed the phrases. Several students were watching. Theophilus took it on himself to correct Amoako; he heard when a drummed phrase was wrong, whereas Mr. Opare did not. So Mr. Opare would keep reading, and Theophilus would tell Amoako to do it again and show him how to drum certain words. At Abɛ Secondary School the music teacher who was helping Reynolds Addo with the drum language told me that he himself could not play the drums, although he claimed he could teach drumming. A man in his late fifties, he said that when he was a child, because of his Catholic missionary education, he was forbidden to go near drums. As a teacher, when he went to specialist music training at Winneba, he avoided drumming class, saying he was sick. I asked if he had done so because of his religious beliefs, and he said no, he did not believe that drums contained anything "fetish," but he did not explain further why he had not wanted to learn to drum (conversation, 8 Mar. 1999). Like Mr. Opare at Gyahene, he relied on written text—in this case, Professor Nketia's book *Ayan* (Drum Language)—to give Reynolds Addo drumming phrases to practice.

In the circumstances, it is surprising that schools did not rely more on outside experts, such as those from chiefly retinues. In both 1999 and 2002, the more prosperous and organized schools worked with Kofi Martin, a graduate of the School of Performing Arts at the University of Ghana and, in 2002, the district cultural officer for the Center for National Culture. Although he was an employee of the state whose job included outreach to schools in the North Akuapem district, he charged schools for his services. (This situation was nonetheless an improvement from the schools' point of view; the previous cultural officer had lived in Koforidua and rarely came to Akuapem at all.) But because Kofi Martin did not always show up as promised, many schools had some misgivings about hiring him, despite his obvious talents. He trained students through a combination of explicit direction and modeling. His own professional training showed up in his productions, which tended to have two distinctive features: a choreography that generates dramatic tension and the use of dances from a variety of different regions. Because showcasing different dances has become an increasingly important feature to the judges in the dance-drama competitions (chapter 3), Kofi Martin's expertise in teaching northern dances, gained through his training at the School of Performing Arts, was particularly appreciated. Local experts, that is, the members of the chiefs' and elders' households, were at a distinct disadvantage because they generally knew only the dances common in Akuapem, such as *adowa, kete,* and *fɔntɔmfrɔm.*

Schools that wanted to participate in the cultural competitions had to make some initial choices, taking into account their staff's personal networks and their own financial resources. They could ask for the help of court personnel or of Kofi Martin or rely on their students' expertise. Because the outside experts required compensation, most schools tended to reject that option and depended instead on their own students' existing skills. One primary school headmistress told me that they chose a drummer for the competition from the chief's court, or *ahemfi,* so he could practice on the drums there. Primary school teachers, explaining why their schools did not participate in the drum-language category at the 2002 circuit cultural competition in Akropong, said that they did not have any students capable of competing: "Yenni ɔkyerɛma" (We don't have a drummer) and "Obiara a onim ayan akɔ JSS" (Everyone who knew drum language went to Junior Secondary School). As for Kofi Martin, because of his unreliability, there continued to be a void in expertise even when a school did hire him. As a result, two changes in the logic of the school occur during rehearsals for the cultural competitions: other styles of learning based on observation, imitation, and participation become available in the school, and second, particularly at the secondary school level, students step into the void created by the lack of adult guidance and begin to assume greater authority.

The Chiefly Court in the School: Obikyerɛ Primary School

Primary schools, more connected to surrounding communities than either junior secondary or secondary schools, were the most likely to use local experts. But even among primary schools, chiefly specialists were not often called on. Only four of the thirteen primary schools in the Larteh and Akropong circuit received such help in the cultural competitions in 2002. Obikyerɛ Primary School in Akropong was one of the four. Five young men between the ages of eighteen and twenty-five, all members of the Krontihene's drumming troupe, came several times to the school to help with that year's drum language and dance-drama performances. These young men behaved very quietly and shyly; they were deferential to the teachers and hung back until the teachers made it clear that they should take over the rehearsal. They acted as if they were intruding on school space; this was the first time they had helped Obikyerɛ school.

The way they taught the children to drum was very similar to the methods I saw in practice sessions during festivals. At a rehearsal four days before the competition, the young men started off by taking over all the school's instruments, expecting the student drummers to stand by and watch them drum. The student drummers, aged ten to twelve, were primarily from royal families. They seemed a little awed by the drummers, but also looked discouraged at not being allowed to join them on the drums. During this demonstration period, the young men switched places regularly. At one switch, a student, Godfried, took over the gong-gong (*dawuru*), the instrument that the youngest members are often given in an ensemble. When I looked back at the drumming troupe again, Peter, a student, was now on one of the drums, and a troupe member had taken over on the *dawuru* again. Then Godfried got the *dawuru* back, and he smiled. He seemed especially excited to be in the company of these men. Next Samuel got to drum. A man showed him how to do it by beating on the drum with him. The main drum was still in the hands of a troupe member. The troupe then took over all the instruments again, including the *dawuru*. A drummer showed Samuel how to use the *dawuru* as Godfried looked on. The *dawuru* was then given back to Godfried. A drummer clapped Godfried's back and shoulders from behind for a little bit, in time with the beat. Now Samuel was also back on the same drum as before, and one of the young men tapped on his back in time for a little while. More students were being incorporated into the drumming all the time (fig. 5). The leader of the troupe took over the *dawuru* and gave it to a boy in the back, having shown him what to do. Another drummer clapped in time, to make the student do it properly. He then took over the drum from Peter.

Figure 5. Boys at Obikyerɛ Primary School being taught to drum by the drumming troupe from the Krontihene court, June 2002

In this process we see constant movement among the drummers in and out of the ensemble and between different instruments, in which the students slowly became part of the ensemble but were also subject to being replaced for further demonstration. After half an hour or so, the students were playing all the instruments. Other members of the drumming troupe taught girls *adowa* dancing during this time as well, also through demonstration, saying very little.

The local experts, then, the people who regularly drummed and danced in the court during festivals, used demonstration as their teaching technique, including drumming while the boy watched, beating the drum with the boy, and beating the rhythm on the boy's back or shoulders while he played. Nothing much was said at all. Students slowly became incorporated into the drumming ensemble as minor members, starting with the *dawuru,* and were continually rotated among the instruments until they were drumming to the satisfaction of the visitors.

"We Did It Ourselves": Horeb Secondary School

In schools that did not rely on chiefly troupes, students attempted to recreate the learning structure that the drummers above provided, although they lacked their expertise. I saw this most prominently at the rehearsals of Horeb Secondary School for the 1999 competition. Here are the remarks of some of the girls three days after the competition:

> DINAH: Culture no nso, drum, dance-drama no nso, yɛn ankasa na yɛyɛɛ, na yeannya obi nkyerɛ yɛn, nti yɛn ankasa na ɛsɛ sɛ yɛforci ara (Culture also—drumming and the dance-drama also—we did it ourselves, and we didn't have anyone to teach us, so we had to force it).
>
> GIFTY: Yɛyɛɛ yɛn adwene nso sɛ yɛbɛyɛ bragoro, nanso bragoro no, yeannya obiara a ɔbɛkyerɛ yɛn the way a yɛbɛyɛ no, nti Agnes de nyansa yi bae sɛ yɛnyɛ "Kwaku Ananse" (We decided also that we would do puberty rites, but we didn't get anyone to teach us the way to do it, so Agnes wisely said we should do "Kwaku Ananse").
>
> [Rosemary then described the story of Kwaku Ananse they performed.]
>
> NORA: Afei nso na yekodu hɔ, nneɛma a ɛsɛ sɛ yɛde yɛ, yenni nneɛma nyinaa nyɛ [to show that they were on a farm]. . . . Tikyafo, obiara mmoa yɛn. Yeannya obiara ammoa yɛn (Then also when we got there, the things that we should use, we didn't have all the things to do it [to show that they were on a farm]. . . . Teachers, no one helped us. We didn't have anyone to help us).
>
> DINAH: Yɛanyɛ ade (We didn't do well [in their performance]).[7]

And indeed, out of six secondary schools participating in the district cultural competition, Horeb came in fifth in the dance-drama category, fourth in poetry recital, and second in drum language. For the Horeb performers, there would be no regional competition that year.

The teacher-organizer for Horeb, Mr. Dartey, was not quite sure what to do for the cultural competition and may not have wanted to participate at all: he had raised objections during Mr. Devoh's workshop about the un-Christian nature of cultural practices.[8] The first the students knew about their school's participation was when Mr. Dartey gathered eighteen to twenty of them in an empty classroom for a rehearsal just a week before the competition. After breaking the news to them, he told them that they would have to put together a dance-drama. As an example, he recited a poem about a dog and then had students act out a little skit about it. The girls told me later, in our group discussion, that they hid their laughter at this point, because the skit was so ridiculous, but they followed his direction until he had given up on the idea. After the skit the students experimented with their own ideas. They danced *kpanlogo,* a sexually explicit dance associated with young people, and then recreated a parade that was part of the Odwira festivities, in which girls, possessed by spirits, carry food to the house of the spirits. After this, Mr. Dartey tried to control the rehearsal again. He asked the girls to dance in a circle. A girl who had come to watch said softly, "Ei! Awurade!" (Oh, Lord!), and there was quiet laughter among the other girls in the audience. He then danced with the boys in a circle and played a game similar to "Duck-duck-goose," in which one boy tapped each of the others on the head, tagging one "it," and the one tagged then chased him around the circle until he reached the spot that the tagged one had vacated. In the meantime the girls were working up their own skit outside, "Bragoro," recreating a dance-drama on puberty rites that they had performed two years before at the last cultural competition for secondary schools.

By the next rehearsal day, the Monday before the cultural competition on Thursday, the students had abandoned the notion of doing "Bragoro" for their dance-drama, because, they told me, they did not know the dances and music that accompanied puberty rites. Both boys and girls experimented with the drums and various dances, trying to build their skills. After they had been playing for a little while, Mr. Dartey asked them to dance. The students—both boys and girls—were teaching one another *kete* dancing on the veranda outside the classroom. There was confusion; they were not getting it. Mr. Dartey said, "Monkɔ so" (Keep at it). Then he told them all, "We are learning by trial and error." By Tuesday the students had decided to do a dance-drama based on an Ananse story called "Kwaku Ananse" that Agnes had seen on TV and set out at once to practice it.

It was clear as early as the first rehearsal that the students had decided to ignore their teacher and his suggestions as much as possible without insulting him. Students practiced, watched one another, and evaluated their own ability and that of their peers. At one point on Tuesday, when students were arguing over how to do something, Mr. Dartey, concerned about the chaos and noise, chastised them. He said that students in other schools, like Abε, listened to their teachers, and that if they would allow themselves to be "manipulated the way the teacher wishes, then we will all succeed." Otherwise, "m'ani awu" (I am ashamed). But he went on to acknowledge that the chance of success rested on their own abilities and expertise, not his leadership: "Asaw biara a wutumi asaw, saw; then it is finished" (Dance anything you can; then we are done). Eveline then asked the drummers to drum *kpanlogo*, and six girls got up to dance. The students continued with their activities of practicing their dancing and drumming skills.

Kpanlogo, although associated with the Gã people along the coast and not local to the area, seemed to be the predominant form in the Akuapem students' repertoire. On a Sunday afternoon, while waiting for Kofi Martin to arrive for a rehearsal, students at Gyahene Secondary School performed several versions of it on their own for over two hours. *Kpanlogo* was the most popular music-dance form performed in school cultural competitions in Akuapem, and if a dance-drama contained only one kind of musical-dance form, it was usually *kpanlogo*.

Of the three secondary schools whose rehearsals I followed, the Horeb students had the most creative control over their performances. This school was the least well regarded of the three, with a poor reputation in examination results, a lack of facilities, and a large proportion of local students. It also did far worse in the competition than the two boarding schools, Gyahene and Abε. At Gyahene the dance-drama was created and directed by Kofi Martin; at Abε it was created and directed by a teacher, Mr. Boateng, with some help from Kofi Martin.[9] Because these schools were wealthier, they were able to hire Kofi Martin to train the students.

The students at Horeb experienced what I saw as their creative control as disenfranchisement. The sentiment among them was that the teachers did not care about traditional culture; rather than enjoying their control over the content and rehearsals, they seemed to feel that the teachers had abandoned them. Left to their own devices, they drew on the cultural resources they had available to them as young people: a children's TV show illustrating an Ananse story that Agnes had seen, the parade down the main street of Akropong of young girls bringing food to the spirits during the annual Odwira festival, and *kpanlogo*. Through their own ideas and resources, they ended up presenting a youthful perspective of culture through their rehearsals and ultimate performance of "Kwaku Ananse." Thus, the students who were least likely to continue on in their education had the greatest opportunity to create a climate of solidarity and mutual support, thereby distancing themselves from the competitiveness demanded by a clientelist state.

Solidarity and the Expansion of Expertise

Just as students whenever they could opened the way for those without access to chiefly rites to learn drumming and other performing arts, so students often helped each other in the classroom. Under the threat of examinations in which only a few would do well, students freely shared knowledge and resources. Many students got through primary school by copying from their fellow students, and as the lessons became more difficult in junior secondary school, copying and sharing became more and more a strategy of survival. During a social studies lesson in Osuafo Junior Secondary School, I watched as students cooperated in answering ten questions from the blackboard under the eye of a bored teacher. Appiah used a textbook,

Social Studies for Junior Secondary Schools, to answer the questions. Dankwa and Aaron used their notes. Abigail borrowed Rosemary's notes. Mavis and Nyankoma were talking and exchanging answers. Eric borrowed Appiah's notes. Abigail borrowed Appiah's textbook from Nyankoma. Rosemary took it from her. It moved around to Christina. Adobea borrowed the book from Ivy. Abigail asked Ivy for an answer. Eric borrowed Appiah's notes again. Deborah took the textbook from Rosemary. Adobea gave Abigail an answer. Abigail underlined something for Appiah in the textbook. Obviously, I could not keep track of the rapid and extensive circulation of materials and notes in this exchange; they moved too rapidly for my eye. The rotation of the notes and textbooks recalls the rotation of the drums, in and out of various students' hands, as these students sought to help everyone to do well on the assignment. Students' interactions with one another were characterized by giving everyone access to information as a survival mechanism. The clientelist state, however, requires competition, in which prestige and resources will be awarded to only a few.

During rehearsals for the cultural competitions, students adopted the teaching strategies of the drumming troupe that visited Obikyere Primary: drummers and dancers moved in and out of performance and among different instruments. Students absented themselves from performance when they felt that they were not competent and reentered the fray after a little more observation or when they had the guidance of more expert peers. There was little verbal instruction; students *showed* each other how to dance and drum. This open structure gave students who did not have the benefit of royal connections the opportunity to drum and dance.

It also gave girls the opportunity to play the drums, as we saw at Horeb Secondary School. On one Saturday afternoon at Gyahene school, the drums were dragged out of their storage room and set out on the veranda outside the room. After a little while, Mr. Opare, the faculty organizer, wandered away, leaving the boys to practice *fɔntɔmfrɔm* drumming. Occasionally some girls would stand up to dance behind the drummers, where the boys could not see them. As this rehearsal wound down, Felicity and Cassandra wanted to take over from Daniel on the *fɔntɔmfrɔm* drum, but he would not let them. When many of the original drummers had left and a new set of boys had replaced them, Felicity beat a rhythm on the small *mmariwa* drum but was not quite sure what she was doing. She had a frown on her face. "O, daabi" (Oh, no), Lucy said to Felicity, who was trying to drum the beginning rhythm of an *adowa* beat. The drummer on the *fɔntɔmfrɔm* drum was beating out something, and Felicity copied what he was doing, but he showed her that she was supposed to drum a different

Figure 6. Girls and boys drumming at Gyahene Secondary School, March 1999

rhythm. Mary took over from Felicity, showing her what to do. Mr. Opare wandered up at about this time and told the girls to stop drumming or they would become infertile. But they did not heed him, and I then distracted them all by asking for their picture (fig. 6).

The girls' opportunity to practice drumming came to a halt as the day of the competition neared. By Tuesday, two days before the competition, only boys were allowed on the drums at the Horeb rehearsal. As one group practiced, a clump of boys stood nearby, watching and waiting for a turn. The drums had been redesignated as male property. At the national cultural competition held in Cape Coast, the audience was surprised and pleased that a girl from Brong-Ahafo region competed and won in the drum-language category, but it turned out that she had been raised in a royal household where she had access to expert help and drums.

More students came to watch than actually participated in the rehearsal sessions. At an early rehearsal at Gyahene on a Wednesday afternoon, I counted twenty-seven people—mainly boys and perhaps three or four girls—standing around the drums, with other students watching from the nearby classroom blocks. At Abε, where dance-drama performers rehearsed late at night by Akuapem standards (8–10 p.m.) in the teachers' lounge, the room was filled every night with perhaps sixty students studying or sleeping; some would occasionally rouse themselves to watch and comment on the performances. During some rehearsals the faculty organizer, Mr. Boateng, threatened to throw the audience out, perhaps afraid that they were making his performers shy. "Anyone not going with us [to the competition] shouldn't be here," he said, to little effect. In fact the audience members were learning by observation, another way that the rehearsals opened access, which faculty organizers tried to limit.

At times these observers practiced on their own at the side or back of the room, imitating the performers, just as the little boy had practiced in the corridor at the Krontihene's court. At the beginning of a rehearsal at Abε school, there was a group of students in the back beating the drums, a girl among them. Shortly after I arrived, she began beating the column of the fɔmtɔmfrɔm drum with a stick as part of the kpanlogo beat, taking over from a boy who was not drumming very well. A boy with glasses was reading a math book as he danced in the aisle. At another rehearsal at Abε, the drummers were beating the music for the opening northern dance, and before the girls who were to perform it started in, the boys in the back of the room and in the aisles were having fun dancing what is, in fact, a male dance.

Students created rehearsal formats in which many of them could learn traditional performing arts through observation and imitation. The primary pedagogy of the rehearsals was based on the ways that young people from royal households learned to drum and dance, although it did not fully reproduce them because of the absence of expert elders. Students' desire to share their expertise and affirm their solidarity, witnessed in the classroom, prompted this style of learning during the rehearsals. These goals put students in conflict with teachers and one another as they experienced pressure to succeed within the competitive constraints the state established, in both school classrooms and cultural competitions.

Discouragement and Talent: Conflicts over Expertise

In the two boarding schools, which had about three weeks to practice under the control of adults, rehearsals in the dance-drama were filled with conflict, rivalry, and competition, among the students themselves and between them and the teachers. Rotation among performers was a feature of festival performances. It allowed more people to participate and gave respite to drummers who inevitably got tired. Mr. Boateng, the faculty sponsor at Abε Secondary School, wanted only "the best" students to perform, and since the rules allowed only a maximum of twenty people, he insisted on limiting all the roles of drummers and dancers/singers to those twenty best even during practice. While Mr. Boateng may represent an extreme in this regard, organizers in general tended to script the performance tightly and discourage improvisation, because the dance-drama performance had to be completed in twenty minutes or less.[10] Thus, the constraints of the competition—limits on time and personnel—ran against the open, accessible nature of the rehearsals that students tried to create.

Mr. Boateng made it abundantly clear to me that the rehearsals were not meant to teach novices how to dance or drum (conversation, 11 Mar. 1998), and this perspective showed in his handling of rehearsals. One night a girl who played a minor dancing role was absent. Floricia said she would go and dance in her place, but Rachel told her, "You can't take two [parts]." Patience told Pamela to get the light-skinned girl sitting nearby.[11] I asked Patience why she pointed her out, and Patience said, "She can do it." But Mr. Boateng asked if the light-skinned girl had been there the night before, and Patience replied that she had not. He said he wanted someone who saw what had happened the previous night so he did not have to teach it again. He told the drummers, "Don't keep changing hands." The next night he said about one boy, "The gentleman is not a dancer. He is just learning. I want people who do it naturally." Mr. Boateng was clearly not interested in giving all students a chance to participate; what he wanted was to create a beautiful performance, which meant allowing only those students who were already most expert to practice and hone their skills.

The roles in the dance-drama at Abɛ shifted constantly, with many hard feelings. The changes were due in part to conflicts with Mr. Boateng, who annoyed many of the students with his insulting comments about their performances and his constant modifications of the storyline and dances. Mr. Boateng wanted the third-year students to perform because, as first-year students, they had come in second at the cultural competition two years before. The third-year students refused to participate because of their irritation with Mr. Boateng's style of leadership. He had become increasingly disengaged from teaching and involved in other projects in the last few years owing to conflicts with the headmaster, and the students had been running the drama club for several years, creating and rehearsing plays in his absence. As older students who had been allowed some freedom of action, they wanted to be treated with more respect. During the group discussion with the boys, when I asked what bothered them about the changes Mr. Boateng made, one boy remarked, "Mr. Boateng wants his decision to be final. As he said, he is not very good in drumming and dancing, so he invites those who were doing it in the JSS to take part. But when we are doing something, maybe he has seen something from somewhere.

He doesn't actually know the full meaning of that, but he will want us to do it as he saw it somewhere. But because maybe we are doing it, we know whether it is wrong or not. But when we try to say it, he doesn't want to respect our views on that particular issue" (20 Mar. 1999).

These tensions were increasingly evident during the rehearsals. Once one of the girls who was dancing onstage stopped and sat down, saying that she could not do it. Another girl stood up to take her place and as she got to the stage, she turned around and said to Mr. Boateng, annoyed, "But you will tell me to sit down again." Students were shocked by the audacity of this comment, but Mr. Boateng remained calm and merely told her she was right. Her boldness obviously did not make enough of an impression on him to make him change his mind, for he did indeed tell her to sit back down. As a result there were only five dancers onstage instead of six, and since they were dancing in pairs, this upset the balance of the dance, confusing the dancers. Students were annoyed with Mr. Boateng's changes, his comments, and his insistence on having only one person to a role.

Although rehearsals increased some students' access to these performance skills, they also privileged the students who were already competent. Those students were assigned the main roles in performance and so got the most opportunities to practice. The emphasis was not on giving everyone a chance to learn local musical and dance forms, but on demonstrating artistic excellence and winning in the competition. Although faculty organizers relied on student expertise, they also wanted to control the creative content and retain authority. These were not student-run productions, by any means, yet students did not feel that teachers had sufficient knowledge in the domain of culture to justify the authority they normally wielded in the classroom.

In many ways these school competitions gave adolescents from royal homes greater opportunities for performance in front of other adults and adolescents, with accompanying adulation or criticism, than they might have experienced otherwise. When I asked Gwendolyn Appiah, from a royal household in Akropong, whose poetry recital on AIDS made it all the way to the national competition, what she had gotten out of the four-month competition process, she replied, "I know I am talented" (conversation, 29 May 1999). These adolescents got validation in front of a larger audience: their talent was recognized, and they had brought honor to the school and themselves in the process. Although only twenty students from each school could actually perform in the dance-drama competition, perhaps fifty more observed or participated during the rehearsals. Even so, at each school only a small proportion of the students were exposed to the lessons to be learned in the rehearsals and performances. These conditions increased rivalry and competition among the students themselves.

Because only a few students could perform, students were continuously evaluating their own performance and that of their peers. At Gyahene Secondary School the conflicts over expertise were more intense between students than between the teacher and students. These evaluations of "talent" and "knowing how to do it," especially negative evaluations, prevented some students from performing at all, as girls at Gyahene commented.

> JOAN: Afei nso obi wɔ hɔ a ɔwɔ ne talent. Obi se, onim yɛ, anaa onnim yɛ. Ɛmma ɔnyɛ. Oyi ne ho fim (Also some people have a talent. Someone says, she knows how to do it, or she doesn't know how to do it. It prevents her from doing it. She withdraws from the activity).[12]
>
> JACQUELINE: Na ɛha nso, yɛyɛ nnamfofo [pause], sɛ woyɛ biribi a, obi wɔ hɔ a (If you do something someone—)
>
> FLORICIA INTERRUPTS: ɔmma ɔnkɔ (she doesn't let her do it).
>
> JACQUELINE: ɔnhyɛ wo nkuran. ɔbɛyɛ no sɛɛ, "Ɛɛ! na wode biribiara na woagyegye agyina mu" (—doesn't encourage you. She will do it like, "Ɛɛ! [a sign of disapproval] and you get involved in everything").
>
> MILLICENT: Yes.
>
> JACQUELINE: Obiara wɔ ne talent. Ɛsɛ sɛ otumi yɛ, du akyiri. Nanso ɛsiane sɛ wɔtan n'ani . . . (Yes, everyone has her talent. She should be able to do it, to become proficient. But because they treat her maliciously . . .).[13]

Although these students talk about talent — natural and innate, perhaps God-given — their comments show how skill depended also on opportunities for participation: Jacqueline said that one should be able to perform so she gets better.

The rehearsals were thus characterized by conflicts over participation in the dance-drama with teachers and between students; expertise became both the basis of authority in those conflicts and the subject of conflict itself. Relations were negotiated through the language of competence, knowledge, and talent, but they were as much about young people's right to participate in state domains, gaining visibility and honors, as about knowledge and learning. The conflicts about participation in the two boarding schools signal their prestige; more than their Horeb confreres, the students in those schools felt pressed to compete for the few privileged slots that the state provides, even as they tried to create more open participation in their rehearsals. Thus, although school cultural competitions allowed greater access to cultural performing skills, this access was limited by the constraints of the competition and by peer rivalry.

Conclusion

This chapter has been concerned with the question: What do the rehearsals for the school cultural competitions reveal about the state's designs for young people and about the students' own expectations of the state? We have seen that, in terms of their organization, the competitions mirror the clientelist state, in which there are far fewer openings to secondary school, university, and good jobs than the number of applicants. The rehearsals create a domain in which students compete against one another to gain recognition and honor, as they do in other state contexts. Because of the lack of time and the competitive aspects of the performances, students who are already relatively competent, primarily those from chiefly households, are favored in the rehearsals and given more opportunity to hone their skills. Unable to provide students with cultural expertise through schools, the state ironically ends up saluting the superior status and knowledge of chiefs and elders.

Yet young people are here less under the supervision and guidance of adults than they generally are either at home or in the classroom. Students, for the most part, ended up creating a youthful representation of culture, based on the forms of culture accessible to them: *kpanlogo,* TV shows, Ananse stories, and the most public aspects of courtly activities. They thus did not gain access to the most respected forms of culture. Because both students and adults recognized that culture in the school is a simplified and youthful version, elders and chiefs continued to be respected for holding the most authentic and deep knowledge. Because young people's forms of culture could be disparaged as "not deep," the students' performances did not change their relations to elders. But their relations with one another and with their teachers did change as students claimed authority and expertise in these youthful cultural forms.

Students tried to create a social space within the constraints of the school, in which they freely shared the knowledge they had and opened participation to all. The rehearsals thus broadened participation in drumming and dancing to those who might not have access to it through chiefs' courts. Girls also had the opportunity—however limited—to experiment with drumming, a practice legitimized by the Arts Council since the 1960s, but still contested in local schools. The openness of rehearsals was heightened by the students drawing on structures of learning used in chiefly courts, in which participants rotate in and out of performance, and in which those who feel less competent watch and imitate those who are more so. Students at Horeb Secondary School had the most open and accessible rehearsals, but they rightly interpreted this situation as one of marginalization and abandonment by their teachers. In the two boarding schools, where teachers tried to help "the best" performers win in the cultural competitions, tensions increased not only between students and teachers but also between students vying for recognition in a system that recognizes and rewards only a few. In these cases the limit on participation and the use of an expert, Kofi Martin, worked: in the district competition both schools took first or second place in most of the categories, allowing them to participate in at least a few categories at the regional level.

Thus, students felt ambivalent about their solidarity and authority. On the one hand, this mode of participation suggested a different model for getting ahead, one in which resources and power would be shared freely. On the other hand, precisely because it was not the mechanism by which state resources were distributed, it took them out of circuits of distribution. These cultural programs have the effect of empowering young people unintentionally relative to their teachers and simultaneously marginalizing them. The rehearsals for the cultural competitions suggest that even in situations of state expansion, students in the wealthier, more prestigious schools are likely to be highly critical of the state for the lack of access to its honors and rewards. As for students in other, poorer schools, as the state increasingly leaves them to their own devices, they draw on strategies of solidarity to broaden access to knowledge and participation among their peers.

Thus, the teaching of culture in the school sometimes, problematically and with tension, gives greater authority and recognition to young people who are eager to take over the positions of honor held by their teachers and elders but who except in rare instances are denied access to the honor and resources accruing to either elders or the state. As Dinah from Horeb Secondary School said when the girls complained that they had to rely on their own skills, "Yɛanyɛ ade" or "We didn't do well." While some students are learning that participation in state events like cultural competitions can lead to honor and personal visibility, others are learning to feel personal disappointment and disenchantment with the mechanisms of a clientelist state.

THIS WORK has focused on the intersection of two state projects in modern Ghana, the production of national culture and schooling. Ghana's use of schools to promote culture is not an isolated experience. When state governments seek to produce a national culture, they usually turn to schools as an organizing apparatus, along with other strategies, like national festivals, to accomplish that end (Aina 1992; Apter 1996). Since the 1970s the United Nations Educational, Scientific, and Cultural Organization has encouraged governments to formulate cultural policies and has organized conferences with some success for that purpose. The Inter-Governmental Conference on Cultural Policies in Africa, held in Accra in 1975, for example, was followed by the publication of numerous cultural policy statements (Aina 1992; UNESCO 1981). In Kenya oral literature is part of the school curriculum (Opondo 2000; Samper 1997); in independent Namibia, performing arts, music, and visual arts are taught in the schools (Mans 2000); "cultural activity" is studied in South Africa under the ANC (UNESCO 1995). In Burkina Faso an organization similar to Ghana's Arts Council teaches theater in schools (UNESCO 1981). Clearly, when African governments decided to engage in cultural interventions, most involved schools in that effort.

The intersection of the two projects—of national heritage and schooling—focuses on young people. Schools are already organizing children, so much so that, in Akuapem today, the proper role of a child is said to be as a student. Akuapem people consider the school to be a separate, somewhat isolated realm for young people. With the expansion of mass education, especially in Ghana, which has a high rate of education for an African country (Clignet and Foster 1971), schools seem to offer a way to reach many of the nation's children and thus many of its future citizens. The schools that are entrusted with

CONCLUSION
Youth, Nationalism, and the Transformation of Knowledge

this task are nominally under government control, so that teachers, as state workers, are vulnerable to political and administrative pressure. Schools are already subject to myriad state policies. Furthermore, during a time of nationalist sentiment in the 1960s and 1970s, cultural revitalization became a project for teachers and students as well, and they turned to state institutions to support them in their local endeavors. During that time in Ghana, a particular definition of culture—as drumming and dancing—became hegemonic, and teachers and students recognized themselves and their dreams in state cultural productions.

It thus seems quite natural for the state to involve schools in the work of producing a national culture. However, Ghana's case shows that the state's use of schools limits its ability to appropriate tradition for the ends of national unity and legitimacy. The hegemony of culture as drumming and dancing was short-lived. Once the state subscribed to neoliberalism, it sought to expand its reach through a new definition of culture as the way of life of a people. The cultural interventions of the (P)NDC government took place within a complex field of discourses and practices about culture, in which multiple government and popular discourses coexisted and interacted. This complex terrain was formed by previous colonial and postcolonial policies that became sedimented in schools and by a missionary legacy that encouraged a particular relationship to cultural traditions of both separation and study, denunciation and documentation. Since the 1970s charismatic Christianity has reinvigorated this contradictory relationship to traditional culture. Charismatic Christians seek to limit and excise the powers of traditional religion, but in the process continue to reveal and document the significant workings of traditional gods and spirits in people's everyday lives. The historical legacy of missionary activity means that education is closely tied to Christian practice. From the start teachers played key roles in the making of good Christians under the guidance and oversight of local pastors. Although schools in Akuapem are now principally under the management of the state, they continue to be Christian institutions in all but name.

Schools are therefore far from being straightforward state institutions in Ghana. Because they are institutions that the state inherited from the church—and not without a struggle—schools produce both national and Christian identifications. National and Christian discourses create different ideas of what it means to be modern, and, as a result, different relationships to tradition. A "rich culture" is seen as integral to a modern nation's identity and strength, yet many Africans, influenced by Christianity's civilizing mission, see traditional culture as a remnant of the past and as inextricably linked to evil and dangerous forces. Because nationalism and Christianity generate two models of modern personhood, teachers and students are particularly affected by the stresses caused by these internal divisions in modernity.

Teachers and students have multiple subject positions from which they interpret government policy and curricula. As they realize government cultural programming in their classrooms and schools, they refract that policy according to their own understandings and identifications. While teachers are state employees, many, particularly women and the younger men, are devout Christians. Those teachers who are committed to a Christianity founded on a rejection of traditional religious practices—equated with culture—work to reconcile the cultural studies curriculum to their beliefs in ways that undermine the government of Ghana's intent to respect and promote its diverse ethnic and religious heritage. Thus, while the state creates the space in which cultural programming happens, the schools produce a multivocal cultural program in which government discourses vie with Christian and popular discourses.

As some students and teachers try to reconcile participation in school cultural activities to their religious beliefs, they find it easier to respond to the government's notion of culture for development than to other meanings of culture. A discourse of development allows Christians to wed their anxieties about personal holiness to national ideologies about progress. In negotiating between the government's promotion of Ghanaian culture for national ends and Christians' rejection of it, students and teachers attempt to reconcile these competing idioms and position themselves as Christians benefiting the moral state of the nation. Combining the discourse of development with that of Christianity, they put on development morality plays condemning teenage pregnancy and drug abuse as ruining not only individual lives but also the nation. School cultural programming produces a wider range of messages than the state intends, some of which result in the undermining of its policy, but all of which result in that policy's transformation.

The state is also limited in its ability to appropriate culture through schools because the modern project of knowledge-transmission in schools goes against the logic of learning practices and knowledge marked as cultural that people generally learn only after they have gained a ritual-political position in their families and towns after middle age. In general school lessons transform the practical into the theoretical, or students' experiential, embodied knowledge (of farming and cooking, for instance) into "school knowledge," into facts that can be memorized and regurgitated on an exam. Schooling is therefore a process of alienating students from what they know as they struggle to articulate their everyday experiences in complicated English in the particular forms required by school knowledge. Teachers, as they do with other kinds of vernacular knowledge, strive to transform cultural knowledge into school knowledge by reducing discussions of, say, libation or the Odwira festival to a series of lists, definitions, and functions, which are written on the blackboard for students to copy into their notebooks. Culture becomes located in the past, distant from the experience of young people as it takes the shape of a codified, standardized school knowledge, circulated verbally and in writing in the classroom. In incorporating the teaching of traditions into schools, the meaning, the location of expertise, and the process of learning those traditions shift.

However, this effort has not been fully successful because the schools' ventures into this domain go against local proscriptions against any sharing of cultural information with the general public, and especially with children and youth. Teachers are the linchpin in the state's strategy to appropriate cultural traditions and make schools the site for their transmission. But for one reason or another—some teachers are too young to know anything about the local traditions or are strangers, others are Christians who reject culture as demonic, and still others have never had access to books or courses on culture—many teachers feel shaky in their grasp of the subject. As a result, when cultural matters come up in the classroom, many teachers can neither retain their role as teachers giving school knowledge nor appropriate the role of traditional elders. Akuapem people thus tend to dismiss the school teaching of culture as appropriate for children and unworthy of respect, pointing to chiefs and elders as the guardians of the ancestors' and the town's traditions. Because the majority of teachers do not feel expert, the state-sponsored competitions, the principal form of school cultural programming, have had the effect of giving students a sense of confidence in themselves they rarely feel in the classroom. That feeling of youthful authority is a double-edged sword for students, however, for it signals their marginalization from the distributive process of the state. The cultural competitions are organized according to the procedures of a clientelist state, in which only a few gain access to the state's patronage and recognition. In their rehearsals for those competitions, students challenged that model by creating learning contexts marked by solidarity and the sharing of information, and by generating a youthful representation of culture, based on TV shows, the accessible and visible rituals of annual festivals, and the youthful and sexualized dance form of *kpanlogo*. Thus, through the cultural competitions, the state has simultaneously empowered and frustrated young people, boding ill for their future participation in its projects. Disappointment with the cultural competition led the main male dancer in Gyahene Secondary School's dance-drama, a first-year student, to say, "Mihuu sɛnea wɔyɛɛ no, enti next time no, biribi ni a, sɛ meyɛ koraa a emfi me komam'" (I saw how they did it, so the next time, if at all, if I do it at all, it won't be with all my heart).[1] Although the state seeks to "capture" young people through its cultural programming in schools, it has so far failed to win them over completely: if students participate in state projects and enterprises at all, as this young man says, they will try to protect themselves from disappointment by being less hopeful and enthusiastic, and a little more cynical and wary.

The findings of chapters 5 and 6 have implications for culturally sensitive curricula and pedagogy produced and taught under the auspices of multiculturalism in the United States, although the politics of knowledge and pedagogy play out in distinctive ways in these two arenas. Multicultural education emerged in the early 1970s from the civil rights movement of the 1960s. Based on the idea that schools reflect dominant cultural practices and are thus monocultural institutions (Nieto 1992), multicultural education is a "reform movement that is trying to change the schools and other educational institutions so that students from all social-class, gender, racial and cultural groups will have an equal opportunity to learn" (Banks 1989, 3). The theoretical work on multicultural education—which suggests changes to institutional practices that create inequality, the involvement of parents and students in school decision-making, and a substantial rethinking of the entire school curriculum through the lens of diversity—is often more sophisticated than its actual implementation in classrooms (Banks 1984; Nieto 1992).

As practiced in classrooms, multicultural education often focuses on cultural representation, particularly through the insertion of bits of "diversity" into existing curricula. Changes in content result in the inclusion of sources and materials from a variety of groups. "The primary goal of these approaches is to incorporate the voices, experiences, cultures, and struggles of [disenfranchised] cultural and gender groups into the curriculum" (Banks 1992, 83). Multicultural education attempts to make all students' cultural experience visible and acceptable within schools by transforming it into school knowledge; thus, in many college courses multiculturalism is taken to mean including new texts that fit within the elite aesthetic traditions central to the received humanistic canon (Turner 1993; Urciuoli 1999). Many multicultural programs take a touristic approach to culture, focusing on the celebrative, performative, or public aspects that are most accessible to outsiders, such as food, dress, and festivals (Coe 1994; Derman-Sparks 1989; Kaomea 2000). Furthermore, the culture that is often represented is "the national culture" of students' countries of origin, rather than their lived experience (Leistyna 2002). These strategies, like the Ghanaian government's attempt to transform cultural knowledge into school knowledge, render "culture" distant from students' lives and vernacular knowledge, although under different auspices. Critics from the left like Tony Platt and Hazel Carby have argued that "'celebrating differences' is a far cry from dismantling inequalities" (Platt 2002, 45), and that learning about others from cultural texts may merely be a substitute for achieving integration through political agitation for civil rights (Carby 1992). Thus, although multicultural education was born from a political movement, the civil rights movement's foray into schools has blunted its critical edge.

Platt and Carby give excellent reasons for depoliticizing multicultural education at a philosophical and macro level, but without exploring what actually happens in lessons and classrooms where cultural diversity is taught. This study of the teaching of culture in Ghana, by examining closely the processes that occur within "the black box" of schooling, helps explain the depoliticizing of culture as it is taught in schools. When cultural traditions are taught in school, their meaning and form are transformed. The teaching of culture in school does not necessarily produce closer connections between the school and the community or result in local styles of learning transforming school pedagogy. Rather, it creates a new form of tradition that is acceptable so long as it is contained within the existing structures and modes of regimentation of schooling. In classroom lessons teachers teach culture in the ways that they do other forms of knowledge, with moderate success; they render it into the more prestigious form of school knowledge, an abstract form of knowledge reproducible in notes and on exams. They thus attempt to adapt traditional knowledge to the logic of the school, alienating students from the practical knowledge they have acquired from experience. The teaching of culture in school can thus change students' relationships to knowledge, rendering experiences that are fluid, contested, and ongoing into more stable, abstract, and codified information.

Yet at the same time, contrary to the progressive critiques of multiculturalism, my research shows that the teaching of culture in Ghana did open up a critical space, however momentarily. In rehearsals for the cultural competitions, ways of learning not associated with the school emerged, the routines of the school were disrupted, and authority relations between teachers and students were challenged. Young people became critical of teachers for denying them the opportunity to participate and learn new skills, and generated solidarity by drawing on pedagogical strategies present in their communities. The blandness and depoliticization of culture through schooling does not necessarily blunt students' voices in negotiating their access to what they feel they deserve within the national space, an inherently political act.

This study shows how schools' incorporation of traditional knowledge transforms the construction of that knowledge, its meanings, the location of expertise, and students' relationship to knowledge-production. Thus, as we analyze the teaching of culture as part of the incorporation of immigrants in Europe, of the empowerment of disenfranchised people in the United States, or in the creation of national culture in Ghana, we need to examine the complex processes that actually take place in schools.

As with multicultural education in the United States, the question arises: Is the Ghana government's cultural program a failure? While it may not accomplish what it is expected to achieve, it has certainly accomplished something. The Ghanaian government's cultural program, as it occurs under the current policy of neoliberalism, turns out to have some unintended results. One is that because schools transform cultural knowledge into either school knowledge or youth knowledge, the school cultural program supports chiefs as cultural authorities knowing the most sacred and secret cultural knowledge. While the state seeks to wrest cultural prestige away from alternative political authorities to prop up its own, that attempt does not seem to be entirely successful at the level of the school cultural program. Second, the school cultural competitions open up, momentarily, a space where young people can claim authority and knowledge, in relation to their teachers and one another, as they compete for the resources the state provides, even though that space is devalued by others and experienced by students as disempowering. For many, the ultimate effect is disenchantment and pessimism about their prospects for participating in the nation-state. Finally, as teachers and students shape the cultural program according to their own identifications and understandings of culture, a fusion between Christian discourse and nationalism appears to be taking place. The political strength of Christians, particularly charismatic Christians, is very much in evidence.

And yet it also seems to me that a half-century of cultural programming in schools has been successful to the extent that it has generated a sense of nationhood that frames and contains local and ethnic loyalties. Thus, when ethnic violence breaks out, it is relatively local and small-scale. The state-sponsored buffet of a variety of ethnic cultures presented in state pageantry and school cultural competitions means that the nation is not associated with one ethnic group, as happened in Côte d'Ivoire with the Akan. Thus, the fact that Ghana has not been plagued by ethnic violence since independence speaks, at least in part, to Ghanaians' feeling of the legitimacy of the nation as a political entity, and school cultural programming has contributed, at least in part, to that attitude. While students and teachers debate the fairness of the judges in the cultural competitions, they do not contest the government's right to organize those competitions, just as localities compete for national prestige and resources within the frame that the government has generated. While culture is not solely associated with the nation, several of its contemporary definitions among the swirl of discussions about the cultural do justify government programming and support of culture. Thus, the state in Ghana has been partially successful in associating culture with the nation, reifying both culture and the nation-state, and as a result, containing the potential challenge of ethnicity as the nation becomes the frame in which ethnicity and town have to compete to be visible.

Attention to the complex social processes that take place in schools reveals that the Ghanaian state's power to appropriate vernacular traditions through schools has been limited by two factors: the proliferation of competing discourses about culture, in which the Christian identities of students and teachers render the teaching of culture associated with the demonic problematic, and the local perception that culture lies in the domain of elders, not young people. The transmission of knowledge and ideology is not straightforward, but bound up in institutions, social relations, and personal identifications. Ghana's citizens have sometimes, briefly, been able to make sense of their lives through state activities. But more often and increasingly so, they cannot, and in that circumstance, they turn to other ideologies that compete with the state's project. The production of national culture in schools in Ghana is therefore an intervention with contradictory effects, through which we can uncover the complex negotiations between a state and its citizens as each seeks to lay claim to the space of the nation.

APPENDIX A

Titles and Themes of 68 Dance-Dramas Performed in School Cultural Competitions, 1997–2002

1997 Basic School Cultural Competitions in Akuapem North District

    Akropong/Abiriw Circuit
      Primary schools (8):   Unity (2)
                                "Send Your Girl Child to School" (2)
                                King Solomon (Biblical story)
                                Water pollution
                                Obedience
                                Funeral

      Junior secondary schools (5):   Teenage pregnancy (2)
                                  "Send Your Girl Child to School"
                                Education of girls
                                Drug abuse

      Adukrom Circuit
      Primary schools (5):   "Send Your Girl Child to School"
                                  The importance of school
                                Teenage pregnancy
                                Drug abuse
                                Greed

1997 Second-Cycle National Cultural Competition

      Ashanti Region
      Secondary school (1):   Respect for the elderly

1999 Second-Cycle National Cultural Competitions
Theme: "Culture: Gateway to the Nation's Prosperity"

      Akuapem North District
      Secondary schools (6):   Women love riches
                                  Puberty rites
                                "Kaya-yoo" (rural-urban migration)
                                Unity
                                "Kwaku Ananse" (folk tale about greed)
                                Occupations

Eastern Region

Secondary schools (9):
Importance of school
Girl-child education
"Kaya-yoo" (carried over from district)
"Greediness" (folk tale)
Importance of writing a will in a matrilineal
society
Land disputes
Women should wear traditional cloth
Environmental awareness and health
Apprenticeship

National Festival

Secondary schools (9):
Ethnic intermarriage
Kindness brings riches
Importance of plant medicine
Showcasing the culture of the region
Problems of Ghana: drinking, sexuality, smuggling,
AIDS, brain drain, madness
Dispute settlement
"The Lazy Girl"
Rape
Killing a wild animal

The school that won the Eastern regional for its dance-drama on land disputes did not have the opportunity to perform at this festival.

2002 Basic School Cultural Competitions in Akuapem North District
Theme: Preserving Our Environment through Our Culture

Akropong/Abiriw Circuit

Primary schools (8):
Tree cutting (2)
"Preserving Our Environment"
Deforestation (2)
"Bush Fire Caused by Palm Wine Tappers in
a Village"
"Preventing Bush Fire"
Misuse of the Sacred Grove

Junior secondary schools (7):
"Yɛ ɔman ba pa" (Be a good citizen)
Teenage pregnancy
"Pollution of Water Source Causes Disease" (2)
"Environmental Degradation"
Different towns have different ways of hunting

Larteh Circuit

Primary schools (6):
Lack of environmental cleanliness causes
illness (3)
Taboos about cutting down trees
A hunter sets a bush fire
Taking a second wife

Junior secondary schools (4):   Mistakes in fetching water
"Smuggling: a social evil"
"*Efiri Tete*" [It is from long ago]: ways to keep the
house and community clean
"*Bɔ Nnua ho ban*" [Protect our trees]

APPENDIX B

The Teaching of Culture in Akuapem Schools, 1998–99

The first table in this appendix, table B.1, is straightforward enough; it is a primary school teacher's plan for the cultural studies subject for one semester. But table B.2, showing the topics that were taught in cultural studies lessons in Akuapem schools that I observed in the school year September 1998–August 1999, needs some explanation. It is first of all important to keep in mind that although the cultural studies subject was officially mandated for the primary and junior secondary schools, none of them taught it routinely; the data for those levels are therefore based on lessons that were specially put on for my benefit. Second, because teachers sometimes treated more than one topic in a lesson, the total number of topics listed (51) is larger than the total number of observations (43). Finally, I have attempted to identify the mode of teaching for each lesson as either theoretical (discussion followed by note-taking) or practical (demonstrations and performances), or a combination of the two. In 29 of the 51 cases (57 percent), the approach was entirely theoretical, and in 8 (16 percent), it was entirely practical; in the other 14 cases (27 percent), the teacher used both approaches.

Table B.1 Primary school teacher's lesson plan for sixth-year students, first semester, by week, Mamfe, 1998–99 (30-minute classes)

Week	Topic	Week	Topic
1–3	Greetings and responses	7	Kinship terms
4	Local festivals	8–9	Extended family system
5	Funerals	10–12	Messages and directions
6	Professions, vocations, and occupations	13–14	Review and examinations

Table B.2   Topics treated in cultural studies lessons, Akropong-Abiriw circuit (topics ordered by frequency of observation)

Topic and school	Year	Mode[a]	Topic and school	Year	Mode[a]
Greetings (*nkyia*)			Kinship system		
Obikyerε Primary	2	T	Obikyerε JSS	8	T
Krata Primary	2	T	Suabea JSS	9	T
Adesua Primary	2	T	Marriage (*awaregye*)		
Suabea Primary	6	T	Obikyerε Primary	3	T
Nhoma Primary	6	T, P	Training college	3	T
Osuafo JSS	8	T	Calendar (*Akanfo nnabu*)		
Libation (*nsagu* or *apaeyi*)			Kenkan JSS	9	T
Adesua Primary	6	T, P	Obikyerε JSS	9	T
Osuafo JSS	9	T, P	Proverbs (*mmεbu*)		
Abε SS	10	T	Nhoma Primary	5	T
Gyahene SS	10	T	Kenkan Primary	5	T
Gyahene SS	11	T	Christianity		
Child-naming ceremony (*abadinto*)			Adesua Primary	3	T
Obikyerε Primary	1	P	Kenkan Primary	5	T
Nhoma Primary	1	T, P	Drumming (*ayan*)		
Suadan Primary	2	D	Kenkan Primary	5	P
Nhoma Primary	3	D	Training college	2	T
Names and appellations (*edin ne mmran*)			Things in the chief's court		
Nhoma Primary	1	T, P	(*nneεma a yehu wɔ ahemfi*)		
Kenkan Primary	1	T, P	Bruku Primary	2	T, P
Krata Primary	6	T	Adesua Primary	4	T
Funeral (*ayiyε*)			Festivals (*afahyε*)		
Adesua Primary	6	P	Bruku Primary	2	T
Kenkan JSS	7	T, P	Obikyerε JSS	9	T
Abε SS	12	T	Dances		
Music and songs			Kenkan Primary	5	P
Adesua Primary	1	T, P	Suabea Primary	6	P
Suabea Primary	6	P	Symbolism		
Suabea JSS	7	T, P	Abε SS	11	T
Ananse stories (*Anansesεm*)			Puberty rites (*bra goro*)		
Kenkan Primary	4	T	Suadan Primary	4	T, P
Osuafo JSS	8	T, P	Divorce (*awaregu*)		
Osuafo JSS	9	T, P	Gyahene SS	12	T
Occupations			Games		
Obikyerε Primary	5	T	Kenkan Primary	5	T, P
Kenkan Primary	5	T			

Note: All school names are pseudonyms.

[a]T = theoretical; P = performance by student; D = demonstration by students.

NOTES

Introduction

1. The list of countries holding cultural competitions comes from conversations with Aurolyn Luykx, Ilana Gershon, Kristen Cheney, and Deborah Durham; and from Straker 2002.

2. The Arts Council and the National Commission on Culture are discussed in detail in chap. 2.

3. I have written more extensively about the process of doing fieldwork in Akuapem elsewhere (Coe 2001).

Chapter 1

1. During the 1830s and 1840s, the urban middle class and the agrarian upper class in Sleswig was divided in nationalist consciousness, turning to either Danish or German nationalism (Wåhlin 1980). Others in Denmark considered Sleswig to be a bulwark against German influence and sought to preserve and revive the Danish language there (Simon 1960). Whether Riis was influenced by these events is uncertain, given that he was working in the Gold Coast from 1832 to 1845.

2. This formulation may have something to do with the fact that Africans in the diaspora have been very supportive of Ghana. Citing the influence of the West Indians is a way present-day Akuapem people can stress their connection to diasporic Africans.

3. "Efise mefwɛ [mehwɛ in modern Twi] m'agya ofi, n'akura, ne yerenom ne ne mma, ne nkoa ne nwowafo, ne kɔree ne bae a, ɛma mibu me ho sɛ meyɛ obi. Dabi mefom so na me yiyeyɛfo yi twee m'aso no, mesɔre mitiaa no sɛ 'Wo akoa ne me na wofwe [wohwe] me sɛ? Mɛsan makɔ m'agya fi.'" Unless otherwise noted, all translations from *Kristofo Senkekafo* are by Afari Amoako and me.

4. According to Kwamena-Poh (1980), *Kristofo Senkekafo* had 2,000 subscribers in 1912. Paul Jenkins (1973) suggests it had a potential readership (the literate population of the Christian community linked to the Basel Mission church) of about 3,500 in 1885, rising to about 10,000 in 1905. But the mission was able to sell only about 360 copies of the Twi edition on average. At the same time, the fact that in the late 1990s I found three people from Akuapem who had copies from 1907 to 1917 speaks to its circulation and its value.

5. In his autobiography (*Kristofo Senkekafo*, May 1916, 11 [5]: 51–53), Opoku describes the mocking and insults he received during his service as pastor in Mamfe (1868–72).

6. "Akuapemfo nyɛ Asantefo, wɔnyɛ Asante Akyemfo, Ɔkwawufo ana Akyemfo, ana Fantefo. Wɔyɛ Akuapemfo, nso wɔnyɛ Akuapemfo. Wɔayɛ 'damusa.' Ɛne dɛn? Ɛne sɛ wofi Akuapem nso wɔatotɔ nsase akodu Asante ne aman a wɔbobɔdin yi nhina so asisi adan atwe wɔn yerenom ne wɔn mma nhina kɔ hɔ. Wɔfrɛ wɔn ho Akuapemfo, nso wɔpɛ wɔn Akuapem a, wonhu wɔn."

7. Birgit Meyer (2002) discusses a parallel case of the Norddeutsche Missionsgesellschaft among the Ewe, although she argues that the linguistic nationalism did not find political expression.

8. The paramount chief (*ɔmanhene*) at the time was Nana Addo Dankwa I. David Asante was the son of Owusu Akyem, the nephew and heir apparent to the Okuapemhene's stool, who played a key role in the political events of the 1840s (Haenger 2000) and had taught Riis Twi (Kwamena-Poh 1980). David Asante was the first African missionary to be trained in Basel.

9. By contrast, the Wesleyan Methodists working among the Fante never undertook to reduce the Fante language to writing; it was left to educated Fantes to take up this project in the 1860s (Kimble 1963; see also P. Foster 1965).

10. In a letter dated 22 May 1852, the missionary Süss said that he was living with five boys, who were also helping him on his farm and learning from his collection of Twi stories, Ananse stories, war stories, prayers, and proverbs (*Heidenbote* 1852, in Ghana Natl. Archives, EC 6/3).

11. Methodist newspapers, centered in Cape Coast, also fostered cultural nationalism (Kimble 1963).

12. The Basel Mission's promotion of the Twi language was not always well received by people in the Gold Coast. Many, because of the increasing trade with and power of the British in the area from the 1870s onward, wanted to learn English. Missionaries and African pastors and teachers complained that parents wanted their children to attend the Methodist schools, where English was given more emphasis. "These days, whether Christian or traditional religious practitioner, all children and adults want to speak English" (*Kristofo Sɛnkekafo,* July 1912, 7 [7]: 79). If in African eyes schools were places to learn new knowledges and the secrets to European power, Twi literacy was not so important.

13. Birgit Meyer (1999b) describes a similar process among the Ewe, in which the Bremen missionaries hoped that unifying the various dialects of the Ewe language would also bring together the various Ewe tribes of the southeastern Gold Coast and Togoland.

14. The missionaries' focus on history for the purposes of nation-building and progress articulated with local interest in history. J. A. Mader said about the Christiansborg Middle School (in Accra) in 1870, "Our Africans study history with great zeal and warmth. The study of world history helps this people to self-confidence. The class is one with the teacher, living the historical events. . . . We must expect a new generation on the Gold Coast after ten years: a nation, called to freedom and independence, able to give political expression to this and gaining its aim in due course" (quoted in Bediako 1995, 47–48). Clearly, Mader had different ideas about the independence of this "nation" than the British, whose rule would continue into the 1950s, showing that the institution of colonialism was shot through with contradictions and conflicts (John Comaroff 1997).

15. Ray Jenkins (1990) argues that despite the Basel Mission's active program of historical research, the Cape Coast intellectuals produced far more history than the Basel Mission intellectuals of Accra and Akropong, because of their fear of losing their historic prominence when the seat of British power moved to Accra.

16. "M'adesre no ne sɛ ehia papapa sɛ yenya Agyinafo anase Fekuw wɔ Akuapem, Akyem, Ɔkwawu, Asante, Asuogya, ne Asante-Akyem. Sa agyinafo yi wɔ hɔ ma Twifo

(Abosomsomfo ne Kristofo ahorow) nhina [nyinaa] nkɔso pa a wɔn botae ne sɛ wɔde mmɔdenbɔ kɛse ne ɔman ho dɔ a emu yɛ den pagyaw wɔn Agyapade man a ɛyɛ akyɛde a efi Nana Nyankopɔn Tweaduapɔn ankasa a ɛsɔ n'ani sɛ yɛyɛ Abibifo nsam."

17. "Ehia sɛ yenya Twi abasɛm a ewie pɛyɛ a obiara kura a ohu Twifo amane ahorow nhina [nyinaa] ne wɔn ho asɛm firefire wɔn afi mu, abusuam' fekuw mu, ahemfi ne amansɛm mu. Yɛn tete agyanom Nyamesom, wɔn gyidi horowɔ, wɔn su, wɔn dwumadi ahorow."

18. In 1924 Ayuw, along with another cocoa farmer from Larteh, traveled to the United States to persuade a manufacturer to buy cocoa from Akuapem farmers, many of whom were dissatisfied with the price they were being paid. Unfortunately, although the manufacturer received 6,000 tons of cocoa, the farmers were not recompensed properly (Brokensha 1966, 40). This was one incident in a long history in which cocoa farmers formed associations to get a better price for cocoa, whose local price fluctuated with the international market (Kimble 1963).

19. "Tete bre [bere] a yɛte Asanteman, Ɔkyemman, Okuapemman, ne Fanteman mu no na yekura yɛn amanne mu dennennen a yɛntoto n'ase."

20. "Agyanom, momma yɛnyɛ yɛn amanne a eye ma yɛn na yenyi brɔfo de a enye mma yɛn no mfim'. Yɛn nananom amanne a wɔde dii ako peree wɔn ho no bi ne atumpan a yɛn de nɛ [nnɛ] yi, sɛbeo, yese ɔpɔw aba nti yemmu no ade titiriw no."

21. The selection process by African Christians, as documented in *Kristofo Sɛnkekafo*, was similar to that of colonial officials in the Gold Coast, which Askew (2002) discusses in the case of Tanzania also.

22. "Biribiara a ɛyɛ Abibifo ade no, ɛyɛ nwonwasɛm no. Asɛm baako ne sɛ, yɛn bere so no, sɛ wɔapɔn sukuu a, na w'ankasa, bere yɛ wo de a, wɔapɔn sukuu, na wufura ntama Abibifo kwan so koraa na wutwam abɔnten so, ɔsɔfo anaasɛ ɔsɔfo panyin, obehu wo a, ɔfrɛ wo, se *'Teacher!* bra. O! Mihui sɛ wutwam wɔ ha na wufura ntama. Aden?' Na ɛyɛ nwomwa. Wo de, ɛnyɛ bone biara wɔ wo tirim. Ɛnyɛ bone biara, nanso mpanyinfo no fa no sɛ wo teacher ni de, sɛ wobɛyɛ no te sɛ Obibini no, ɛyɛ nwonwasɛm."

23. The most common reason for demotion or suspension was a sexual relationship outside of marriage, whether with a schoolgirl or with a woman in the town where the teacher was posted.

24. Amu attributed Ferguson's interest in this song to an article about it by W. E. F. Ward, music master at the government school of Achimota, for the government magazine *Gold Coast Review*.

25. Otto Boateng, another of Amu's students and founder of the singing band in the Larteh Presbyterian Church, wrote that except for songs (*mmoguo*) embodied in folk stories, Christians were not allowed to sing, hum, or whistle African songs until 1939 (1963, 81).

26. Boafo Akuffo later became the state *ɔkyeame* for Nkrumah (Agyemang 1988, 44).

27. Up until the 1930s the whole congregation had sung songs; there was no choir (Okae-Anti interview, 23 Oct. 1998). The songs were European hymns translated into Twi, whose tonal pattern had to be distorted to fit the musical rhythm.

28. The Basel Mission was not pleased with the 1887 Educational Ordinance for its emphasis on English, its indifference to religion, and the introduction of an English primary school into Africa without regard for African conditions (Smith 1966, 166). It campaigned strongly for the use of the vernacular as the medium of instruction in pri-

mary schools and for English to be used only in middle schools. The 1925 Education Ordinance restored the use of the vernacular for primary students, and some ten years later, the Education Committee recommended that classes on local languages in two-year training colleges include the study of the "pure, rich, idiomatic vernacular which in the Gold Coast is sometimes called 'deep,'" and the study of proverbs and folklore (*Report* 1942, 32). The committee felt that the colleges should encourage the production of original work in the vernacular.

Chapter 2

1. The format of the school plays at Achimota has many similarities with the genre of the concert party, a variety show of music and humorous drama (Barber et al. 1997; Cole 2001).

2. I am indebted to Catherine Newling for the felicitous phrase "buffet of culture."

3. In the 1930s and 1940s, the increased importance the colonial government placed on the vernacular, including its codification in writing, did indeed give rise to heightened ethnic consciousness and conflict. The Nzema Literature Association in the late 1930s argued against the teaching of Fante in the schools, preferring English to Fante if Nzema could not be taught for lack of reading materials. Later, in 1945, after the association succeeded in persuading local schools to teach Nzema literacy, the paramount chief of Axim protested against "the Nzima [Nzema] literature being established in the schools," because the local language was Evalue; if anything, his people would prefer Fante in the schools (Ghana Natl. Archives, RG 3/1/205). The teaching of a particular vernacular language in the schools was therefore taken to express the dominance and status of a particular linguistic, ethnic, and regional group.

4. In contrast, Independence Day celebrations today in Akropong are characterized by "the march past," in which students and occupational groups (e.g., seamstresses) march past the stand of officials and dignitaries. This is competitive, with the best marching group at each level rewarded.

5. In his speech inaugurating the IAS, Nkrumah said that by "the African Genius" he meant "our socialist conception of society, the efficiency and validity of our traditional statecraft, our highly developed code of morals, our hospitality, and our purposeful energy" (University of Ghana 1992).

6. Mike Oquaye (1996) says that Nkrumah used the ideological institutes to combat the growing student activism to his regime. In 1964 the government made admission to any university in Ghana conditional on two weeks of ideological orientation at the institute at Winneba.

7. Many YP records and other materials were destroyed, and because of the fear and repression associated with the YP era, people were reluctant to talk about the group or lead me to organizers. With information on the subject so hard to come by, it was my good fortune to find that the Akuapem district records were preserved in the Eastern Regional Archives; they are in fact the only district records to have survived.

8. The following list replicates the YP program for June 1962 in Akuapem (Eastern Regional Archives, ADM KD 33/6/215). There was also an older group called the Kwame Nkrumah Youth, for youth aged 17–25.

African Personality (aged 3–7)	*Young Pioneers (aged 8–16)*
Action Songs	Nkrumahism (Economic Aspects)
Foot-drill and Games	Discipline Code

Osagyefo [Nkrumah] in Pictures
History of Lumumba
Discipline Code
Hiking in the [Aburi] Gardens
Songs and Games
Modeling
Pictures of Great African Leaders
Aims and Codes
Developments in Ghana
Craft
Picture Study
Sports
History of [Aburi] Botanical Gardens
Folklore and Dancing

Current Affairs
Physical Display [Marching?]
Topography
Folklore and Dancing
Foot-drill Formation
Craft
Tradition of Drumming and Dancing

9. There is some evidence that the local YP organizers and volunteers, aside from Mr. Nyante, were connected to chiefs' houses. William Opare in Aburi worked with the YP and was later ɔkyeame to the chief there (Adi-Dako interview, 7 June 1999). A YP organizer in Larteh had been a youth leader in the Presbyterian Church there, in charge of its singing band and boys' brigade. In Akropong a maternal nephew of Okyeame Akuffo, Kwesi Akuffo, took over when Mr. Nyante was injured in an accident in 1965.

10. The adenkum singing group in Akropong is now defunct.

11. As early as the 1950s, schoolgoing, at least to primary school, was considered normal for children in southern Ghana (F. Boateng 1975).

12. The YP organizer Nyante started a club at Okuapemman Secondary School in Akropong, with 80 members, and pressure was put on Presbyterian Teachers College to start a Kwame Nkrumah Youth group. The inauguration of the Okuapemman YP group on 6 July 1963 included a flag procession ceremony, a song called "Pan African Socialist Students," a drama about Kwame Nkrumah, a recitation of the appellations and wise sayings of Nkrumah, and a demonstration of traditional drumming and dancing (program, Eastern Regional Archives, ADM KD 33/6/215). However, the headmaster of Okuapemman seemed to have doubts about the CPP and the Young Pioneers; a year later, the district commissioner chastised him for not talking about the inculcation of party ideology in the students at the annual speech and prize-giving day and wanted "a firm branch" of the Ghana Young Pioneers established at the school (District Commissioner to Headmaster of Okuapemman, 30 June 1964, ADM KD 33/6/215).

13. Ohum is usually considered a Guan, not an Akan, festival. I assume that this student or one of his friends was from Aburi, and that it was picked as a site to do cultural research on that account.

14. St. Andrews was a Certificate "B," two-year teacher training college at this time, meaning that its graduates were certified to teach primary and middle school.

15. Cultural studies had been previously proposed (and rejected) as a subject for primary, middle, and secondary schools by the Education Review Committee appointed by the military government of the National Liberation Council in 1967 (Chinebuah 1970; Ghana 1967).

16. The idea of replacing bells in schools with drums has a long history. It was proposed as early as 1932 by E. R. Addow, a drumming teacher at Achimota, in an article in the Teachers' Journal. Drums were used to summon children to class before 1987,

though perhaps not in Akropong; there is a picture showing this use of drums in a report on Komenda Teacher Training College in the April 1967 *Ghana Teachers' Journal* (no. 54). But I believe Professor Sutherland-Addy's statement that the (P)NDC government institutionalized the replacement of bells by drums to signal class changes, and that previously the use of drums had been dependent on individual teachers' initiative (pers. comm., 9 Aug. 1999).

17. As in Tanzania, the section in charge of culture frequently moved from one bureaucracy to another (Askew 2002).

18. One letter writer to an opposition paper joked that the Educational Reform Programme (ERP) should be called the "Educational Ruining Programme" (*Ghanaian Chronicle* 28 Oct. 1998, 2). For further criticism, see Morna 1989; Scadding 1989; and Sefa Dei 1993.

19. Here, for example, are the assigned points on the judges' sheet for the dance-drama category in 2002: (1) dance type: suitability, appropriate occasion, etc. (15 points); (2) blending and mastery of dances: use of instruments and voice, etc., including form and structure (35 points); (3) dynamics and aesthetics: appropriate movements, loud/soft, fast/slow, etc., including emotions and general style (25 points); and (4) general impression: costume involved, general discipline (25 points). For drum language the categories of evaluation were (1) technique: holding the sticks, use of palm and wrist, etc. (20 points); (2) accuracy (30 points); (3) fluency, including pacing (30 points); (4) general impression: attire, introduction, etc. (20 points).

Chapter 3

1. *Adwere* is a plant used in purifying the soul.

2. Teachers told me that themes for school cultural competitions were first used in 1997. In 2002 the theme was "Preserving Our Environment through Our Culture," a theme very much in the culture for development mode.

3. The speaker, the Apesemakahene of Akropong, served as master of ceremonies for the paramount chief of Akuapem on public occasions, such as during the Odwira festivals. A masterly speaker, he had been a delegate to the United Nations under Nkrumah.

4. Ghana and Malaysia engaged in a South-South exchange program, in which Ghana sought to adapt the Malaysian model of development.

5. In 1998 some 300,000 visitors came to Ghana, compared with just 80,000 the previous year, and the Ministry of Tourism realized $300 million as a result (*Daily Graphic*, 10 June 1999, 24). Tourism became the third-highest foreign exchange earner that year (*Daily Graphic*, 20 Nov. 1998, 1, 3). By 2010 Ghana hopes to have 1,000,000 visitors annually for earnings of up to $1.6 billion (*Daily Graphic*, 24 Oct. 1998, 15).

6. The poem in the text was recited by Abigail Mintaah, representing Kwawu South district in the Eastern regional second-cycle cultural competition, 16 April 1999. Translations of this and the earlier cited poems are by Afari Amoako and me.

7. "The Cultural Policy of Ghana" bears many similarities in wording and sentiment to "The Cultural Policy of Tanzania" (Askew 2002, 189).

8. Although Gyahene's dance-drama involved a "national" issue and could have taken place anywhere in Ghana, one judge interpreted it as referring to a local issue: the dissolution of Akuapem and ethnic conflict between Guans and Akans. During a rehearsal the faculty sponsor, Mr. Opare, told students that the dance-drama was "about

ethnic unity" and "national unity." It represented ethnic conflict, like the one between the Abiriws and the Akropongs, in which two people lost their lives in 1994. Or the one between five ethnic groups in the north, in which thousands of people lost their lives, and property losses ran into the millions. This dance-drama was about "the unity of all the ethnic tribes," he said.

9. The earliest evidence I found for this view of culture as inheritance was from Bennett Akuffo's *Ahemfi Adesua*, written in 1945, in which he explicitly argues that cultural traditions belong to the chiefs, and that they should not be lost, so that Akan wisdom may be preserved and elders and chiefs respected.

10. Text drummed on the *ntumpan* drums by Akua Yeboa and recited by Kwame Ababio at the national secondary school cultural competition, 4 May 1999.

11. Translation by Kobina Ofosu-Donkoh and me.

12. "Twifo afahyɛ mmienu a ɛsɛ sɛ Ɔkanni ba biara bɔ mmɔden hwɛ ne Adɛɛ ne Odwira. Nanso nnipa pii wɔ hɔ a, sɛ wɔahu saa afahyɛ yi mpo a, na ɛyɛ ɔfa ne fa bi kwa. Efise emu adeyɛ turodoo no de, gye tiri-ho-nam nkutoo na wonya kwan hu. . . . Wo nso a woyɛ ɔman ba, tɔ bi kenkan, na wunim wo man ho ahintasɛm a, wonkyi."

13. "Depth" indexes a sacred significance and has a double connotation in that it is used pejoratively by Christians to dismiss chiefly activities as spirit-worship, as I discuss further in the next chapter.

Chapter 4

1. An Akan language teacher at a secondary school in Adukrom told me that the Scripture Union there had given him and the participants trouble during the secondary school cultural festival in 2001, but he then joined the Scripture Union and was able to convince them that taking part in the competition was all right.

2. Paul Gifford (1998) shows that Pentecostalism was present in Africa for most of the twentieth century, in what are usually called African Independent Churches. The "new wave" of Pentecostalism that gained strength in the 1970s was quite different in theology and practice, and it is sometimes labeled "charismatic" to distinguish it from the earlier Pentecostal manifestations (33), but in Ghana these churches are called "new churches" or "young people's churches."

3. Birgit Meyer (1999b) describes the process by which some of these groups were rejected by the orthodox church and went on to form their own independent churches; others were accepted and formed Bible study and prayer groups inside the church (see also Omenyo 1994).

4. If one became possessed and then did not want to become a ɔkɔmfo, one could go through a series of rituals that would placate the spirits. However, the rituals were expensive and to be avoided if possible.

5. It was not uncommon for paintings to be done on the outside walls of schools. I heard that there had been similar murals at Mampong Junior Secondary School, but they had been painted over when it had become a secondary school several years ago.

6. On the success of evangelical churches in Africa in raising money from the sale of musical cassettes, publishing, and overseas contacts, see Gifford 1998.

7. In an extensive conversation with a presbyter at Grace Presbyterian Church who was also a teacher at Abɛ Secondary School, I was told that the lack of music and dance in Presbyterian churches in earlier times was the result of missionary culture, and that Ghanaians are "ebullient." The tune sung in church could be the same as a traditional

one, but the words had to praise God, he said, and the drums must not have undergone any traditional ritual (as is usually done in making drums). He had no problem with putting on cloth, but would not participate in puberty rites or libation pouring. Nor would he attend festivals because they were inextricably connected to the worship of traditional gods. He himself had been involved in the Scripture Union as a schoolboy.

8. Toward the end of my stay in 1999, Kofi Martin, who had been hired by schools as an expert in drumming and dancing, began attending Grace Presbyterian Church, singing songs to give thanks for God's grace. When I saw him there, I wondered whether this graduate of the School of Performing Arts and talented artist was finding a socially acceptable performance space in church, since the "traditional" performance spaces were deemed disreputable.

9. I heard, but do not know for certain, that some schools prohibit their students from attending festivals. The churches also provide alternative entertainment for children during festival time.

10. As noted in chapter 3, religious and moral education was one of three subjects covered in cultural studies until 1998, when, under pressure from Christians, it was made a separate subject.

11. Although Samuel Adubofuor (1994) says that children are seen as especially susceptible to spirit possession, many young children and babies attended the deliverance services at Grace Presbyterian Church (unlike the regular Sunday worship services, where children and youth were separated from the adults), perhaps because so many of the attendees were young women, and therefore young mothers. People in Akuapem, when I asked, had differing opinions about whether children could be possessed by spirits or not. From stories and conversations, however, it seemed that girls and young women were more susceptible to spirit possession (most traditional priests, or akɔmfo, in Akuapem were women), and adolescence was often the time they would have their first possession and be initiated into the priesthood. The most prominent ɔkɔmfo in Abiriw was a young woman who had first been possessed as a schoolgirl.

12. The School of Ghana Languages primarily gives teachers further training after teacher training college; it awards diplomas and degrees in languages and linguistics.

13. She had been asked to participate because she was Gã and knew Accra dances.

14. The 200-person attendance for the SU meeting represented about one-fifth of Abɛ school's student population.

15. Sexuality is not openly discussed in Akuapem; here too, the students refer to it either obliquely (without naming it, as Patience does) or euphemistically, by discussing teenage pregnancy.

Chapter 5

1. Cultural knowledge is not associated with witchcraft in Ghana, as it is in Botswana (Burke 2000).

2. Kwawu South poetry recital, 16 April 1999. Translation by Afari Amoako and me.

3. My discussion of the secrecy of elders is necessarily an overview, giving context to the educational reform. I hope that those more knowledgeable than myself, such as Professor Yirenkyi, publish their insights and findings on this subject.

4. A study of constraints on schooling placements in Ghana showed that attendance through junior secondary school is driven by parents' perceptions of the avail-

ability or possibility of the child attending secondary school and beyond (Lavy 1996). This has some historical depth: during the 1950s middle school teachers prepared students for the Common Entrance Exam for secondary school, rather than teaching the middle school course itself (Odamtten 1993).

5. In 1998 only about 18.5 percent of the total number of candidates for the Secondary School Certificate Examination passed in six or more of the nine subjects needed to get into secondary school. Only 4 percent passed in all nine, against a 21 percent rate of failure in all nine (A. Kofoya-Tetteh, "Reform Programme Didn't Achieve Results," *Daily Graphic*, 2 Oct. 1998, 3). That year's Basic Education Certificate Examination produced even more dismal results, especially in rural areas. The Manya Krobo district in the Eastern Region, for example, reported that only 11 percent of 1,800 candidates obtained aggregate scores that would allow them to continue to secondary school ("Manya Krobo Records Poor Results in BECE," *Daily Graphic*, 27 May 1999, 17). In other places, such as Sefwi Wiaso in the Western Region, 57 percent of BECE candidates qualified for admission to secondary school ("Teachers Asked to Raise Standard," *Daily Graphic*, 23 Feb. 1999, 16). In Akuapem North in 1998, 1,350 (79 percent) of children passed the BECE, and 354 (22 percent) failed, the district chief executive, E. Tony Gyampo, reported in a speech at PTC, but he did not say how many scored high enough to continue to secondary school.

6. In the President's Sessional Address to Parliament in January 1999, Rawlings reported that between 35 and 40 percent of junior secondary school graduates currently gained admission to secondary schools, and that the secondary school population was 194,785 (*Daily Graphic*, 15 Jan. 1999, 11). However, at a meeting of secondary school headmasters in the same month, it was estimated that "vacancies existed for only 53% of *successful* candidates" (Damasus Tuurosong, "The Scramble for Schools," *Daily Graphic*, 30 Jan. 1999, 9; my emphasis). The transition from secondary school to university was even more difficult. By one estimate, only about 5,000 of 70,000–80,000 students who qualified actually gained admission to a tertiary institution (Francis Kwarteng, "Accessing Tertiary Education: Methodist University to the Rescue," *Daily Graphic*, 6 May 1999, 7). Only 374 of the 1,451 secondary school students who applied to study science at the University of Ghana at Legon in 1998 were admitted because of limited science equipment (Ibrahim Awal, "Lack of Facilities Hamper Intake of Science Students at Legon," *Daily Graphic*, 22 Jan. 1999, 12–13; see also Daddieh 1995).

7. Examinations had always been important in Ghanaian schooling; not only did the elite seek to pass the examinations administered by overseas (British) examination bodies to gain admission to British universities, but for a few years (1902–9) the amount of government assistance to a school (and therefore the teachers' salaries) depended on how many students passed the annual examination (McWilliam and Kwamena-Poh 1975, 41).

8. An editorial in the *Daily Graphic* noted that "reports from examiners continue to indicate that most candidates perform poorly due to their inability to comprehend the questions" and called for schools to place greater emphasis on English language reading ("Promoting Reading in Basic Schools," 25 June 1999, 7). In a letter to the *Ghanaian Chronicle* (10–11 May 1999, 4), Isaac Owusu-Ansah, of St. George's Junior Secondary School in Kumase, argued that English language was "the backbone of almost all the subjects in the curriculum" and should be made compulsory in junior and senior secondary schools. Shortly thereafter, "Oral English" was made compulsory for all candi-

dates sitting for the SSCE, beginning that November ("Oral English Compulsory for SSS," *Daily Graphic*, 31 May 1999, 30).

9. To cite some examples of the deficiencies of rural schools: a junior secondary school in the Upper West Region reported it had only two teachers to handle 12 subjects and 111 students ("Kani JSS Has Only 2 Teachers," *Ghanaian Times*, 22 Sept. 1998, 1); in the Eastern Region, a primary school in Birim South district had two teachers for 87 pupils ("Two Teachers Handle Asikaso Primary," *Daily Graphic*, 5 Jan. 1999, 15); and three primary schools in Birim North district had only one teacher each ("Birim Schools Lack Teachers," *Daily Graphic*, 23 Jan. 1999, 18). Not one of the students of the community school at Likpe Nkwanta in the Volta Region passed the BECE in 1999, causing "most parents to withdraw their wards from the community school to the urban areas for quality education" (Alexander Kukah, "Education Reform Has Not Benefitted People," *Independent* 22 Apr. 1999, 6).

10. In a letter to the *Daily Graphic*, Samuel Adadi Akapule wrote that "public education is becoming less attractive to Ghanaians. . . . Many Ghanaian parents are prepared to go on empty stomach and sacrifice large sums of money to send their wards to private schools. Mr. Adu, a parent[,] lamented: 'I earn only 100,000 cedis a month, how am I going to get 600,000 cedis to pay my four kids' school fees?'" (4 Nov. 1998, 9).

11. In 1999 Cape Coast's seven top schools (Mfantsipim, Adisadel, St. Augustine's, Wesley Girls, Holy Child, Aggrey Memorial, and Ghana National College) reported that they were under more pressure than usual to admit students because the pass rate on the BECE had been higher in 1998 than in 1997 ("SSS Selection Begins Today," *Daily Graphic*, 14 Jan. 1999, 24). There is always a crush of students wanting admission at top schools like these. For instance, in 1998, according to the same newspaper story, St. Mary's Secondary School got 1,150 applications for its 240 vacancies; Presec at Legon got 1,200 for 520; and Accra Academy got 1,477 for 400.

12. Unfortunately, I do not have statistics on student origin and residence for the three secondary schools I studied in Akuapem, because the schools themselves did not have that information. The text here is based on anecdotal evidence: my observations and statements by students and teachers.

13. The Ministry of Education and Culture put it this way: "The participation of every Ghanaian is extremely important if this country is to develop but sadly, the majority of Ghanaians are cut off from participation because they are either not literate at all, partially literate or have been miseducated and therefore are not able to realise their potentials either for themselves or their society" (Ghana 1988b, 3). I disagree with the assumption of this statement. Many of the people who contribute to "development" are illiterate or partially literate. But this is the modernist stance: that literacy is intimately connected to individual and social progress.

14. Asare interview, 24 October 1998. Translation by Kobina Ofosu-Donkoh and me.

15. The rote-learning system has a long history. Inspectors of Achimota College during the 1930s repeatedly complained about the emphasis on notes; in 1933 they said that "occasionally, a lesson consisted of a lecture, punctuated by the dictation of notes," a process that they feared the teachers-in-training would imitate in their own classrooms (Report on Teacher-Training, Ghana Natl. Archives, CSO 18/6/92; see also CSO 18/6/93 and CSO 18/6/97). Similarly, one goal of the 1986 reforms was "to ensure that teaching at the basic level does not degenerate again into rote learning and memorization of fact and that teaching encourages inquiry, creativity, and manipula-

tion and manual skills" (Ghana 1988b, 6). Yet clearly teachers consider the system a tried-and-true teaching method.

16. The exams generally ask for the kind of information generated in classroom lessons. In the August 1999 BECE, each subject exam consisted of two parts, a multiple choice section and a section of open-ended questions. For example, in the open-ended section: for the social studies exam, students were asked to read a map and to list the four achievements of Dr. Kwame Nkrumah, together with the four main reasons for his overthrow; and for English and Twi language, they were asked to write a composition. In science they were asked to define a lever and give two examples of second-class levers. My thanks to Patience Ohene for providing me with her 1999 BECE exam questions. The end-of-term exams are similarly organized into two parts.

17. At Abε, with about 1,000 students, only 20 were taking Akan. At Gyahene, where the headmaster was an Akan language teacher and writer, Akan was required for students taking the general arts track. Approximately 100 of its 900 students were taking Akan, compared with some 300 taking French.

Chapter 6

1. Although the school cultural competitions were organized annually, primary and junior secondary schools competed alternately with secondary schools, so these were every-other-year events for individual schools.

2. Group discussion, 22 March 1999. Translation by Afari Amoako and me.

3. Group discussion, 22 March 1999. Translation by Afari Amoako and me.

4. John Chernoff (1979) described how he learned to play drums: "I imitated what my teachers played, and I attempted to follow them through their changes by responding to their gestures and bodily cues. I understood what to do before I learned how to think or talk about it" (21).

5. On Saturday nights on the government TV channel, there was a game show ("Agorɔ") in which three contestants picked from the audience were asked questions about culture (proverbs, riddles, Twi kinship terms, etc.) and Ghanaian history, politics, and geography. When I watched with the family of the queen mother, the men of the family eagerly participated and answered the questions. If a particular contestant on TV seemed especially knowledgeable about proverbs, rituals, and history, they would agree that he was an ɔheneba, the child of a royal family.

6. Interview, 8 March 1999. Translation by Kobina Ofosu-Donkoh and me.

7. Group discussion, 22 March 1999. Translation by Kobina Ofosu-Donkoh and me.

8. Horeb was the one school where I worried that the school authorities might have decided to participate in the cultural competitions only because I had asked to attend rehearsals.

9. At Abε Secondary School, there was some room for student input and improvisation because Mr. Boateng felt that he did not know about culture. For their dance-drama on kaya-yoo labor, the students learned how to perform the northern dance from a girl from the north.

10. Ngoma performances for the state also discouraged improvisation, a key element of traditional forms (Askew 2002).

11. Ghanaians often characterize people by skin color: "kɔkɔɔ" (fair or red) or "tuntum" (dark).

12. The pronouns in Twi could refer to either male or female.

13. Group discussion, 21 March 1999. Translations by Afari Amoako, Kobina Ofosu-Donkoh, and me.

Conclusion

1. Boys' group discussion, 21 March 1999. Translation by Afari Amoako and me.

GLOSSARY

The translations in this book are transcribed from the dialect of Twi spoken in Akuapem and are based on the Basel missionary J. G. Christaller's dictionary (1933). Akan is the umbrella term given to all Twi and Fante dialects, and much work since the 1940s has gone into unifying the different orthographies for Akuapem Twi, Asante Twi, and Fante into a single orthography:

ɛ is a short *e* as in *let*

ɔ is a short *o* as in *not*

hw is a slightly nasal *shw*

ky is like *ch* as in *cheer*

Words, as here, are conventionally arranged alphabetically by the first consonant, with the singular form followed by the plural form.

bambaya	a northern dance characterized by athletic and leaping movements
batakari	a long, loose shirt made of woven cloth associated with the north and warfare
ɔbonsam	in Christian discourse, the devil
ɔbosom, abosom	a traditional god, usually associated with a family, area, or natural object (rock, stream, tree, etc.); also called a spirit in the text; translated by many Ghanaians today and missionaries previously as "a fetish"
bra goro	Akan ceremony celebrating the onset of a girl's puberty and transition to womanhood
abusua	the extended family
abusuapanyin	the head of the extended family, almost always male
Adae	festivals that occur twice every forty days, one of which is called Awukudae because it falls on a Wednesday and the other Akwasidae because it falls on a Sunday
dawuru	gong-gong, an instrument made of two joined prongs of iron that is beaten with a stick
adenkum	a women's musical form named after a small calabash with a long neck
adowa	a dance and music form associated with Asante, Kwawu, and Akyem people

adwerɛ	a kind of herb that is mixed with water to be sprinkled for purification in religious ceremonies
Odwira	an annual week-long festival held in September or October to celebrate the coming of the new yam; also marks the beginning of the new year in Akuapem and other Akan areas
fɔntɔmfrɔm	a large, long drum; also a type of drumming used for a symbolic political dance performed by individuals (male and female) in the chief's court
agbaja	a dance and music form associated with the Ewe people
agorɔ	an all-purpose term for entertainment, encompassing instrumental music, dance, and song
ahemfi	the chief's court
ɔheneba	the "child" or descendant of a royal family
hu	to perceive visually; to understand or recognize
hwɛ	to deliberately direct the eye toward; to look at or observe carefully; to watch in order to imitate
juju	charms or amulets; now extended to mean witchcraft and even the practices of akɔmfo (see ɔkɔmfo)
kaya-yoo	the job of carrying bags full of produce and purchases in the marketplace; particularly done by girls in the cities for women who are doing their shopping
kente	an expensive, prestigious cloth sewn from woven strips, from southern Ghana
kete	a music and dance form associated with Akan peoples; named for the opening staccato rhythm
ɔkɔmfo, akɔmfo	a religious specialist (male or female) who is possessed by a god or spirit (ɔbosom) and delivers prophecies and heals spiritual ailments (often with physical manifestations); although often called traditional priests or priestesses, they are really mediums
kpanlogo	a flirtatious dance performed by boy-girl pairs with sexually explicit moves; a music and dance form associated with young people and the Gã people
Kronti division	a royal division held by the town of Akropong; one of the most important divisions, whose head serves as regent in the ɔmanhene's absence
ɔkyeame, akyeame	often translated as "linguist," but really the spokesman and mouthpiece for chiefs; because the chief is regarded as sacred, the ɔkyeame serves as a spiritual buffer between him and others
kyerɛ	initially, to show or to demonstrate, but also used as the equivalent of the English "to teach"
amammrɛ	literally, the customs of the traditional state (see ɔman), but also used as the equivalent to the English word "culture"

ɔman, aman	historically referred to a traditional state like Akuapem or Asante; today also used to refer to the nation-state
ɔmanhene	the paramount chief, or highest chief, of a traditional state
mmariwa	a small set of drums in a drum ensemble
nana, nananom	grandparent, ancestor; also used as a title of respect for a chief
Anansesɛm	literally, stories about Ananse the Spider; used more broadly for all fables and folktales, whether Ananse appears in them or not
asafo	an association of nonroyal men, formerly connected with warfare; most prominent in Fante areas
Sankɔfa	literally, "Go back for it"; a proverbial phrase of respect for the past
sua	to learn; to imitate
atɛntɛbɛn	a type of bamboo flute
tie	to perceive through the ear; to hear or listen
toto	to roast over the fire (as with plantain or yam)
atumpan, ntumpan	the talking drum(s) used in a form of drumming that imitates the tonal quality of Twi speech (*ayan*); of the pair, one drum plays a high note (the female), and the other a low one (the male)
Awukudae	see Adae
ayan	the kind of drumming performed on the talking drums (see *atumpan*)

REFERENCES

This list is divided into two main sections. For convenience of citation, I have chosen to lump all official government documents, both published and unpublished, together in the main section, though they obviously qualify as primary sources. In the interview subsection, unless otherwise noted, the interviews were taped.

Primary Sources

Interviews

Abavon, Mensah, Boy Scout leader, jointly with Mr. Duah, teacher, Awukugua, 30 July 1999

Addo-Fening, Robert, professor of history, Legon, 27 Sept. 1998

Adi-Dako, Mansfield Bediako, retired arts and crafts teacher and artist, Akropong, 9, 16, 23, 29 Sept. 1998, 7 June 1999 (untaped)

Akuffo, Obuobi Atiemo (Teacher Okyen), teacher and drummer, Akropong, 21 Sept. 1998

Ampene, Afua, secondary school teacher and TV host, interview, Tema, 12 June 1999

Ampene, Kwame, retired teacher and founder of Guan Congress, Anyinasu, Central Region, 3 Mar. 1999

Anim, Albert, cultural studies officer in Eastern Regional Ghana Education Service, jointly with Esther Otoo, Koforidua, 26 Apr. 1999

Appaenti, Maxwell Amoh, Twi teacher, Akropong, 12 Oct. 1998, 31 Dec. 1998

Asare, Kobina, art teacher, Kaneshie-Accra, 24 Oct. 1998

Asiedu Darko, Nana E. (Teacher Darko), retired music teacher, judge at cultural festivals and ɔkyeame, Larteh, 29 Dec. 1998, 19, 26 Feb. 1999, 9, 29 Mar. 1999, 2 July 1999

Duah, Mr., teacher, jointly with Mensah Abavon, Awukugua, 30 July 1999

Gyampo, F. A., retired arts and crafts teacher and painter, Accra, 12 Sept. 1998

Larbi, Yaw, teacher and judge at cultural festivals, Koforidua, 23 Mar. 1999, 20 July 1999

Mawεre-Opoku, A., professor of dance, Legon, 4, 6 Aug. 1997, 29 Oct. 1998, 10 Nov. 1998, 8 Dec. 1998, 11 Jan. 1999 (the three interviews in Oct.-Dec. 1998 were not taped)

Offei, Beatrice Duodua, teacher and chorister, Abiriw, 28 July 1999

Okae-Anti, W. E., retired Presbyterian minister and teacher, Tutu, 23 Oct. 1998, 27 Nov. 1998

Osei-Awuku, Mr., teacher, Awukugua, 10 Aug. 1999

Otoo, Esther, cultural studies officer, Eastern Regional Ghana Education Service, jointly with Albert Anim, Koforidua, 26 Apr. 1999

Reynolds, Gilbert Ofosu, retired teacher and musician, Mamfe, 24 Sept. 1998, 6 Oct. 1998, 2 Dec. 1998, 19 Jan. 1999, 3 June 1999

Sedofu, Stephen, judge at cultural festivals and dance officer at the Center for National Culture, Koforidua, 23 Mar. 1999

Tetteh, Margaret Rose, circuit supervisor, Twi teacher, and judge at cultural festivals, Akropong, 19 July 1999

Archival Records

Basel Mission Archives (microfilm), Yale University, Divinity School Library, New Haven, Conn.

D-10.4, 6. Nine school essays on the gods and fetishes of the Accra natives, 1875

D-10.4, 7. Essays on Homowo, 1876

D-10.4, 8. Erzählungen von Afrikaner/African Folk Tales. Ten school essays, ca. 1875 or 1876?

D-12, 1. English transcriptions of the documents in series D-1, 1828–51, translated by Dr. Hans Debrunner, 1956

Eastern Regional Archives, Koforidua

ADM KD 33/6/215. Young Pioneers, Eastern Region, 1962–66

ADM KD 33/6/466. Ghana Young Pioneers, 1966

ADM KD 33/6/503. Permits to drum, 1962–64

ERG 1/13/234. Festivals—General, 1964–1970

ERG 1/14/11. Ghana Young Pioneers, 1960–63

ERG 1/14/12. Arts Council reports, 1961–76

ERG 1/14/14. Disbanded Young Pioneers

Ghana National Archives, Accra

CSO 18/6/62. *Achimota Review, 1927–1937.* 1937. Achimota: Achimota Press

CSO 18/6/92. Report on Teacher Training, Achimota, 1933

CSO 18/6/93. Report on Teacher Training, Achimota, 1934

CSO 18/6/97. Teacher Training classes, Achimota, 1935

EC 6/3. Digest of articles on Ghana in the Basel Mission periodicals, 1828–51

RG 3/1/74. Advisory Committee on Vernacular Orthography, agenda and minutes, 1959–60

RG 3/1/205. Language in African education. Memorandum by H. S. Scott

RG 3/1/217. Educational policy of the Presbyterian Church of Ghana

RG 3/1/447. Young Pioneers, 1960

RG 3/1/590. Young Pioneers, 1962–65

RG 3/7/55. Eastern Region Arts Committee activities, 1961–63

RG 3/7/60. Drama—General, 1959–63

RG 3/7/146. Drumming and dancing, 1967–68

RG 3/7/250. Drumming and dancing, 1970–72

Other Published and Unpublished Works

Abrahams, Roger. 1993. Phantoms of Romantic Nationalism in Folkloristics. *Journal of American Folklore* 106:3–37.

Abu-Lughod, Lila. 1986. *Veiled Sentiments: Honor and Poetry in a Bedouin Society*. Berkeley: University of California Press.

Achimota College. 1932. *Report of the* [Achimota College] *Committee*. London: Government of the Gold Coast.

Addo-Fening, Robert. 1980. Akyem Abuakwa, 1874–1943: A Study of the Impact of Missionary Activities and Colonial Rule on a Traditional State. Ph.D. thesis, University of Ghana.

Addow, E. R. 1932–33. Native Drumming. 3 parts. *Teacher's Journal* 4:99–102, 181–87, 5:39–44.

Adinku, W. Ofotsu. 1996. Justifying Dance Education in Ghana. *Journal of Performing Arts* (Legon) 2 (1): 1–6.

Adjakly, Edoh. 1985. Practique de la Tradition Religieuse et Reproduction Sociale chez la Guen/Mina du Sud-Est du Togo. Geneva: Institut Universitaire d'Études du Développement.

Adubofuor, Samuel Brefo. 1994. Evangelical Parachurch Movements in Ghanaian Christianity, c. 1950–early 1990s. Ph.D. thesis, University of Edinburgh.

Agbodeka, Francis. 1977. *Achimota in the National Setting: A Unique Educational Experiment in West Africa*. Accra: Afram Publications.

Agyemang, Fred. 1988. *Amu the African: A Study in Vision and Courage*. Accra: Asempa Publications.

———. 1978. *We Presbyterians: Yɛn Presbyterianfo, wɔ Presbyterianbii, mi Presbyterianɔwo: 150th Anniversary of the Presbyterian Church of Ghana, 1828–1978*. Accra-North: Select Publications.

———. N.d. *Christian Messenger Centenary, 1883–1983*. Accra: Christian Messenger.

Ahearn, Laura. 2001. *Invitations to Love: Literacy, Love Letters, and Social Change in Nepal*. Ann Arbor: University of Michigan Press.

Aina, Tade Akin. 1992. Culture in the Context of National Development: The Nigerian Case. In *Culture and Nation Building*, ed. Ebun Clark and Dele Jegede. Lagos: National Council for Arts and Culture.

Allman, Jean Marie. 1990. The Youngmen and the Porcupine: Class, Nationalism and Asante's Struggle for Self-Determination, 1954–57. *Journal of African History* 31:263–79.

Alver, Brynjulf. 1989. Folklore and National Identity. In *Nordic Folklore: Recent Studies*, ed. Reimund Kvideland and Henning K. Sehmsdorf. Bloomington: Indiana University Press.

Amuwo, Ade Kunle. 2002. Nigeria's Academic Political Scientists Under the Babangida Military Junta. *African Studies Review* 45 (2): 93–121.

Anderson, Benedict. 1991. *Imagined Communities: Reflections on the Origin and Spread of Nationalism*. New York: Verso.

Anderson-Levitt, Kathryn, ed. 2003. *Local Meanings, Global Schooling: Anthropology and World Culture Theory*. New York: Palgrave.

Appadurai, Arjun. 1996. *Modernity at Large: Cultural Dimensions of Globalization*. Minneapolis: University of Minnesota Press.

Apter, Andrew. 1996. The Pan-African Nation: Oil Money and the Spectacle of Culture in Nigeria. *Public Culture* 8 (3): 441–66.

Arhin, Kwame. 1981. *Cultural Values and Religious Education. A Lecture to the Ghana National Association of Teachers, Seminar on Religious Education in Ghanaian Schools and Colleges*. 27 May. Pamphlet.

Ariès, Philippe. 1962. *Centuries of Childhood: A Social History of Family Life*, tr. Robert Baldick. New York: Vintage.

Asad, Talal, ed. 1973. *Anthropology and the Colonial Encounter*. Atlantic Highlands: Humanities Press.

Askew, Kelly M. 2002. *Performing the Nation: Swahili Music and Cultural Politics in Tanzania*. Chicago: University of Chicago Press.

Austin, Dennis. 1964. *Politics in Ghana, 1946–1960*. Oxford: Oxford University Press.

Bakhtin, M. M. 1984. *The Dialogic Imagination: Four Essays*, ed. Michael Holquist, tr. Caryl Emerson and Michael Holquist. Austin: University of Texas Press.

Ball, Stephen J. 1983. Imperialism, Social Control and the Colonial Curriculum in Africa. *Journal of Curriculum Studies* 15 (3): 237–63.

Banks, James. 1992. Multicultural Education: Approaches, Development, and Dimensions. In *Cultural Diversity and the Schools*, vol. 1, ed. James Lynch, Celia Modgil, and Sohan Modgil. London: Falmer Press.

———. 1989. Multicultural Education: Characteristics and Goals. In *Multicultural Education: Issues and Perspectives*, ed. James Banks and Cherry A. McGee Banks. Boston: Allyn & Bacon.

———. 1984. *Teaching Strategies for Ethnic Studies*. 3rd ed. Boston: Allyn & Bacon.

Barber, Karin. 2000. *The Generation of Plays: Yoruba Popular Life in Theater*. Bloomington: Indiana University Press.

Barber, Karin, John Collins, and Alain Ricard. 1997. *West African Popular Theatre*. Bloomington: Indiana University Press.

Bayart, Jean-François. 1993. *The State in Africa: The Politics of the Belly*, tr. Mary Harper and Christopher and Elizabeth Harrison. London: Longman.

Bearth, Thomas. 1998. J. G. Christaller, A Holistic View of Language and Culture, and C. C. Reindorf's History. In The Recovery of the West African Past: African Pastors and African History in the Nineteenth Century, C. C. Reindorf and Samuel Johnson, ed. Paul Jenkins. Basel: Basler Afrika Bibliographien.

Bediako, Kwame. 1995. Christianity in Africa: The Revival of a Non-Western Religion. Edinburgh: Edinburgh University Press.

Beidelman, Thomas O. 1981. Contradictions Between the Sacred and the Secular Life: The Church Missionary Society in Ukaguru, Tanzania, East Africa, 1876–1914. Comparative Studies in Society and History 23 (Jan.): 73–95.

Bellman, Beryl. 1984. The Language of Secrecy: Symbols and Metaphors in Poro Ritual. New Brunswick, N.J.: Rutgers University Press.

Ben Abdallah, Mohammed, and Margaret A. Novicki. 1987. Interview with Mohammed Ben Abdallah, Secretary of Education and Culture, Ghana. Africa Report 32 (4): 14–18.

Bendix, Regina. 1997. In Search of Authenticity: The Formation of Folklore Studies. Madison: University of Wisconsin Press.

———. 1992. National Sentiment in the Enactment and Discourse of Swiss Political Ritual. American Ethnologist 19 (4): 768–90.

Bledsoe, Caroline. 1990. School Fees and the Marriage Process for Mende Girls in Sierra Leone. In Beyond the Second Sex: New Directions in the Anthropology of Gender, ed. Peggy Reeves Sanday and Ruth Gallagher Goodenough. Philadelphia: University of Pennsylvania Press.

Bloch, Maurice. 1993. The Uses of Schooling and Literacy in a Zafimaniry village. In Cross-cultural Approaches to Literacy, ed. Brian Street. Cambridge: Cambridge University Press.

Boama, I. E. 1954. Reviews of Adɛɛ by J. H. K. Nketia and Odwiratwa by E. A. Tabi. Kristofo Sɛnkekafo 44 (Sept.): 12.

Boateng, F. Yao. 1975. The Catechism and the Rod: Presbyterian Education in Ghana. In African Reactions to Mission Education, ed. Edward H. Berman. New York: Teachers' College Press.

Boateng, Otto Ampofo. 1963. An Insight into the Musical Culture of Africa Through Ghana Gates. Ph.D. dissertation, Hochwürdigen Theologischen Fakultät der Martin-Luther Universität.

Boli, John, Francisco O. Ramirez, and John W. Meyer. 1985. Explaining the Origins and Expansion of Mass Education. Comparative Education Review 29 (2): 145–70.

Bourdieu, Pierre, and Jean-Claude Passeron. 1990. Reproduction in Education: Society and Culture, tr. Richard Nice. 2nd ed. London: Sage.

Boyer, Dominic C. 2000. On the Sedimentation and Accreditation of Social Knowledges of Difference: Mass Media, Journalism, and the Reproduction of East/West Alterities in Unified Germany. Cultural Anthropology 15 (4): 459–91.

Briggs, Charles L. 1986. *Learning How to Ask: A Sociolinguistic Appraisal of the Role of the Interview in Social Science Research*. Cambridge: Cambridge University Press.

Brokensha, David. 1966. *Social Change at Larteh, Ghana*. Oxford: Clarendon Press.

Burchell, Graham. 1996. Liberal Government and Techniques of the Self. In *Foucault and Political Reason: Liberalism, Neo-liberalism, and the Rationalities of Government*, ed. Andrew Barry, Thomas Osborne, and Nikolas Rose. Chicago: University of Chicago Press.

Burke, Charlanne. 2000. They Cut Segametsi into Parts: Ritual Murder, Youth, and the Politics of Knowledge in Botswana. *Anthropological Quarterly* 73 (4): 204–14.

Cantwell, Robert. 1999. Habitus, Ethnomimesis: A Note on the Logic of Practice. *Journal of Folklore Research* 36 (2/3): 219–34.

Carby, Hazel. 1992. The Multicultural Wars. In *Black Popular Culture*, ed. Gina Dent. Seattle: Bay Press.

Carlson, Marvin. 1990. *Theatre Semiotics: Signs of Life*. Bloomington: Indiana University Press.

Certeau, Michel de. 1984. *The Practice of Everyday Life*, tr. Steven F. Randall. Berkeley: University of California Press.

Chabal, Patrick. 1992. *Power in Africa: An Essay in Political Interpretation*. New York: St. Martin's Press.

Chatterjee, Partha. 1999. The Nation and Its Fragments: Colonial and Postcolonial Histories. In *The Partha Chatterjee Omnibus*. New Delhi: Oxford University Press.

Chazan, Naomi. 1983. *An Anatomy of Ghanaian Politics: Managing Political Recession, 1969–1982*. Boulder, Colo.: Westview Press.

Chernoff, John Miller. 1979. *African Rhythm and African Sensibility: Aesthetics and Social Action in African Musical Idioms*. Chicago: University of Chicago Press.

Chinebuah, I. K. 1970. The Education Review Report and the Study of Ghanaian Languages. *Ghana Teacher's Journal* 1 (2): 22–45.

Christaller, J. G. 1933. *Dictionary of the Asante and Fante Language Called Tshi* [Twi]. 2nd ed. Basel: Basel Evangelical Missionary Society.

Chun, Allen. 2000. From Text to Context: How Anthropology Makes Its Subject. *Cultural Anthropology* 15 (4): 570–95.

Clarke, John. 2002. Turning Inside Out? Globalisation, Neo-liberalism, and Welfare States. Paper presented at the joint CASCA/SANA conference, Windsor, Ontario.

Clignet, Remi, and Philip Foster. 1971. Convergence and Divergence in Educational Development in Ghana and the Ivory Coast. In *Ghana and the Ivory Coast: Perspectives on Modernization*, ed. Philip Foster and Aristide R. Zolberg. Chicago: University of Chicago Press.

Cocchiara, Guiseppe. 1981. *The History of Folklore in Europe*, tr. John H. McDaniel. Philadelphia: Institute for the Study of Human Issues.

Coe, Cati. 2002. Educating an African Leadership: Achimota and the Teaching of African Culture in the Gold Coast. *Africa Today* 49 (3): 23–46.

———. 2001. Learning How to Find Out: Theories of Knowledge and Learning in Field Research. *Field Methods* 13 (4): 392–411.

———. 1999. The Education of the Folk: Peasant Schools and Folklore Scholarship. *Journal of American Folklore* 113 (447): 20–43.

———. 1994. Caught Between Two Worlds: A Professional Development Initiative in Multicultural Education. Report for PATHS/PRISM.

Cohen, Abner. 1981. *The Politics of Elite Culture.* Berkeley: University of California Press.

Cohn, Bernard S. 1984. The Census, Social Structure and Objectification in South Asia. *Folk* 26:25–49.

Cole, Catherine M. 2001. *Ghana's Concert Party Theatre.* Bloomington: Indiana University Press.

Colonna, Fanny. 1997. Educating Conformity in French Colonial Algeria, tr. Barbara Harshaw. In *Tensions of Empire: Colonial Culture in a Bourgeois World,* ed. Frederick Cooper and Ann Laura Stoler. Berkeley: University of California Press.

Comaroff, Jean. 1985. *Body of Power, Spirit of Resistance: The Culture and History of a South African People.* Chicago: University of Chicago Press.

Comaroff, Jean, and John Comaroff. 1991. *Of Revelation and Revolution: Christianity, Colonialism and Consciousness in South Africa,* vol. 1. Chicago: University of Chicago Press.

Comaroff, John L. 1997. Images of Empire, Contests of Conscience: Models of Colonial Domination in South Africa. In *Tensions of Empire: Colonial Culture in a Bourgeois World,* ed. Frederick Cooper and Ann Laura Stoler. Berkeley: University of California Press.

Cruise O'Brien, Donal B. 1996. A Lost Generation? Youth Identity and State Decay in West Africa. In *Postcolonial Identities in Africa,* ed. Richard Werbner and Terence Ranger. London: Zed Books.

Daddieh, Cyril. 1995. Education Adjustment Under Severe Recessionary Pressures: The Case of Ghana. In *Beyond Economic Liberalization in Africa: Structural Adjustment and the Alternatives,* ed. Kidane Mengisteab and B. Ikubolajah Logan. London: Zed Books.

Dah, Jonas N. 1983. Missionary Motivations and Methods: A Critical Examination of the Basel Mission in Cameroon, 1886–1914. Ph.D. dissertation, University of Basel.

De Boeck, Filip. 1996. Postcolonialism, Power and Identity: Local and Global Perspectives from Zaire. In *Postcolonial Identities in Africa,* ed. Richard Werbner and Terence Ranger. London: Zed Books.

Debrunner, Hans W. 1967. *A History of Christianity in Ghana.* Accra: Waterville Publishing.

Dedy, Séri. 1984. Musique Traditionnelle et Développement National en Côte-d'Ivoire. *Tiers Monde* 25 (97): 109–24.

Derman-Sparks, Louise, and the ABC Task Force. 1989. *Anti-Bias Curriculum: Tools for Empowering Young Children.* Washington, D.C.: National Association for the Education of Young Children.

Dominguez, Virginia R. 1992. Invoking Culture: The Messy Side of "Cultural Politics." *South Atlantic Quarterly* 91 (1): 19–42.

Dunn, John, and A. F. Robertson. 1973. *Dependence and Opportunity: Political Change in Ahafo.* Cambridge: Cambridge University Press.

Durham, Deborah. 2000. Youth and the Social Imagination in Africa. *Anthropological Quarterly* 73 (3): 113–20.

Ebron, Paulla. 2002. *Performing Africa.* Princeton, N.J.: Princeton University Press.

Eckert, Penelope. 1989. *Jocks and Burnouts: Social Categories and Identities in the High School.* New York: Teachers College Press.

Egblewogbe, E. Y. 1975. *Games and Songs as Education Media (A Case Study among the Ewes of Ghana).* Accra-Tema: Ghana Publishing Co.

Fabian, Johannes. 1983. Missions and the Colonization of African Languages: Developments in the Former Belgian Congo. *Canadian Journal of African Studies* 17 (2): 165–87.

———. 1971. *Jamaa: A Charismatic Movement in Katanga.* Evanston, Ill.: Northwestern University Press.

Falnes, Oscar J. 1933. *National Romanticism in Norway.* New York: Columbia University Press.

Ferguson, James. 1999. *Expectations of Modernity: Myths and Meanings of Urban Life on the Zambian Copperbelt.* Berkeley: University of California Press.

———. 1994. *The Anti-Politics Machine: "Development," Depoliticization, and Bureaucratic Power in Lesotho.* Minneapolis: University of Minnesota Press.

Ferme, Mariane C. 2001. *The Underneath of Things: Violence, History, and the Everyday in Sierra Leone.* Berkeley: University of California Press.

Fiedler, Klaus. 1996. *Christianity and African Culture: Conservative German Protestant Missions in Tanzania, 1900–1940.* Leiden: E. J. Brill.

Foley, Douglas E. 1990. *Learning Capitalist Culture: Deep in the Heart of Tejas.* Philadelphia: University of Pennsylvania.

Ford, Rosalee. 1997. Educational Anthropology: Early History and Educationalist Contributors. In *Education and Cultural Process: Anthropological Approaches,* ed. George D. Spindler. Prospect Heights, Ill.: Waveland Press.

Foster, Philip. 1965. *Education and Social Change in Ghana.* Chicago: University of Chicago Press.

Foster, Robert J. 1991. Making National Cultures in the Global Ecumene. *Annual Review of Anthropology* 20:235–60.

Foucault, Michel. 1979. *Discipline and Punish: The Birth of the Prison.* New York: Vintage.

Friedman, Jonathan. 2003. Modernity and Other Traditions. In *Critically Modern: Alternatives, Alterities, and Anthropologies*, ed. Bruce Knauft. Bloomington: Indiana University Press.

Gable, Eric. 2000. The Culture Development Club: Youth, Neo-Tradition, and the Construction of Youth in Guinea-Bissau. *Anthropological Quarterly* 73 (4): 195–203.

Gamble, Harry. 2002. Developing Cultures: Debates over Education in French West Africa, 1930–1950. Ph.D. dissertation, New York University.

Geertz, Clifford. 1963. The Integrative Revolution: Primordial Sentiments and Civil Politics in the New States. In *Old Societies and New States: The Quest for Modernity in Asia and Africa*, ed. Geertz. London: Free Press of Glencoe.

Ghana, Republic of. 1998. Ministry of Education and Culture. *Ghanaian Languages and Culture (Basic Stages 7–9)*. Accra.

———. 1997. National Commission on Children. *State of the Child Report: Akuapem North District*. Accra.

———. 1996. S. K. Obeng, director-general, Ghana Education Service, letter of 2 Oct.: Guidelines for the Implementation of Improved School Education Reforms.

———. [1995?]. Ministry of Education and Culture. Update on the Educational Reform Programme. Unpublished document.

———. 1991. National Commission on Culture. The Cultural Policy of Ghana. Unpublished document.

———. 1989a. Curriculum Research and Development Division. *Cultural Studies for Junior Secondary Schools: Pupil's Book 1–3*. Legon-Accra: Adwinsa Publications.

———. 1989b. Statistical Service. *Population Census of Ghana: Special Report on Localities by Local Authorities, Eastern Region*. Accra.

———. 1988a. *Cultural Studies Syllabus for Primary Schools*. Legon-Accra: Adwinsa Publications.

———. 1988b. Ministry of Education and Culture. The Educational Reform Programme: Policy Guidelines on Basic Education. Unpublished document, 17 Aug.

———. 1984. Statistical Service. *Population Census of Ghana: Special Report on Localities by Local Authorities, Eastern Region*. Accra.

———. 1974. Ministry of Education. *The New Structure and Education of Ghana*. Accra.

———. 1967. Ministry of Information. *Report of the Education Review Committee, Appointed by the National Liberation Council*. Accra.

———. N.d. Ghana Education Service, Cultural Studies Division. Achievements of the PNDC Government in the Field of Cultural Studies. Unpublished document.

Gifford, Paul. 1998. *African Christianity: Its Public Role*. Bloomington: Indiana University Press.

Gilbert, Michelle. 1997. "No Condition Is Permanent": Ethnic Construction and the Use of History in Akuapem. *Africa* 67 (4): 501–33.

Gramsci, Antonio. 1988. *An Antonio Gramsci Reader: Selected Writings, 1916–1935*, ed. David Forgacs. New York: Schocken Books.

Grindal, Bruce T. 1972. *Growing Up in Two Worlds: Education and Transition among the Sisala of Northern Ghana*. Case Studies in Education and Culture. New York: Holt, Rinehart & Winston.

Guss, David M. 2000. *The Festive State: Race, Ethnicity, and Nationalism as Cultural Performance*. Berkeley: University of California Press.

Guthrie, Grace Pung. 1985. *A School Divided: An Ethnography of Bilingual Education in a Chinese Community*. Hillsdale, N.J.: Lawrence Erlbaum Associates.

Haenger, Peter. 2000. *Slaves and Slave Holders on the Gold Coast: Towards an Understanding of Social Bondage in West Africa*. Basel: P. Schlettwein.

Hagan, George P. 1993. Nkrumah's Cultural Policy. In *The Life and Work of Kwame Nkrumah*, ed. Kwame Arhin. Trenton, N.J.: Africa World Press.

Hall, Peter. 1965. *Autobiography of Reverend Peter Hall, Moderator of the Presbyterian Church of Ghana*. Accra: Waterville Press.

Halldén, Erik. 1968. *The Culture Policy of the Basel Mission in the Cameroons, 1886–1905*. Lund: Berlingska Boktryckeriet.

Handler, Richard. 1988. *Nationalism and the Politics of Culture in Quebec*. Madison: University of Wisconsin Press.

Hayes, Carlton J. H. 1927. Contributions of Herder to the Doctrine of Nationalism. *American Historical Review* 32 (4): 719–36.

Heath, Shirley Brice. 1983. *Ways with Words: Language, Life, and Work in Communities and Classrooms*. Cambridge: Cambridge University Press.

Herzfeld, Michael. 1997. *Cultural Intimacy: Social Poetics of the Nation-State*. New York: Routledge.

Hess, Janet. 2001. Exhibiting Ghana: Display, Documentary, and "National" Art in the Nkrumah Era. *African Studies Review* 44 (1): 59–77.

Hill, Polly. 1972. The Migration of Cocoa Farmers, 1890–1914. In *Akwapim Handbook*, ed. David Brokensha. Accra-Tema: Ghana Publishing Corp.

———. 1963. *The Migrant Cocoa-farmers of Southern Ghana: A Study in Rural Capitalism*. Cambridge: Cambridge University Press.

Holland, Dorothy, William Lachicotte Jr., Debra Skinner, and Carole Cain. 1998. *Identity and Agency in Cultural Worlds*. Cambridge, Mass.: Harvard University Press.

Hornberger, Nancy H. 1988. *Bilingual Education and Language Maintenance: A Southern Peruvian Quechua Case*. Dordrecht, Holland: Foris Publications.

Hutchful, Eboe. 2002. *Ghana's Adjustment Experience: The Paradox of Reform*. Geneva: United Nations Research Institute for Social Development.

Institute of African Studies. 1989. *Memorandum on Cultural Studies in Ghanaian Secondary Schools*. Pamphlet.

Jega, Attahiru. 1995. Nigerian Universities and Academic Staff Under Academic Rule. *Committee for Academic Freedom in Africa Newsletter* 8: 7–11.

Jenkins, Paul. 1980. Villagers as Missionaries: Württemberg Pietism as a 19th Century Missionary Movement. *Missology: An International Review* 8 (4): 425–32.

————. 1973. A Forgotten Vernacular Periodical. *Mitteilungen der Basler Afrika Bibliographien* 9:27–33.

Jenkins, Ray P. 1998. C. C. Reindorf's "Traditions and Historical Facts": From Gesichte des Volkes der Goldküste to a Provisional National History of the Gold Coast, 1889–1895. In *The Recovery of the West African Past: African Pastors and African History in the Nineteenth Century, C. C. Reindorf and Samuel Johnson*, ed. Paul Jenkins. Basel: Basler Afrika Bibliographien.

————. 1990. Intellectuals, Publication Outlets and "Past-Relationships": Some Observations on the Emergence of Early Gold Coast/Ghanaian Historiography in the Cape Coast-Accra-Akropong Triangle, c. 1880–1917. In *Self Assertion and Brokerage: Early Cultural Nationalism in West Africa*, ed. P. F. de Moraes Farias and Karin Barber. Birmingham: Centre of West African Studies, University of Birmingham.

Johnson, Marion. 1972. The Migration. In *Akwapim Handbook*, ed. David Brokensha. Accra-Tema: Ghana Publishing Corp.

Jones, Adam. 1998. Reindorf the Historian. In *The Recovery of the West African Past: African Pastors and African History in the Nineteenth Century, C. C. Reindorf and Samuel Johnson*, ed. Paul Jenkins. Basel: Basler Afrika Bibliographien.

Kaomea, Julie. 2000. A Curriculum of Aloha? Colonialism and Tourism in Hawai'i's Elementary Textbooks. *Curriculum Inquiry* 30 (3): 319–44.

Kaspin, Deborah. 1993. Chewa Visions and Revisions of Power: Transformations of the Nyau Dance in Central Malawi. In *Modernity and Its Malcontents: Ritual and Power in Postcolonial Africa*, ed. Jean Comaroff and John Comaroff. Chicago: University of Chicago Press.

Kavanagh, James H. 1995. Ideology. In *Critical Terms for Literary Study*, ed. Frank Lentricchia and Thomas McLaughlin. Chicago: University of Chicago Press.

Kerr, David. 1995. *African Popular Theatre*. London: James Currey.

Kimble, David. 1963. *A Political History of Ghana: The Rise of Gold Coast Nationalism, 1850–1928*. Oxford: Clarendon Press.

Kirshenblatt-Gimblett, Barbara. 2000. Folklorists in Public: Reflections on Cultural Brokerage in the United States and Germany. *Journal of Folklore Research* 37 (1): 1–21.

Knauft, Bruce, ed. 2002. *Critically Modern: Alternatives, Alterities, Anthropologies*. Bloomington: Indiana University Press.

Kruger, Loren. 1992. *The National Stage: Theatre and Cultural Legitimation in England, France, and America*. Chicago: University of Chicago Press.

Kwamena-Poh, M. A. 1980. Vision and Achievement: A Hundred and Fifty Years of the Presbyterian Church in Ghana, 1828–1978. Unpublished manuscript.

————. 1973. *Government and Politics in the Akuapem State, 1730–1850*. Evanston, Ill.: Northwestern University Press.

———. 1972. History. In *Akwapim Handbook*, ed. David Brokensha. Accra-Tema: Ghana Publishing Corp.

Ladouceur, Paul André. 1979. *Chiefs and Politicians: The Politics of Regionalism in Northern Ghana*. London: Longman.

Lave, Jean. 1993. The Practice of Learning. In *Understanding Practice: Perspectives on Activity and Context*, ed. Seth Chaiklin and Jean Lave. Cambridge: Cambridge University Press.

Lave, Jean, and Etienne Wenger. 1991. *Situated Learning: Legitimate Peripheral Participation*. Cambridge: Cambridge University Press.

Lavy, Victor. 1996. School Supply Constraints and Children's Educational Outcomes in Rural Ghana. *Journal of Development Economics* 51:291–314.

Leis, Philip E. 1972. *Enculturation and Socialization in an Ijaw Village*. New York: Holt, Rinehart & Winston.

Leistyna, Pepi. 2002. *Defining and Designing Multiculturalism: One School System's Efforts*. Albany: State University of New York Press.

Lentz, Carola, and Paul Nugent, eds. 2000. *Ethnicity in Ghana: The Limits of Invention*. London: Macmillan.

Levinson, Bradley A. 1999. Resituating the Place of Educational Discourse in Anthropology. *American Anthropologist* 101 (3): 594–604.

Levinson, Bradley A., and Dorothy Holland. 1996. The Cultural Production of the Educated Person: An Introduction. In *The Cultural Production of the Educated Person: Critical Ethnographies of Schooling and Local Practice*, ed. Bradley A. Levinson, Douglas E. Foley, and Dorothy C. Holland. Albany: State University of New York Press.

Löfgren, Orvar. 1989. The Nationalization of Culture. *Ethnologia Europaea* 19 (1): 5–24.

Luykx, Aurolyn. 1999. *The Citizen Factory: Schooling and Cultural Production in Bolivia*. Albany: State University of New York Press.

MacGaffey, Janet, and Rémy Bazenguissa-Ganga. 2000. *Congo-Paris: Transnational Traders on the Margins of the Law*. Oxford: James Currey.

Mahmood, Saba. 2001. Feminist Theory, Embodiment, and the Docile Agent: Some Reflections on the Egyptian Islamic Revival. *Cultural Anthropology* 16 (2): 202–36.

Mamdani, Mahmood. 1996. *Citizen and Subject: Contemporary Africa and the Legacy of Late Colonialism*. Princeton, N.J.: Princeton University Press.

Mans, Minette. 2000. Creating a Cultural Policy for Namibia. *Arts Education Policy Review* 101 (2): 11–17.

Marshall, Ruth. 1993. "Power in the Name of Jesus": Social Transformation and Pentecostalism in Western Nigeria "Revisited." In *Legitimacy and the State in Twentieth-Century Africa*, ed. Terence Ranger and Olufemi Vaughn. Hampshire: Macmillan.

Masemann, Vandra. 1974. The "Hidden Curriculum" of a West African Girls' Boarding School. *Canadian Journal of African Studies* 8 (3): 479–94.

Mawere-Opoku, A. N.d. African Dance Perspectives: A Review of Basic Dance Concepts: The Dance in Traditional African Societies. Unpublished manuscript.

Mbembe, Achille. 1992. Provisional Notes on the Postcolony. *Africa* 62 (1): 3–37.

McNeil, Linda M. 1986. *Contradictions of Control: School Structure and School Knowledge*. London: Routledge & Kegan Paul.

McWilliam, H. O. A., and M. A. Kwamena-Poh. 1975. *The Development of Education in Ghana: An Outline*. 3rd ed. London: Longman.

Meyer, Birgit. 2002. Christianity and the Ewe Nation: German Pietist Missionaries, Ewe Converts, and the Politics of Culture. *Journal of Religion in Africa* 32 (2): 167–99.

———. 1999a. Popular Ghanaian Cinema and "African Heritage." *Africa Today* 46 (2): 93–116.

———. 1999b. *Translating the Devil: Religion and Modernity among the Ewe in Ghana*. London: Edinburgh University Press.

Meyer, John W., David H. Kamens, and Aaron Benavot. 1992. *School Knowledge for the Masses: World Models and National Primary Curricular Categories in the Twentieth Century*. Washington, D.C.: Falmer Press.

Middleton, John. 1983. One Hundred and Fifty Years of Christianity in a Ghanaian Town. *Africa* 53 (3): 2–19.

Modell, John. 1994. The Developing Schoolchild as Historical Actor. *Comparative Education Review* 38 (1): 1–9.

Morna, Colleen Lowe. 1989. An Exercise in Educational Reform. *Africa Report* 34 (6): 34–37.

Mosse, George L. 1964. *The Crisis of German Ideology: Intellectual Origins of the Third Reich*. New York: Grosset & Dunlap.

Murphy, William P. 1980. Secret Knowledge as Property and Power in Kpelle Society: Elders Versus Youth. *Africa* 56 (2): 193–207.

Nieto, Sonia. 1992. *Affirming Diversity: The Sociopolitical Context of Multicultural Education*. New York: Longman.

Nigerian Folklore Society, ed. 1987. *Folklore and the Challenge of National Integration*. Proceedings of the 5th annual congress of the Folklore Society, 1985. Ile-Ife: Folklore Society.

———, ed. 1985. *Folklore and National Development*. Proceedings of the 4th annual congress of the Folklore Society, 1984. Ile-Ife: Folklore Society.

Nketia, J. H. Kwabena. 1997. The Importance of Language as an Aspect of Culture. Address given at the launching of *Akan Orthography* and *Akan Wordlist* by the Bureau of Ghana Languages, Ghana National Association of Teachers' Hall, Accra, Ghana, 12 June.

———. 1974. *The Music of Africa*. New York: W. W. Norton.

———. 1963a. *African Music in Ghana*. Evanston, Ill.: Northwestern University Press.

————. 1963b. *Folk Songs of Ghana*. London: Oxford University Press.

Odamtten, S. K. 1993. *The Search for Educational Goals in Independent Ghana*. Accra: Waterville Press.

Ofei, Yirenkyi. N.d. *Akropong Nnwontofo Fekuw Abakɔsɛm, 1930–1973*. Ghana: Presbyterian Press.

Oku-Ampofo, Nyamekye. 1981. The Missionary Role of Selected West Indian Families of the Basel Mission in Ghana. M.A. thesis, University of Ghana.

Omenyo, Cephas Narh. 1994. Charismatic Revival in the Mainline Churches: The Case of the Bible and Study Prayer Group of the Presbyterian Church of Ghana. M.A. thesis, University of Ghana.

Ong, Walter J. 1982. *Orality and Literacy: The Technologizing of the Word*. New York: Routledge.

Opoku, A. A. 1970. *Festivals of Ghana*. Accra: Ghana Publishing Corp.

Opondo, Patricia A. 2000. Arts Education in Kenya. *Arts Education Policy Review* 101 (3): 18–24.

Oquaye, Mike. 1996. Youth, Politics, and Society in Ghana. In *Civil Society in Ghana*, ed. F. K. Drah and Mike Oquaye. Accra: Friedrich Ebert Stiftung.

Osofisan, Babefemi Adeyemi. 1974. The Origins of Drama in West Africa: A Study of the Development of Drama from the Traditional Forms to the Modern Theatre in English and French. Ph.D. dissertation, University of Ibadan.

Peasah, J. A. 1975. Politics in Abuakwa. In *Politicians and Soldiers in Ghana, 1966–1972*, ed. Dennis Austin and Robin Luckham. London: Frank Cass.

Peil, Margaret. 1995. Ghanaian Education as Seen from an Accra Suburb. *International Journal of Educational Development* 15 (3): 289–305.

Pelissier, Catherine. 1991. The Anthropology of Teaching and Learning. *Annual Review of Anthropology* 20: 75–95.

Peshkin, Alan. 1972. *Kanuri Schoolchildren: Education and Social Mobilization in Nigeria*. New York: Holt, Rinehart & Winston.

Phelps-Stokes Commission. 1922. *Education in Africa*. New York: Phelps-Stokes Fund.

Philips, Susan Urmston. 1983. *Invisible Culture: Communication in Classroom and Community on the Warm Springs Reservation*. New York: Longman.

Platt, Tony. 2002. Desegregating Multiculturalism. *Social Justice* 29 (4): 41–46.

Pobee, John S. 1977. *Kwame Nkrumah and the Church in Ghana, 1949–1966*. Accra: Asempa Publishers.

Ranger, Terence O. 1986. Religious Movements and Politics in Sub-Saharan Africa. *African Studies Review* 29 (2): 1–69.

Rathbone, Richard. 2000. *Nkrumah and the Chiefs: The Politics of Chieftaincy in Ghana, 1951–1960*. Accra: F. Reimmer.

Rattray, R. S. 1929. *Ashanti Law and Constitution*. London: Oxford University Press.

————. 1923. *Ashanti*. Oxford: Clarendon Press.

Raum, O. F. 1940. *Chaga Childhood: A Description of Indigenous Education in an East African Tribe*. London: Oxford University Press.

Read, Margaret. 1987 [1968]. Children of Their Fathers: Growing Up among the Ngoni of Malawi. Prospect Heights, Ill.: Waveland Press.

Reed-Danahay, Deborah. 1996. *Education and Identity in Rural France: The Politics of Schooling*. Cambridge: Cambridge University Press.

Report of the Education Committee, 1937–41. 1942. Accra: Gold Coast Government Printer.

Reynolds, Rev. Edward. N.d. *Akropong Akuapem Presbyterian Church: 1835–1985*. Accra: Presbyterian Press.

Richards, Paul. 1996. *Fighting for the Rain Forest: War, Youth, and Resources in Sierra Leone*. Portsmouth, Eng.: Heinemann.

Rockwell, Elsie. 1994. Schools of the Revolution: Enacting and Contesting State Forms in Tlaxcala, 1910–1930. In *Everyday Forms of State Formation: Revolution and the Negotiation of Rule in Modern Mexico*, ed. Gilbert M. Joseph and Daniel Nugent. Durham, N.C.: Duke University Press.

Rofel, Lisa. 1999. *Other Modernities: Gendered Yearnings in China After Socialism*. Berkeley: University of California Press.

Samper, David. 1997. "Love, Peace, and Unity": Romantic Nationalism and the Role of Oral Literature in Kenya's Secondary Schools. *Folklore Forum* 28 (1): 29–47.

Scadding, Helen. 1989. Junior Secondary Schools: An Educational Initiative in Ghana. *Compare* 19 (1): 43–48.

Scanlon, David G. 1966. Introduction. In *Church, State, and Education in Africa*, ed. Scanlon. New York: Teachers' College Press.

Scott, James. 1998. *Seeing Like a State: How Certain Schemes to Improve the Human Condition Have Failed*. New Haven, Conn.: Yale University Press.

———. 1985. *Weapons of the Weak: Everyday Forms of Peasant Resistance*. New Haven, Conn.: Yale University Press.

Sefa Dei, George J. 1993. Learning in the Time of Structural Adjustment Policies: The Ghanaian Experience. *Canadian and International Education* 22 (1): 43–65.

Sekyi, Kobina. 1997. *"The Blinkards," a Comedy, and "The Anglo-Fante," a Short Story*. Osu-Accra: Readwide/Heinemann Publications.

Sharp, Lesley Alexandra. 2002. *The Sacrificed Generation: Youth, History, and the Colonized Mind in Madagascar*. Berkeley: University of California Press.

Shaw, Rosalind. 2002. *Memories of the Slave Trade: Ritual and the Historical Imagination in Sierra Leone*. Chicago: University of Chicago Press.

Shore, Cris, and Susan Wright. 1997. Policy: A New Field for Anthropology. In *Anthropology of Policy: Critical Perspectives on Governance and Power*, ed. Shore and Wright. London: Routledge.

Simon, Erica. 1960. *Réveil National et Culture Populaire en Scandinavia: La Genèse de la Højskole Nordique, 1848–1878*. Copenhagen: Scandinavian University Books.

Smith, Noel. 1966. *The Presbyterian Church of Ghana, 1835–1960: A Younger Church in a Changing Society*. Accra: Ghana Universities Press.

Stambach, Amy. 2000. *Lessons from Mount Kilimanjaro: Schooling, Community, and Gender in East Africa*. New York: Routledge.

Stoler, Ann Laura, and Frederick Cooper. 1997. Between Metropole and Colony: Rethinking a Research Agenda. In *Tensions of Empire: Colonial Culture in a Bourgeois World*, ed. Cooper and Stoler. Berkeley: University of California Press.

Straker, James. 2002. Ideologies of Schooling and "Cultural Revolution" in Guinea: Revisiting the Emergence of Centres d'Enseignement Revolutionnaires. Paper presented at the annual African Studies Association meeting, Washington, D.C.

Street, Brian V., ed. 1993. *Cross-Cultural Approaches to Literacy*. Cambridge: Cambridge University Press.

———. 1984. *Literacy in Theory and Practice*. Cambridge: Cambridge University Press.

Stuiver, Jochem Hans. 1995. Gospel, Context and Confidence: The Quest for Power. Paper for Ministerial Training of Netherlands Reformed Church, University of Utrecht.

Thomas, Nicholas. 1994. *Colonialism's Culture: Anthropology, Travel and Government*. Princeton, N.J.: Princeton University Press.

Thorne, Susan. 1997. "The Conversion of Englishmen and the Conversion of World Inseparable": Missionary Imperialism and the Language of Class in Early Industrial Britain. In *Tensions of Empire: Colonial Culture in a Bourgeois World*, ed. Frederick Cooper and Ann Laura Stoler. Berkeley: University of California Press.

Todorov, Tzvetan. 1984. *Mikhail Bakhtin: The Dialogical Principle*. Minneapolis: University of Minnesota Press.

Turino, Thomas. 2000. *Nationalists, Cosmopolitans, and Popular Music*. Chicago: University of Chicago Press.

Turner, Terence. 1993. Anthropology and Multiculturalism: What Is Anthropology That Multiculturalists Should Be Mindful of It? *Cultural Anthropology* 8 (4): 411–29.

UNESCO. 1995. *Looking Backwards, Looking Forwards: Culture and Development Conference, Johannesburg, April–May 1993*. Bellville: Mayibuye Books.

———. 1981. *Cultural Development: Some Regional Experiences*. Paris: UNESCO Press.

University of Ghana. 1992. *African Studies: The Vision and the Reality. Open Day of the Institute of African Studies and the School of Performing Arts*. 13 March. Pamphlet.

Urciuoli, Bonnie. 1999. Producing Multiculturalism in Higher Education: Who's Producing What for Whom? *Qualitative Studies in Education* 12 (3): 287–98.

Vail, Leroy, ed. 1989. *The Creation of Tribalism in Southern Africa*. London: James Currey.

Vaughn, Mary Kay. 1997. *Cultural Politics in Revolution: Teachers, Peasants, and Schools in Mexico, 1930–1940*. Tucson: University of Arizona Press.

Verdery, Katherine. 1990. The Production and Defense of "The Romanian Nation," 1900 to World War II. In *Nationalist Ideologies and the Production of National Cultures*, ed. Richard G. Fox. Washington, D.C.: American Anthropological Association.

Wåhlin, Vagn. 1980. The Growth of Bourgeois and Popular Movements in Denmark, ca. 1830–1870. *Scandinavian Journal of History* 5 : 151–83.

Weber, Eugen. 1976. *Peasants into Frenchmen: The Modernization of Rural France, 1870–1914*. Stanford, Calif.: Stanford University Press.

Weber, Max. 1958. *The Protestant Ethic and the Spirit of Capitalism*, tr. Talcott Parsons. New York: Charles Scribner's Sons.

Weis, Lois. 1979. Education and the Reproduction of Inequality. *Comparative Education Review*, February, 41–51.

Whisnant, David. 1983. *All That Is Native and Fine: The Politics of Culture in an American Region*. Chapel Hill: University of North Carolina Press.

Willis, Paul. 1981. *Learning to Labour: How Working Class Kids Get Working Class Jobs*. New York: Columbia University Press.

Wilson, William A. 1976. *Folklore and Nationalism in Modern Finland*. Bloomington: Indiana University Press.

Wirz, Albert. 1998. Bridging the Gulf Between Centuries, Continents, and Professions: An Encounter with C. C. Reindorf's History. In *The Recovery of the West African Past: African Pastors and African History in the Nineteenth Century, C. C. Reindorf and Samuel Johnson*, ed. Paul Jenkins. Basel: Basler Afrika Bibliographien.

Yankah, Kwesi. 1995. *Speaking for the Chief: Okyeame and the Politics of Akan Royal Oratory*. Bloomington: Indiana University Press.

———. 1985. The Making and Breaking of Kwame Nkrumah: The Role of Oral Poetry. *Journal of African Studies* 12 (2): 86–92.

Zachernuk, P. S. 1998. African History and Imperial Culture in Colonial Nigerian Schools. *Africa* 68 (4): 484–505.

Zipes, Jack. 1987. Once There Were Two Brothers Named Grimm. In *The Complete Fairy Tales of the Brothers Grimm*, vol. 1. New York: Bantam Books.

INDEX

Note: *Page numbers in italic refer to definitions.*

Abiriw: conflict with Akropong, 11, 14, 204n8; cultural competitions in, 193–94; fieldwork in, 18, 145; Presbyterian Church in, 123; schools in, 15, 19, 103; teaching of culture in schools of, 103–5, 197; traditional priests in, 206n11

Abrahams, Roger, 32, 33

Abuakwa State College, 71

Abu-Lughod, Lila, 111

Aburi: conflict in Akuapem, 15; Presbyterian Women's Training College in, 66; traditions in, 71, 89, 203n13; West Indians in, 35

Accra: Basel Mission in, 29, 34, 200n14; connections to Akuapem, 15–16, 50, 113; festivals in, 29, 30, 117; fieldwork in, 22; schools in, 16, 70, 143; state presence in, 65, 96; students in Akuapem, 144. *See also* Greater Accra region

Achimota school: African culture and, 57–60, 202n1, 203n16; Ephraim Amu and, 51, 201n24; founding of, 49, 51, 57, 58; influence in other colonies of, 8–9; pedagogy and, 208n15

Ada (Volta Region), 71

Adaye, J. J., 43–44

Addo-Fening, Robert, 38, 67, 69, 141

adenkum (singing), 66, 70, 72, 203n10, *211*

Adinku, W. Ofotsu, 64

Adjakly, Edoh, 61

adowa (dance), 63, 71–73, 99–101, 170, *211*

Adubofuor, Samuel Brefo, 125, 206n11

Adukrom, 3, 15, 21, 123, 131, 205n1

Africa: cultural policies in, 184; culture in schools in, 8, 10, 184

agbaja (dance), 73, 99, 100, *212*

Agyemang, Fred: on Ephraim Amu, 49, 50; on

Presbyterian church history, 34, 42, 45; on Young Pioneers, 65

Ahearn, Laura, 111

AIDS, 180

Aina, Tade Akin, 184

Akan language: in Akuapem secondary schools, 209n17; cultural study in, 77–78; development of, 61–62; lessons on, 104–5, 152–53, 155, 157; teachers of, 107, 152, 154–55, 157, 205n1. *See also* Ghanaian languages; Twi language

Akropong: Basel Mission in, 34–40, 41, 43; chiefs in, 49; Christianity in, 125–26; conflict with Abiriw, 11, 14–15, 204n8; cultural competitions in, 131, 170, 193–94; description of, 11–17; festivals in, 66, 107, 165–67; history of, 13–17; Pentecostal church in, 124; Presbyterian Church in, 49, 112, 113–16; schools in, 15–16, 115–16, 143, 168; teaching of culture in schools of, 79, 103–5, 197; West Indians in, 35, 49; Young Pioneers in, 66–67, 68, 203n9

Akuapem: Basel Mission and, 30, 31–32, 34–40, 41, 112; chiefs in, 14, 89, 106, 135, 140; Christianity and, 15, 34–40, 106, 113, 119–20, 123; conflict in, 14–15, 204n8; description of, 11–17; education and, 15, 16, 35–39, 134, 141–44, 151, 156, 159, 184, 207n5, 208n12; history of, 13–16, 18, 34–40; migration and, 12, 15–16, 40; slavery and, 35–36; as traditional kingdom, 14; West Indians and, 35, 199n2; Young Pioneer movement in, 66–69, 202n7–8, 203n9, 203n12. *See also* Akuapem North district

Akuapem North district: cultural competi-